THE POLAR BEAR CATASTROPHE
THAT NEVER HAPPENED

The Polar Bear Catastrophe That Never Happened

Susan J Crockford

GWPF

ISBN 978-0-9931190-8-8
Set in Minion.
Cover design by David Gifford.
Printed by KDP
Published by The Global Warming Policy Foundation.

Contents

List of Figures

List of Tables

Preface

The polar bear is a powerful animal that inspires a conflicting mix of awe and fear. Its life on the sea ice, dictated by one of the harshest environments on earth, is unlike that of any other top predator. We are fascinated by the polar bear's ability to live off its fat, but tend to forget that such an existence is possible only because it is such a proficient and formidable killer. Endearing polar bear cubs, with their virginal white coats and intense dark eyes, evoke a different emotion when covered in bright red blood from a recent meal. Adored by those who view the Arctic from afar, those who live amongst these apex predators cannot afford that luxury of emotion: polar bears can kill humans in the blink of an eye, if the right situation presents itself.

In sub-Arctic regions, where it is possible for domestic livestock to be kept, horses, sheep, pigs, and ducks have also fallen victim to polar bears' predatory skills, but sled dogs, which are still an essential support animal across much of the Arctic, are by far the human companion taken most often. Even well-fed polar bears, always looking for ways to top up their fat stores, will destroy seasonal cabins and cause havoc in small remote communities where people only survive because they can store enough food to last them through the long, dark winters.

This combination of hunting and scavenging behaviour hints at polar bears' resourcefulness and adaptability. Researchers have learned a lot over the last two decades about bears' ability to thrive in the Arctic and to take dramatic changes in that hostile environment in their stride – in particular changes in sea ice levels. Unfortunately, that understanding came too late to prevent the polar bear becoming listed as a species threatened with extinction because of future climate changes.

This is the story of how the polar bear came to be considered 'Threatened' with extinction, and its subsequent rise and fall as an icon of the global warming movement. This also happens to be the tale of why the catastrophic decline in polar bear numbers we were promised in 2007 failed to materialise. It is also, in part, the story of my role in bringing that failure to public attention, and the backlash against me that ensued.

It is a story of scientific hubris and of scientific failure, of researchers staking their careers on untested computer simulations and the attempts to obfuscate inconvenient facts. Polar bear scientists were responsible for elevating the polar bear to climate-change-icon status in the first place, actively promoting the idea of a catastrophic future due to man-made global warming. The failure of their predictions has resulted in a loss of public trust that they entirely deserve.

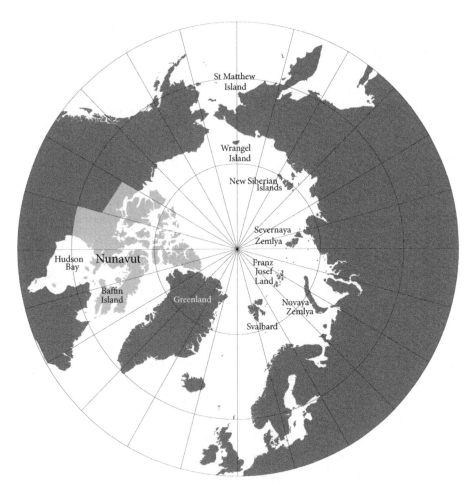

Arctic geography.

Chapter 1

Introduction

By the turn of this century, the polar bear had become an icon for promoting the idea of catastrophic effects of manmade global warming. A polar bear graced the cover of the early September 2000 issue of *Time* magazine; inside, a report from Churchill in the Canadian Arctic – accompanied by a photo of a wet, skinny bear – painted a picture of a gut-wrenching animal struggle:

> The ice forms as much as two weeks later in the autumn than it used to in Hudson Bay, creating a bewildering situation for some of the local wildlife. Polar bears that ordinarily emerge from their summer dens and walk north up Cape Churchill before proceeding directly onto the ice now arrive at their customary departure point and find open water. Unable to move forward, the bears turn left and continue walking right into town, arriving emaciated and hungry.[1]

Let's have a close look at this bit of journalism. Does it really reflect what we know about polar bears? Seeing a polar bear heading for a human settlement to look for food is nothing out of the ordinary. Polar bears are always looking for food, especially when they've taken refuge on land for the summer and have no seals to eat.

But what about its emaciated state? Did all Western Hudson Bay polar bears really arrive in Churchill in that condition? Of course not: this statement is journalistic hyperbole meant to elicit an emotional response from the reader. A photographer was able to capture a shot of one thin polar bear. However, there are always a few of those around in any given year because starvation is the leading natural cause of death for these top predators,[2] especially for young bears aged from two to five years. In fact, most of the polar bears converging on Churchill in the year 2000 would have had plenty of fat reserves, since according to published research reports, it was a relatively good year for body condition.[3]

And was sea ice freeze-up really two weeks later than usual? The fall freeze-up and spring ice break-up dates are important because they determine when the bears can be on the ice to feed. They can get a small amount of food on land in summer, but most of their calories come from the seal pups they catch on the ice in spring. So an earlier ice break-up could mean a shorter hunting season, and a later freeze-up means a longer wait before they can take to the ice again.

But in 2000, the freeze-up date was little different from the average, at least when the term is defined in relation to when bears are able to leave the shore. In other words, 'freeze-up' for polar bears occurs when the available open water is 5–10% covered by ice, rather than the 50% coverage that is standard for meteorological uses.[4] This is an important distinction: Western Hudson Bay polar bears leave the ice as soon as they are able: they don't wait until the bay is 50% covered in ice. Data from the scientific literature shows that after about 1995 (up to 2015), freeze-up in Western Hudson Bay came about one week later than it did from 1979–1989,[*] although the date is highly variable from year to year.[5]

So the situation in Churchill in 2000 was nothing out of the ordinary. There had certainly been much worse years for polar bears in the area. In 1983, many bears came ashore in summer in poor condition, rather than fat and sassy, as was usual. The freeze-up that year was the latest on record, so it was early December before the bears were able to take to the ice again. By this point, they were like 'walking skeletons'.[6] Desperately hungry bears in summer can mean problems for people, and there were also two attacks by bears on people that year in Churchill, one of them fatal.[7]

The 1980s and early 1990s are now mostly touted as 'the good old days' for sea ice conditions worldwide, but the polar bears of Western Hudson Bay were an exception. In the 1980s, average weights of polar bears in the area had declined, and cub mortality increased, with a marked increase in the loss of whole litters over what had been documented in the 1960s and 1970s.[8] Canadian biologist Ian Stirling, who worked for the Canadian Wildlife Service, was Canada's senior polar bear researcher at the time, and he struggled to explain what was going on.

Part of his difficulty arose because of certain assumptions he and other Arctic researchers had made. Their theories about polar bears assumed that the environment they depended on – sea ice – was uniform and stable. It should therefore support an ever-increasing population of polar bears and their prey.[9] This made the difficulties of bears in Western Hudson Bay and other regions where population fluctuations had been observed, such as the Southern Beaufort Sea, hard to understand.[10]

Stirling had been looking at natural fluctuations in 'ecosystem parameters', such as sea ice thickness, snow depth over ice, seal ecology, and primary productivity of the ocean region, as possible causes; ways to explain why polar bear health and survival was affected in some years but not others. But none of these explanations really worked because not enough detailed information was available. He just couldn't find any variations that would scientifically explain the

---

[*] Breakup was about two weeks earlier.

periodic declines in polar bear condition and cub survival in the Southern Beaufort and Western Hudson Bay that he had documented.

This must have been a huge frustration for him as a researcher. But more importantly it may have threatened his career. Working as a researcher in what was then an obscure specialty that required expensive field work, and with little by way of results to show for his efforts, the possibility of his funding drying up must have been an ever-present worry.

But then, in 1988, James Hansen gave his infamous testimony to a US Senate committee on climate change,[11] declaring that mankind was warming the planet and that environmental disaster loomed. Suddenly, a new focus for research in Western Hudson Bay – sea ice decline blamed on human-caused global warming – seemed extremely palatable. Ian Stirling certainly embraced the idea. In 1993, he and his student, Andrew Derocher, published a paper describing how changes in sea ice might have affected polar bears in Hudson Bay, although they had no evidence to support their claims.[12] This paper was, however, a turning point, as Stirling explained in a 2016 interview:

> Leading up to the 1993 paper, I was originally interested in natural fluctuations in ecosystems. It didn't have anything to do with climate change. One day after looking at our long-term population-monitoring data from my project in Western Hudson Bay, I said to Andy [Derocher, then his PhD student, now a full professor at the University of Alberta], 'You know, there are some longer-term things going on underneath what we're seeing up front'. I had set out to look at some completely legitimate but totally different questions, and climate change forced its way onto the agenda.[13]

It quickly became apparent that climate change was a lifeboat that could rescue Stirling's career. In a follow-up paper in 1999, he and a group of colleagues showed that sea ice coverage on Hudson Bay had indeed declined by the late 1990s. However, the correlation with polar bear survival and productivity was weak and not statistically significant,[14] and they had to somewhat gloss over the 1980s' decline in survival of Western Hudson Bay polar bear cubs, which had been documented before any marked changes in sea ice break-up or freeze-up dates had occurred.

Nevertheless, by that time, climate change had become a prominent topic within the scientific community and the media:[15] Stirling's paper therefore came at just the right time. Apparently showing a link between manmade global warming and harm to a charismatic beast like the polar bear, it became the basis of a frenzy of global warming agitation. Soon the polar bear had been hoisted to the top of the climate change flagpole, making it the most easily-recognizable symbol of all that mankind was doing wrong in the world.

This then was the situation when the *Time* magazine article appeared, just a year later. The way the article plays fast and loose with the scientific facts shows that from the moment polar bears became an icon of global warming, the media were willing to stretch the truth (aided and abetted by polar bear scientists) in order to convey a convincing message of looming catastrophe.

And the hype only got worse. From 2004, there were the drowning polar bear stories out of Alaska – including Al Gore's *An Inconvenient Truth* documentary and others[16] – that turned out to be great exaggerations at best, if not outright fabrications. Next were the cannibal stories: polar bears were alleged to be eating each other in their desperation to survive and it was said that it was only going to get worse. In reality, these were just anecdotes without any scientific standing.

By 2006, before sea ice had even begun to decline to any serious degree, a winter solstice gardening article in the *New York Times*[17] imagined polar bears dying in droves amid an endless supply of spinach:

> It's not that I don't like 60-degree days and eating fresh spinach right out of my garden in December. But the extended growing season is one of the signs of global warming. It goes hand in hand with polar bears dying in the Arctic as the sea ice shrinks.

It might be difficult in 2019 to believe the extent of the media hyperbole back then. But it was serious business at the time. The alarm bells of the polar bear apocalypse were pealing across the planet. Scientists, conservation activists, and the media worked together to get everyone wound up, setting the scene for polar bears to be classified as 'Threatened' with extinction.

Chapter 2

Conservation background

Polar bears were classified as 'Threatened' both by the International Union for Conservation of Nature (IUCN), the body that maintains the official 'Red List' of endangered species, and by the US government, under the Endangered Species Act. Before we look at how this happened, we need to understand a little about the natural history of polar bears, and some of the recent history of their relationship with human beings.

Polar bears and sea ice

The polar bear (*Ursus maritimus*) is the top predator of the Arctic ecosystem and is found in five nations with ice-covered polar seas (Figure 2.1). Polar bears are almost entirely carnivorous, having evolved from their nearest omnivorous relative, the brown bear (or grizzly, *Ursus arctos*), perhaps 600,000 years ago.[18] The 2012 study by Miller and colleagues, which suggested an origin for polar bears 4–5 million years ago,[19] is often quoted, but is now an outlier amongst many others that indicate a much later date.[20]

However, in their behaviour towards humans, polar bears are more like black bears than grizzlies. While grizzlies are hyper-protective of their cubs and food when people are around, polar bears are more tolerant, but still make predatory attacks on humans much more often than grizzlies or even black bears. Not surprisingly, then, in encounters between polar bears and grizzlies in the wild, grizzlies (especially females) push polar bears around. Grizzlies are more aggressive, despite their smaller size.[21]

The life history of polar bears is dictated by the changes in sea ice that occur routinely over the seasons, and by the seals that this ice supports. The presence of ice and therefore seals has allowed polar bears to flourish in the Arctic for hundreds of thousands of years.[*,22]

Arctic seals (mostly ringed seals, *Phoca hispida*, and bearded seals, *Erignatha barbatus*, but also harp, ribbon and spotted seals) give birth on the sea

---

[*]The bears are newcomers: the ice algae, zooplankton, fish, and clams that thrive under the ice have supported Arctic seals, walrus, and whales for millions of years.

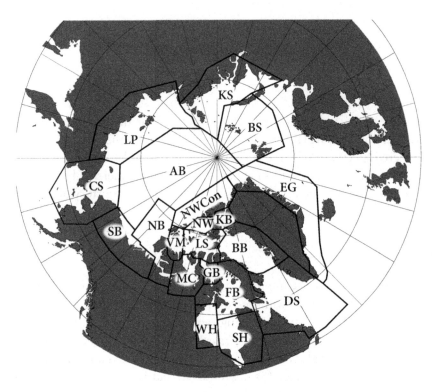

AB	Arctic Basin	FB	Foxe Basin	MC	M'Clintock Channel
BB	Baffin Bay	GB	Gulf of Boothia	NB	Northern Beaufort
BS	Barents Sea	KB	Kane Basin	NW	Norwegian Bay
CS	Chukchi Sea	KS	Kara Sea	SB	Southern Beaufort
DS	Davis Strait	LP	Laptev Sea	SH	Southern Hudson Bay
EG	East Greenland	LS	Lancaster Sound	VM	Viscount Melville
				WH	Western Hudson Bay

Figure 2.1: Global polar bear subpopulations.

As defined by the IUCN Polar Bear Specialist Group. The areas are managed by
five nations (Canada, Russia, Norway, United States of America, and Denmark
(for Greenland). NWCon (also known as 'Queen Elizabeth') is not a recognised
polar bear subpopulation. Redrawn from Environment Canada map.

ice from late winter to early spring. The pups are fat and helpless and therefore much more accessible at this time, so polar bears take advantage of the bounty in order to survive. In spring, polar bears eat as much as possible before the young seals leave the ice (usually around mid-May, depending on the latitude). They put on hundreds of pounds of fat during this 3–4 month period. Older seals that bask on the ice over the summer are wary and much harder to catch: many bears don't even bother trying to catch them, even if they remain on the ice. However, so long as a bear has eaten sufficiently in the spring, its evolved adaptations – storing large quantities of fat and metabolising them slowly – mean it can go without food entirely until fall.[23]

As as consequence, well-fed polar bears truly do not need ice during the summer. Bears in some areas – such as Hudson Bay – spend the summer on land and wait for the ice to reform in the fall. In other regions – such as the Southern Beaufort Sea – most bears stay on the polar pack ice as it retreats away from the shore, although some come ashore for the summer.[24]

Then, in the fall, newly formed ice attracts seals of all ages, including naïve youngsters, to feed at the edges, where they are easy prey for bears. Pregnant females, however, do not resume feeding in fall, but make snug earth/snow or ice/snow dens in which to give birth to tiny cubs in about late December. The cubs are nursed inside the den all winter and emerge at the age of 3–4 months in March or April. After a few days or more at the den site, the cubs follow their mother to the ice, where she will start hunting the latest crop of young seals. A new mother may not have eaten for eight months or more by this time, so a timely and successful spring hunt is crucial to the survival of the family unit.[25]

The slaughter of polar bears that's rarely mentioned

The early slaughter

As is true for whales and walrus, the story of polar bear conservation begins with the history of commercial hunting by European nations in the Arctic. While aboriginal peoples across the Arctic had hunted polar bears in a sustainable fashion for centuries, the species could hardly withstand the wanton slaughter that followed on the heels of a dying whaling industry. As whales in the Arctic became scarce, whalers went after other species, including walrus and polar bears. The slaughter took place across the Arctic, but eastern Canada, Greenland, western Russia and the Svalbard archipelago north of Norway were hit especially hard.

An early 1990s Master's thesis by James Honderich[26] summarised polar bear harvests in Canada from about 4000 years ago to 1935, based on archaeological analysis of pre-European household refuse, records left by Arctic explorers (1594 to mid-1900s), accounts of Hudson's Bay Company fur traders (from 1670 to 1935) and logbooks kept by Arctic whalers (1820s to 1935). The period 1850–1935 was especially devastating: after at least a century of concerted effort to remove as many bowhead whales as possible from eastern Canadian waters – starting in about 1820 in Baffin Bay – commercial whalers increasingly sought seals, beluga and walrus for their oil, and polar bears for their skins, in order to boost their revenues. Some of these polar bears were killed by the whalers themselves (sometimes for food), but the skins of many others were taken in trade with local Inuit hunters at shore-based whaling stations. Unfortunately, according to Honderich:[27]

> ... by the 1890s, polar bears had become a primary resource in their own right and their harvest was no longer an aside to whaling.

Honderich calculated that between 1850 and 1930, between 400–800 bears were taken *every year* from whaling ships, with a peak in the 1890s of 800 or more, primarily from the eastern and central Canadian Arctic, especially Davis Strait, all of Hudson Bay, Baffin Bay and Lancaster Sound. Altogether, it was estimated that about 37,500 bears were harvested over that period, with an additional 40,000 or more taken from the Beaufort and Chukchi Seas.[28] However, Honderich stated that actual harvests may have been 50% higher or more, and that similar amounts were taken from Eurasian polar seas (the western Soviet Arctic plus Svalbard in the Barents Sea). Commercial sealers across the Arctic also took polar bears to augment their revenues and Honderich was not able to account for how many they might have taken. Figure 2.2 shows photographs from the pioneering expeditions of Fridjof Nansen and Roald Amudsen, demonstrating that bears were almost certainly abundant a century ago.

One local example shows the effect of this relentless carnage. Hundreds of polar bears that spent summers on St Matthew Island in the Bering Sea – many of them pregnant females – were wiped out during the period 1875–1899, probably by fur seal hunters rather than whalers.[29] Polar bears never re-colonised the island before sea ice changes made it impossible.

A passage translated from a paper by Russian researcher Savva Uspenski shows that there was some awareness of a similarly large harvest taking place in northern Eurasia:[30]

> Estimates of total historical harvest suggest that from the beginning of the 18th century, roughly 400 to 500 animals were being harvested annually in northern Eurasia, reaching a peak of 1,300 to 1,500 animals in the early 20th century, and falling off as the numbers began dwindling.

This is confirmed by Ian Stirling, in his latest polar bear book, in which he provides detail on polar bear harvests in the Norwegian sector of the Barents Sea, comparing these to other Arctic regions:[31]

> Estimates based on admittedly incomplete information indicate that between 1875 and 1892, the average annual Norwegian harvest at Svalbard was 144 polar bears [total 2,448], increasing to 415 between 1893 and 1908 [total 6,225]. The kill averaged 355 per year from 1924 through 1939 [total 5,325] and, after World War II, dropped to 324 per year from 1945 to 1970 [total 8,100]. Altogether, over 22,000 polar bears were killed during this period. Most of these (60–65%) were taken in the western parts of the Barents Sea [i.e. Franz Josef Land] including the archipelago of Svalbard. Twenty to 25% were estimated to have been killed in the Chukchi Sea, and only 10–20% in the Kara, Laptev, East Siberian and Bering seas.

The late slaughter

Mind-boggling numbers of bears were taken annually in Svalbard by whalers and traders in the 40 years prior to 1930, presumably causing a dramatic drop in population. However, with only a relatively short respite while the Second World War raged in Europe, polar bear numbers were able to make a remarkable recovery. By the late 1940s, hundreds of bears were again being taken annually by sport hunters, and this harvest was to continue for three decades. Norwegian polar bear specialist Thor Larsen has estimated that more than 8000 bears were killed by sport-hunters between 1945 and 1970 in the Svalbard area alone.[32]

It's odd that a marked population decline was not readily apparent around Svalbard when sport-hunting resumed after the war. After being massively overharvested for so many decades prior to 1930, surely polar bear numbers were noticably depleted by the late 1940s? Or had the virtual cessation of hunting during the war years given Barents Sea polar bears enough time to recover significantly from the slaughter during previous decades? It appears so, because there were enough bears in the late 1940s for hundreds of bears per year to be killed and a new period of carnage began.

It was a similar story to the east. Soviet military personnel stationed in the Arctic after World War II were probably responsible for a good proportion of kills in the eastern Barents Sea (for example, around Franz Josef Land) and the Kara Sea. As in Svalbard, bears were chased down with snowmobiles and airplanes, shot from ships, and slaughtered relentlessly. But this intensive sport hunting came only a few decades after almost 1000 bears had been killed *every year for sixteen years straight* from 1908–1923 from the same region. Polar bears must almost certainly have been phenomenally abundant in the Barents and Kara Seas in the late 1800s for that intensity of harvest to have taken place without a serious decline being patently obvious just before the Second World War.

It is possible that bear populations were maintained against the hunters' onslaught by bears redistributing themselves across the Arctic, expanding into depleted areas from regions that had been virtually untouched by hunting. However, results of a genetic study undertaken in the early 1990s suggest that this was not the case and that local populations simply rebounded.[33] Thor Larsen estimated that after Norwegian protective regulations were put in place in 1970, the polar bear population of Svalbard had doubled by the mid-1980s; this pattern was repeated elsewhere across the Arctic.[34]

The silence of the researchers

A recent summary article by Magnus Andersen and Jon Aars discusses harvests since the late 1800s in light of the 2004 population estimate of 1900–3600 bears:[35]

> This implies that the [pre-harvest] Barents Sea population should have numbered at least 10 000 polar bears to have sustained the recorded harvest. The harvest obviously was not sustainable, but the calculation still indicates that the historical population size must have been significantly higher than the current size. The large difference between this number and the upper confidence limit (3600) of our estimate in 2004, after 40 years of protection, is noteworthy. Larsen (1986) indicated that the population approximately doubled in size over a decade after protection in 1973 and suggested that there were close to 2000 bears in the Svalbard area and [a total of] 3000–6700 in the area between East Greenland and Franz Josef Land in 1980. The growth rate from then and up to 2004 is unknown.

As this indicates, knowing the extent of the bear harvest in the period prior to the 1930s can give us some idea of how large polar bear populations must have been before commercial exploitation began: a large harvest implies a large population.

It also tells us about the potential of these populations to recover, a topic I discuss in more detail in Chapter 11.

You would therefore expect these issues to be hot topics for polar bear researchers. However, surprisingly, Stirling's academic papers make no mention of the slaughter by whalers, even though he was a co-supervisor of Honderich's thesis and therefore must have known about the findings since at least 1990. As noted above, he does discuss the issue in his recent book for general readers,[36] but apart from that, virtually the only mention of the slaughter of polar bears in the decades before the Second World War is a paper by Anderson and

Aars.[†] Elsewhere, there is nothing. For example, the US Fish and Wildlife Service (USFWS) polar bear status assessment report for 2006 described pre-1950s harvests as subsistence hunts by indigenous people, without a single mention of the early period of slaughter by whalers and sealers:[39]

> Prior to the 1950s most hunting was done by indigenous people for subsistence purposes. However, population declines due to sport hunting became an increasing international concern during the 1950s and 1960s.

Similarly, the latest Canadian report on the status of polar bears makes no mention of those intensive pre-1930s harvests, nor do any of the fifteen meeting reports (1965–2009) of the IUCN Polar Bear Specialist Group (PBSG).[40] That's a lot of important history ignored.

Time and again, polar bear researchers choose only to mention the post-war harvest. For example, in their paper on polar bear research in Western Hudson Bay from 1966–1992, Derocher and Stirling stated:[41]

> Throughout the 1950s, 50–100 polar bears, including many adult females with cubs, were harvested annually... we suspect that the population size was markedly reduced by the late 1960s.

A recent book chapter on the harvest of polar bears by former US Geological Survey (USGS) biologist Lily Peacock, for example, does not mention that period at all, as if the history of over-hunting began in the mid-20th century.[42]

The silence from scientists regarding that early period of over-harvesting has also impacted other areas of research. An eighty-year-long decimation of polar bear numbers worldwide almost certainly reduced the genetic diversity of polar bears living today, important information for polar bear geneticists trying to unravel polar bear population dynamics and evolutionary history. However, I am almost certain that polar bear geneticists have no idea that such a marked population decline occurred between 1890 and 1930, since none of the standard reference works or status reports they would naturally turn to for that information mention the carnage. They are seemingly only aware of the post-war period of polar bear over-hunting. For example, a paper published by David Paetkau and colleagues in 1999 was the first large-scale genetic study of polar bears, and Ian Stirling was a co-author.[43] Yet the paper mentioned only the 1960s' over-harvests as leading to international concern over polar bear numbers, citing the first PBSG meeting report (1965). More recently, a polar bear evolution paper

---

[†] The *Monitoring of Svalbard and Jan Mayen* website, which has been maintained in recent years by Norwegian government scientists, and which currently lists the number of bears taken in historical harvests back to 1871,[37] could be considered a third example. Most of the data is the work of a Norwegian polar bear researcher named Odd Lønø,[38] and was published in a Norwegian Polar Institute monograph in1970. This was recently made available online as a scanned document, but prior to 2011 would have been difficult to find.

(a) Norwegian explorer Fridtjof Nansen (left), on his first voyage to the Arctic, with the captain of the sealing vessel *Viking*, sitting on two polar bears they had just shot in the West Ice polynya in the Greenland Sea. Another photo (not shown) has Nansen posing in front of the *Viking* crew over another very fat bear he had just shot. Taken March–July 1882.

(b) Two of Roald Amundsen's crew-mates preparing polar bear skins at their camp at Cape Chelyuskin, at the tip of the Taimyr Peninsula between the Kara and Laptev Seas. The number of skins suggests bears were locally abundant and hunting them a common pastime for expedition members. The previous winter, Amundsen had been mauled by a bear, but was saved at the last minute. Taken 19 June 1919.

Figure 2.2: Evidence from early photographs.
Sources: Blix (2016); Fram Museum, no date.

by Webb Miller and colleagues investigated natural population declines over time associated with glacial and interglacial conditions,[44] but failed to mention the significant human-caused decline in polar bear numbers between 1890 and 1970.

It is hard not to wonder why polar bear experts have been so reticent about that black period of the late 19th and early 20th centuries. The professional silence of these biologists about the largest slaughter of polar bears ever known, as reflected in easily available peer-reviewed scientific papers and reports, stands in marked contrast to the wealth of information forthcoming about the many other marine mammals (including bowhead and humpback whales, sea otters, fur seals, and walrus) that share a similarly devastating history.[45]

Conservation status history

It is against this background of two intensive periods of over-harvesting that Arctic nations finally became concerned about the survival of polar bears as a species. The Soviet Union banned hunting in 1956, as did Norway in 1972. Also in 1972, the US Marine Mammal Protection Act introduced broad safeguards for polar bears, sea otters, walrus, whales, fur seals and sea lions in American waters. And finally, an international treaty, signed in 1973 by all Arctic nations, put an end to unregulated hunting of polar bears across their range.[46] It also led to the formation in 1968 of the Polar Bear Specialist Group (PBSG), an agency of the IUCN, tasked with coordinating the research necessary for assessing polar bear health and population size worldwide.[47]

Next, attempts were made to move polar bears towards protected status. The IUCN Red List classified the polar bear as 'Vulnerable' to extinction in 1982, but by 1996 the bears had been up-listed to 'Least concern' because numbers had risen markedly in areas where they were well studied, such as the Southern Beaufort Sea, Svalbard, and Western Hudson Bay. Early concerns regarding polar bear survival were dominated by over-hunting, but oil exploration and extraction was also a worry.[48]

The IUCN listing

However, by 2005, at the height of this newly politicised climate, the PBSG held one of their formal 'working group' meetings. Keep in mind that in 1996, polar bear numbers had been considered robust enough that the IUCN Red List status of 'Vulnerable' had been downgraded to 'Least concern'.[‡] However, it is clear from the minutes of their 2005 meeting that some PBSG members were not happy with that situation.[49]

According to the minutes of that meeting, a few of these members suggested to their PBSG colleagues that if computer-predicted losses of sea ice were considered a threat to polar bear numbers within three generations (a generation considered at that time to be 15 years), the status of 'Vulnerable' could be reinstated. With virtually no further analysis, after being shown the sea ice projections from the just-published summary document of the *Arctic Climate Impact Assessment 2005*,[50] the PBSG recommended that the IUCN Red List committee accept their collective opinion that the polar bear be listed as 'Vulnerable'; and they told the IUCN that the global population was likely to decline by 'more than 30% within the next 35–50 years'.[51]

The following year, the IUCN added polar bears to its Red List, categorising them as being of 'Threatened' status, thus reversing the status of 'Lower risk/Conservation dependent'[§] that polar bears had been assigned in 1996 to reflect their recovery from previous decades of over-hunting.[52] It was as easy and science-light as that.[53] And this is how the polar bear (*Ursus maritimus*) became the first species ever to be classified as threatened with extinction based on predictions of future climate change rather than current population status.

The ESA decision

Getting polar bears listed as 'Threatened' under the US Endangered Species Act (ESA) was a much tougher proposition. The Republican Party, under the leadership of George W. Bush, was in power at the time and they had no love of the ESA. However, emboldened by the Red List success, conservation activists were quick to take advantage. After the 2005 PBSG meeting, they poured on the rhetoric of starving, drowning bears in order to increase financial donations. But more importantly, they took advantage of a provision of the ESA that allowed anyone to sue the government for failing to protect a species.

Kassie Siegel, a lawyer for the Center for Biological Diversity (CBD), spearheaded the ESA campaign.[54] It was launched in late December 2005, with a CBD lawsuit accusing the US government of failing to adequately protect polar bears from known threats to survival. This allowed biologists from the USFWS and the USGS, several of whom were also PBSG members, to begin making a

---

[‡] Polar bears were considered of 'Least concern' for ten years and had therefore been 'saved' from the threat of unregulated hunting.

[§] Now called 'Least concern'.

scientific case for the proposition that human-caused global warming presented a serious threat to polar bear survival.[55]

But it had to be an extremely strong case, because it was likely to face serious political opposition from Republicans and their supporters. In other words, there was a huge incentive for government biologists to over-egg the pudding: to make the threat to polar bears seem as dire as possible.

This was achieved in part by elevating anecdotal incidents to the status of scientific evidence. For example, in one particularly dubious incident, some dead polar bears, spotted in September 2004 off the coast of Alaska, having supposedly drowned in a storm, got huge media attention.[56] Even though there were plenty of questions about the veracity of the claim and its possible significance, it was used as scientifically valid evidence for the ESA case that was being built.

The same approach was taken with cannibalism. Anecdotal reports of polar bears consuming each other in Alaska in the early 2000s were published by Steven Amstrup and colleagues at the USGS.[57] Three apparent incidents of cannibalism in the Southern Beaufort Sea in 2004 were said to be just the tip of the iceberg that was coming for polar bears: soon bears would be so ravaged by hunger they would be eating each other to survive. It mattered not that there was evidence in the literature that cannibalism was relatively common in polar bears, even when sea ice conditions were good.[58] Nor did anyone seem to have noticed the admission in Amstrup's paper that a single rogue bear could have been responsible for all three incidences of cannabilism. The media and conservation organizations helped Amstrup publicise these incidents as more evidence for the ESA case: increased cannibalism was indeed listed as a specific scientific concern in the final ESA determination.[59]

Here is an example of the kind of hyperbole that the media was serving up at the time. A *Washington Post* report[60] on Amstrup's 2006 paper on the cannibalism incidents turned to Kassie Siegel at the CBD for comment:

> 'Cannibalism demonstrates the effect on bears,' said Kassie Siegel, lead author of the petition.
>
> 'It's very important new information,' she said. 'It shows in a really graphic way how severe the problem of global warming is for polar bears.'
>
> Deborah Williams of Alaska Conservation Solutions, a group aimed at pursuing solutions for climate change, said the study represents the 'bloody fingerprints' of global warming.

In 2007, Al Gore's Oscar-winning documentary, *An Inconvenient Truth*, featured Alaska's drowning polar bears, allegedly doomed to extinction because of human fossil-fuel use. Few could manage to talk about global warming without mentioning polar bears or at least include an image of one.[||] By the time the ESA decision was finalised in mid-May 2008 (almost a full year before Barack Obama took over as President), polar bears were everywhere, and polar bear specialists were being quoted *ad nauseum.*

Finally, in 2008, the USFWS, in response to the petition filed by the CBD and two other not-for-profit conservation organizations,[62] similarly declared polar bears 'Threatened'.[¶] Invoking the ESA to protect polar bears,[63] the USFWS explained:

> We find, based upon the best available scientific and commercial information, that polar bear habitat – principally sea ice – is declining throughout the species' range, that this decline is expected to continue for the foreseeable future, and that this loss threatens the species throughout all of its range. Therefore, we find that the polar bear is likely to become an endangered species within the foreseeable future throughout all of its range.

So remarkably, both the USFWS and IUCN listing decisions, granted polar bears in 2006 and 2008, respectively, referred *exclusively* to what might occur in the future if sea ice were to continue to decline in response to rising carbon dioxide levels in the atmosphere.[64] In other words, this was about population declines that were *anticipated* to occur as a result of predicted habitat loss, rather than on current circumstances.[65] This had never happened before.

As Jonathan Adler pointed out in an excellent article that appeared on the heels of the ESA listing decision:[66]

> Insofar as the listing is based upon climate models, ice-melt projections, and assumptions about the effects of habitat loss on the bear's prospects for survival in the wild, its scientific basis is quite speculative.

But at that time it was hard to argue with the researchers, their case laid out in considerable detail in a number of non-peer-reviewed internal government reports produced by the USGS.[67] It was all based on computer-modelled predictions of sea ice loss and a set of assumptions regarding polar bear responses to that habitat loss.

And the conclusions were stark. The authors predicted potentially catastrophic declines in the global population of polar bears by 2050 as a direct effect of crossing a particular threshold of sea ice loss. Summing up the case for the ESA polar bear decision, Amstrup and colleagues stated:[68]

[||] In a later example, to illustrate a letter about climate change and the integrity of science in their May 2010 issue,[61] *Science* magazine included a dramatic image of a thin polar bear on an ice floe. A week later, it apologised and replaced the purchased image because it had been clearly marked as a photoshopped collage.

[¶] Note that the Red List status term 'Vulnerable' is equivalent to the ESA term 'Threatened' (indicating a species likely to become endangered); both use the term 'Endangered' to indicate a higher-risk status.

Our modeling suggests that realization of the sea ice future which is currently projected would mean loss of ≈2/3 of the world's current polar bear population by mid-century.

Chapter 3

Sea ice and population predictions

Polar Bear Numbers Set to Fall
Last autumn, the US Geological Survey concluded that the animals [polar bears] are likely to lose 42% of their summer sea ice habitat by mid-century, cutting the world's polar bear population – estimated at 25,000 – by two-thirds.

Nature, 22 May 2008[69]

Predictions of sea ice decline

In 2002, the NASA Earth Observatory reported that summer sea ice extent had reached a new low, below the long-term median for 1979–2000. This report had researchers worried about the future.[70] The commentary on NASA's 'image of the day' for 16 May 2009 had this to say about that memorable moment back in September 2002:[71]

> Since the satellite record began in late 1978, Arctic sea ice showed an overall decline, but the rate of decline was relatively small through the twentieth century. The record low from 2002 was only barely below previous record lows from the 1990s, and sea ice rebounded to 15.5 million square kilometers the following March. But the 2002 September low was the beginning of a series of record- or near-record-low sea ice extents in the Arctic. This series of record lows, combined with poor wintertime recoveries starting in the winter of 2004–2005, marked a sharpening in the rate of decline in Arctic sea ice. Sea ice did not return to anything approaching long-term average values after 2002.

By 2005, this decline in ice had become more pronounced and it was suggested by a few researchers that an Arctic sea ice 'tipping point' had been reached.[72] The US National Snow and Ice Data Center (NSIDC) issued a press release at the end of September that showed the summer ice extent for 2005 was below the 2002 level and included an anecdote from the director that touched upon the potential fate of polar bears:[73]

In mid-September, NSIDC Director Roger Barry spent time in the Laptev Sea on an Arctic icebreaker. The ship entered only one area of continuous ice to the east of Severnaya Zemvya, one of the most northern island chains of Russia. 'That whole area was covered in thick multiyear ice last year, in September of 2004.' The Northeast Passage, north of the Siberian coast, was completely ice-free from August 15 through September 28.

Barry mused about the possible effects of the sea ice decline, including the impact on Arctic animals. 'We saw several polar bears quite close to the ship,' he said. 'Polar bears must wait out the summer melt season on land, using their stored fat until they can return to the ice. But if winter recovery and sea ice extent continue to decline, how will these beasts survive?

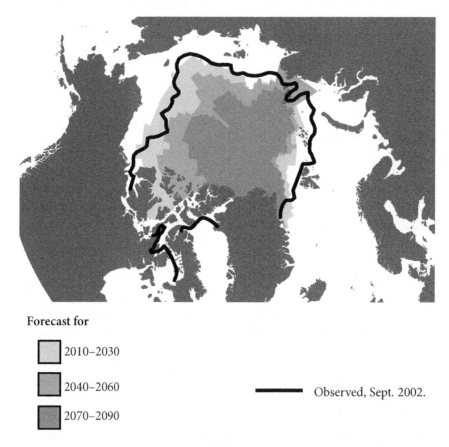

Forecast for

2010–2030

2040–2060   ▬▬▬ Observed, Sept. 2002.

2070–2090

Figure 3.1: Projected September sea ice extents compared to 2002.
Redrawn from ACIA (2005). See also Hassol.[74]

This was the situation for Arctic sea ice that researchers were facing at the start of the 21st century. The state of the ice spawned a number of pessimistic

reports, as well as predictions of further declines.[75] It was these predictions of
habitat loss that underpinned the decision to list polar bears as 'Threatened'. In
order to understand what went wrong, we need to understand the basis of these
predictions of sea ice loss and the level of ice that was supposed to cause the loss
of two thirds of the polar bear population. And in order to do that, we also need
to be clear about what definition of sea ice extent the scientists were referring to,
and for what period of the year. These issues are considered in the rest of this
chapter.

The basis of the ice predictions

The report supporting the 2006 Red List decision,[76] as well as the updates that
followed,[77] were based on the simple modelled declines in sea ice coverage published in the synthesis report of the Arctic Climate Impact Assessment[78](see
Figure 3.1).* In contrast, the ESA decision was based on population predictions
outlined in a detailed report by Steven Amstrup and colleagues at the USGS.[80]
Amstrup in turn used sea ice predictions in a separate USGS paper, by George
Durner et al.[81] This utilised an ensemble of ten of the 'business as usual' (otherwise known as 'worst case scenario') sea ice models† prepared for the Fourth Assessment Report of the Intergovernmental Panel on Climate Change (IPCC).[82]

Sea-ice concentrations

Climate scientists – and in particular the NSIDC and NOAA‡ – use a concentration threshold of >15% for official sea ice extent, while polar bear specialists
use a concentration of >50% for their predictive work. For example, the USGS's
definition of 'preferred habitat' was ' Ice of >50% concentration over continental
shelves'.

The two figures will always be different. For example, for 16 September 2007
(the seasonal minimum), the extent based on >15% sea ice, was 4.15m km² but
only about 3.4m km² at >50% ice concentration. This can complicate things
when analysing readily available sea ice data with respect to polar bears, because
the data that is generally available is at the 'wrong' concentration (15%).

However, it has been shown that in most Arctic regions, the observed differences due to ice concentration thresholds are minimal.[83] This suggests that
published sea ice data based on 15% ice concentration can be used to broadly

---

*The same sea ice projection was also used to assess future polar bear conservation status at
the local level for the province of Newfoundland and Labrador, Canada.[79]
† SRES A1B.
‡ The National Oceanic and Atmospheric Administration.

delimit the critical threshold of ice expected at mid-century as between 3.0m and 5.0m km^2 for both the 2006 Red List assessment and the 2008 ESA decision. This is because the ice level at 50% concentration ('optimal polar bear habitat') will be slightly lower.[§]

Sea ice levels when?

It is clear that the concern for polar bears arose because of possible future loss of *summer* sea ice (i.e. the amount of ice at the annual minimum in September). This is obvious because sea ice coverage in winter (March) and spring (June) was not predicted to change appreciably.[84] In the event, this has turned out to be broadly correct: despite a slight decline of sea ice in other months of the year, including March and June, it is mostly summer ice that has declined,[85] and there has been no evidence presented to suggest that slight declines of global sea ice coverage in winter or spring have negatively affected polar bears.[86] In part, this is because much of the global decline in ice levels in those seasons has occurred in areas such as the Sea of Okhotsk and the Gulf of St. Lawrence, where polar bears do not live.[87]

However, some of the wording in the reports underlying the assessments can be misleading. For example, in the Amstrup *et al.* paper behind the ESA decision, the term 'summer' is used to encompass the July–September melt season, but summer is still represented by the average for September alone, with the September minimum mentioned for emphasis. And Amstrup and his colleagues explained why the sea ice projections used in their model were likely to be conservative:[88]

> In conclusion, to see any qualitative change in the probability of extinction…, even in year 45, sea ice projections would need to leave more sea ice than the maximum [global climate model] projection we used… As of 23 August 2007 declines in Arctic sea ice extent in 2007 have set a new record for the available time series from 1979–2006…But, the sea ice in 2007 already has declined below the level projected for mid century by the 4 most conservative models in our ensemble…This seems to be compelling evidence that we are not likely to see more ice than our models have suggested at any of the future time steps we evaluated.

Throughout their report, Amstrup and colleagues showed their tendency to say 'sea ice loss' when they meant 'summer sea ice loss' and to say 'summer' when they meant 'September.' However, the paper by Julienne Stroeve and colleagues

---

[§] According to NSIDC, in 2012 the difference between the September average (3.61m km^2) and the September minimum (3.41m km^2) was 0.2m km^2. For 2016, it was 0.58 (4.14 vs. 4.72m km^2), for 2015, 0.22 (4.41 vs. 4.63m km^2) and for 2013, 0.25 (5.10 vs. 5.35m km^2). For other years, see http://nsidc.org/arcticseaicenews.

that is their source[89] only reports ice projections for summer, represented by the monthly average for September (winter, represented by the monthly average for March, is discussed briefly but not shown). Also, their detailed description of why the 2007 summer minimum was an important observation cements the notion that this metric was critical in relation to their model.

And while it is certainly true that the complex USGS models incorporated multiple aspects of sea ice, including 'optimum polar bear habitat', when it came down to explaining the results in simple language, the September average was a critical determinant, almost certainly because metrics like length of the ice-free season and extent of sea ice >50% concentration are largely determined by the lowest extent reached in September (in other words, 'summer'). For example, the executive summary of the 2007 USGS reports stated (in the next two quotations the emphasis is mine):

> Ultimately, we projected a 42% loss of optimal polar bear habitat during *summer* in the polar basin by mid century.

Similarly, the abstract for the report by Durner and colleagues stated:[90]

> The ten [global climate models] we used had high concordance between their simulations of 20th century *summer* sea ice extent and the actual ice extent derived from passive microwave satellite observations.

Thus we can be reasonably sure that the predictions of disaster for polar bears depended on predictions of sea ice extent for September, and at 50% concentration.

How much ice causes disaster?

However, the *actual* value of the ice extent involved was not defined numerically in either the Red List or the ESA assessment. Fortunately, a review of the reports associated with each assessment allows us to ascertain this value: 3–5m km^2 (at 50% concentration). For example, for the Red List assessment, an ice forecast graph published in the underlying Arctic Climate Impact Assessment scientific report[91] shows two out of five models consistently predicted September ice below 5.0m km^2 (but above 3.0m km^2) after 2045. Three out of five models consistently predicted 3–5m km^2 after 2060. Similarly for the ESA assessment, the peer-reviewed version of Amstrup's paper shows that the average of the mid-century ice extent in the models used was in a similar range (see Figure 3.2). ‖

‖ This value is confirmed by the so-called 'resource selection function' (RSF) future polar bear habitat maps for September generated by George Durner and colleagues for various decades from 2046–2099. Durner and colleagues' 2007 description of this threshold is explicit in predicting that the Barents, Kara, Laptev, Chukchi and Southern Beaufort Sea would have 'very little' optimal polar bear habitat in summer.[92]

However, there was a significant problem with predicting disaster for polar bears based on this level of sea ice. As Figure 3.3 shows, even before the IUCN and ESA assessments, sea ice levels had already fallen below the sea ice levels predicted by the models.

But in fact the problem was even more extraordinary: as Figure 3.2b shows, the actual value of the September minimum at the time of the ESA decision was already below the predicted sea ice level *for mid-century* in five of the ten models.[93] These were levels that were supposed to bring about disaster for polar bears (Figure 3.3).[94] And we know that Amstrup noticed this extraordinary finding because he commented in his USGS report and to the media after its release, saying that the 2007 sea ice data suggested that the verdict for polar bears was probably 'too conservative' and that the situation was 'worse than we thought.'

Polar bear populations and predictions of decline

In order to understand what polar bear scientists were saying about future population declines, we first need to understand their starting point for the predictions: the population at the time.

Counting polar bears

For management purposes, the PBSG divides polar bears into more than a dozen discrete geographical subpopulations. The boundaries of these areas have been changed somewhat over the years; but at present there are 19 of them, covering all the available Arctic sea ice habitat (Figure 2.1).¶

Because of the nature of the Arctic environment, only estimates of polar bear numbers are available. Some of these are less than satisfactory, being decades-old, and based on limited studies rather than comprehensive survey counts. Consider, for example, the estimate for the Laptev Sea population prepared by the PBSG for the IUCN assessment. The estimate of 1000 polar bears (a range of 800–1200) has not changed since 1993, even though decades of protection from over-hunting should have led to a higher population. Meanwhile, the PBSG's tentative estimate for East Greenland – 2,000 bears – was the low end of an estimate of 2,000–4,000, also proposed in 1993. This had been justified at the time by a mere suggestion that a minimum population size of about 2000 – but perhaps as large as 2,500 – would be required to support the intensity of harvest observed in the 1990s.[95]

¶See p. 6.

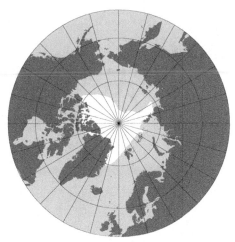

(a) Sea ice extent (>50% ice concentration) on 16 September 2007.

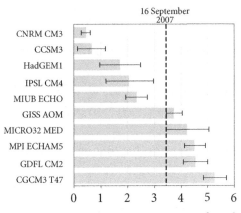

(b) Ten predictions of ice concentrations at 2045–2054.

Figure 3.2: Amstrup was aware that sea ice had already declined.
Redrawn from Amstrup *et al.* (2008). Original caption: 'Area of sea ice extent (>50% ice concentration) on 16 September 2007, compared to 10 Intergovernmental Panel on Climate Change Fourth Assessment Report GCM mid century projections of ice extent for September 2045–2054 (mean 1 standard deviation, $n = 10$ years). Ice extent for 16 September 2007 was calculated using near-real-time ice concentration estimates derived with the NASA Team algorithm and distributed by the National Snow and Ice Data Center (http://nsidc.org). Note that five of the models we used in our analyses project more perennial sea ice at mid century than was observed in 2007. This suggests our projections for the future status of polar bears may be conservative.'

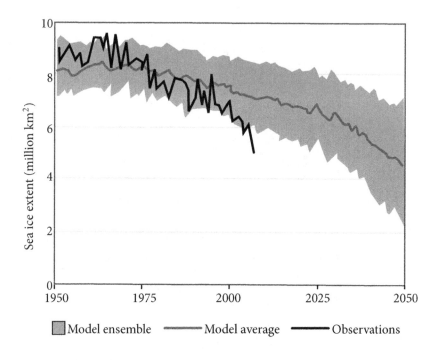

Figure 3.3: Predictions of Arctic sea ice extent vs. observations.
Redrawn from ACIA 2004.

There were other oddities with the PBSG figures too. The estimate for the Chukchi Sea, of 3,000–5,000, as assessed by Belikov in 1993, had became 2000–5,000 in the 1993 PBSG meeting report, 2,000 in the 2005 report, and 'unknown' thereafter.[96] And a preliminary estimate of 2,997 bears for the 2004 Barents Sea subpopulation, which had appeared in the 2005 PBSG meeting report,[97] was later amended to 2,644 by the original investigators, and then simplified to 2,650. However, it appears that the preliminary estimate of '2,997' was the one used in the assessments.[98,**]

The ESA predictions

Rather than prepare predictions for all 19 subpopulations, the USGS predictive models summarised these into four newly-defined sea ice 'ecoregions' (see Table 3.1).

Sea ice ecoregions were a new concept developed for this analysis and were based on 'current and projected sea ice conditions'.[99] For example, the 'Sea-

---

** The 2015 IUCN assessment used the 2,644 figure.

Table 3.1: Polar bear subpopulations within USGS-defined sea ice ecoregions.

Sea ice ecoregion	Subpopulation
Seasonal	
	W. Hudson Bay
	S. Hudson Bay
	Foxe Basin
	Davis Strait
	Baffin Bay
Divergent	
	Barents Sea
	Kara Sea
	Laptev Sea
	Chukchi Sea
	Southern Beaufort Sea
Convergent	
	Northern Beaufort Sea
	East Greenland
Archipelago	
	Kane Basin
	M'Clintock Channel
	Viscount Melville
	Gulf of Boothia
	Lancaster Sound
	Norwegian Bay

Note the Arctic Basin, while considered a subpopulation region by the PBSG, was not considered an ecotype by the USGS. See text for definitions of each ecotype.

sonal' ice ecoregion comprises all subpopulation regions where sea ice melts completely during the summer, stranding polar bears onshore (Western Hudson Bay, Southern Hudson Bay, Foxe Basin, Davis Strait, and Baffin Bay). The 'Divergent' ecoregion comprises all subpopulation regions where sea ice recedes from the coast into the Arctic Basin during the summer, leaving bears the option of staying onshore or remaining on the sea ice (Southern Beaufort Sea, Chukchi Sea, Laptev Sea, Kara Sea, Barents Sea). The geography of the ecoregions is shown in Figure 3.4.

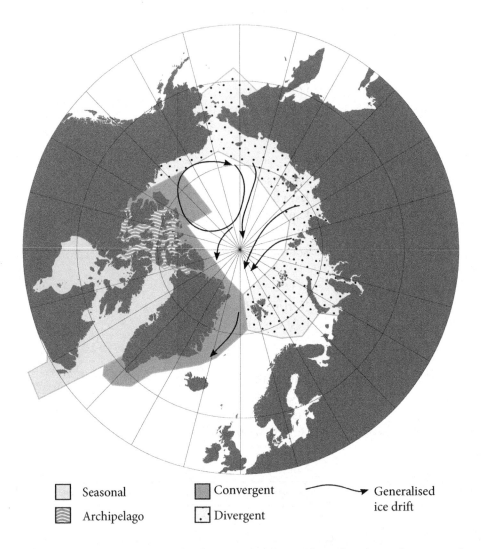

Seasonal	Convergent	Generalised ice drift
Archipelago	Divergent	

Figure 3.4: Boundaries of polar bear ecoregions and predominant direction of sea ice drift.

All polar bears in Seasonal and Divergent sea ice regions (two thirds of the world total) were predicted by computer models to be wiped out by 2050.[100] Redrawn from: US Geological Survey image.

The ESA predictive method used a statistical approach called 'Bayesian forecasting' (sometimes called a 'belief network'), a method that attempts to use subjective beliefs or assumptions in place of facts when the facts necessary are not available. In this case, it involved taking one person's subjective opinion about how polar bears in different ecoregions would respond to various sea ice changes. That person was USGS biologist, Steven Amstrup,[101] whose beliefs were fed into a computer model of polar bear survival that used predicted ice conditions up to the year 2100 to see how populations in each ecoregion might fare.

Although the polar bear habitat predictive model used to support the ESA decision utilised only data from the Divergent and Convergent ecoregions, summer sea ice coverage in the Seasonal ecoregion was also forecast to decline, although without being specifically discussed.[102] It seems to have been assumed that if models predicted Divergent ecoregion populations of polar bears would be wiped out by 2050 based on sea ice declines, those in the Seasonal ecoregion would disappear as well.

The starting point for the predictions was an estimated total of 17,300 bears in the Seasonal and Divergent ecoregions together (7,800 in Seasonal plus 9,500 in Divergent), and a global total of 24,500 bears,[103] somewhat higher than the global total of 22,500 (20,000–25,000) offered by the PBSG at the time.[104,††]

Forty-five years from 2005 (that is, 2050 or 2045–2054) was considered the 'foreseeable future', representing three generations of polar bears at fifteen years each.[106] Within this foreseeable future, the USGS models predicted that if minimum sea ice conditions in 8 out of 10 years (or even 4 out of 5 years) declined to about 3–5m km^2,[107] extirpation[‡‡] of polar bears from all subpopulations within the vulnerable 'Seasonal' ice and 'Divergent' ice ecoregions was 'most likely'.[108] In other words, ten subpopulations, amounting to a total of 17,300 polar bears, would be wiped out completely by 2050, leaving only about 8,100 bears remaining.

Bears in the Archipelago ecoregion were predicted to persist at 2050, but to possibly decline in population size by 2100, while bears in the Convergent ecoregion were predicted to persist through 2050 but would 'most probably' be extirpated by 2080.

If the global population at that time was indeed around 24,500, this consti-

---

††Since they did not state what figure they used for the Kara Sea (which had no estimate at all in the 2005 PBSG report), 2,000 was assumed in my comparisons because only this figure generates the ecoregion total used by the USGS researchers.[105]

‡‡'Extirpation' means a subpopulation (or 'ecoregion') is reduced to zero, while 'extinction' means the entire species (the global population) is reduced to zero.

tuted a predicted decline of approximately 67%.*

The Red List predictions

The Red List assessors took a more generalised approach than the USGS researchers who prepared the ESA assessment,[109] although they too considered what would happen over three polar bear generations of 15 years each.[110] However, conclusions reached were similar, if only slightly less alarming: they predicted a decline in the global polar bear population of more than 30% by 2050, based on forecast sea ice declines to about 3–5m km^2.

The hypothesis

Thus both agencies agreed that a significant decline in polar bear numbers was highly likely to occur by 2050, given the sea ice predictions made in 2005/2006. Their claims thus represent clear hypotheses that can be tested.

---

*Actually 71%, or about two thirds of the total.

Chapter 4

Testing the hypotheses

Arctic Sea Ice Melting Faster Than Predicted

Arctic sea ice is melting at a significantly faster rate than projected by even the most advanced computer models, a new study concludes. 'While the ice is disappearing faster than the computer models indicate, both observations and the models point in the same direction: The Arctic is losing ice at an increasingly rapid pace and the impact of greenhouse gases is growing,' said study team member Marika Holland of the National Center for Atmospheric Research ... The shrinking ice may actually be about 30 years ahead of model predictions....'

LiveScience, 11 January 2008[111]

The consensus among polar bear scientists was that large declines in sea ice habitat would lead to a dramatic reduction of polar bear numbers. How have those predictions turned out in practice? In this chapter, I consider what has actually happened to sea ice in the intervening years, and what has happened to polar bear populations.

Sea ice observations

Records of sea ice for the period 2007–2016 (see, for example, Figure 4.1) show that coverage for September has been well below 6m km^2 since 2007, and fell to 3–5m km^2 in eight of those ten years.

Examination of the records for particular Arctic locations highlights these dramatic changes (Table 4.1). Published analyses for the Beaufort Sea, for example, show that during the period 2007–2015, the length of the ice-free season over the continental shelf area was more than 127 days, a level said to be critical for polar bears.[113] Meanwhile, subpopulations in the Seasonal ecoregion also experienced significant losses of summer sea ice after 2006. Observations for Foxe Basin, a subpopulation with seasonal ice in the northern portion of Hudson Bay, showed that the length of the season with the least favourable habitat for

31

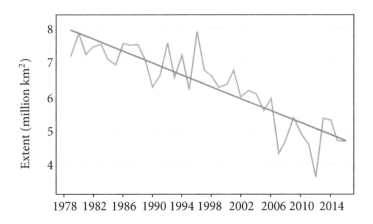

Figure 4.1: Average ice extent for September, 1979–2016, concentration >15%.
Redrawn from NASA's NSIDC Sea Ice Index.[112]

polar bears (≤30% ice concentration, in summer) increased from three months to five,[114] while in the rest of Hudson Bay the ice-free season increased by approximately three weeks in the late 1990s, leaving Southern Hudson Bay and Western Hudson Bay bears onshore for almost five months compared to about four months previously.[115] In Baffin Bay and Davis Strait (west of Greenland), there has been a significant decrease in sea ice concentrations preferred by polar bears between 15 May and 15 October.[116]

Other measures of ice cover tell a similar story. Recently, Harry Stern and Kristin Laidre devised a method for describing sea ice habitat similarly across all 19 polar bear subpopulations.[117] Their method, which tracks the calendar date when the area of 15% ice concentration rises above (or falls below) a midpoint threshold in winter or summer, respectively, showed a marked decline in summer sea ice since 2007 within all USGS-defined polar bear ecoregions. Even allowing for the uncertainties in the sea ice computer models used by USGS analysts* – and the fact that most agencies track ice concentrations of >15% (rather than the >50% concentration used by USGS biologists) – it is clear that conditions not anticipated until mid-century had become reality by 2007.

Here's the bottom line. The ESA decision of 2008 predicted a catastrophic decline in the global population of polar bears by 2050, as a direct effect of sea ice losses hitting a particular threshold. But *when* the threshold is breached is irrelevant. If summer sea ice drops abruptly below the critical level, and remains that low year after year, polar bear numbers should still drop by such a large

---

*Discussed in DeWeaver (2007).

Table 4.1: Sea ice loss 1979–2014, by subpopulation and ecoregion.

Subpopulation by sea ice ecoregion	Days lost* per year (1979–2014)
Seasonal	
Baffin Bay	1.27
Davis Strait	1.71
Foxe Basin	1.15
Western Hudson Bay	0.86
Southern Hudson Bay	0.68
Divergent	
Barents Sea	4.11
Kara Sea	1.70
Laptev Sea	1.35
Chukchi Sea	0.90
Southern Beaufort Sea	1.75
Convergent	
East Greenland	1.07
Northern Beaufort Sea	0.93
Archipelago	
Kane Basin	1.44
MClintock Channel	1.12
Viscount Melville	1.26
Gulf of Bothia	1.88
Lancaster Sound	1.08
Norwegian Bay	0.73

*Change in number of days with ice cover of >15% concentration per year. Lowest and highest values are shaded. Source: Regehr *et al.* (2016).

amount that polar bears would become truly 'Endangered' (at high risk of extinction). So a dramatic decline in polar bear number was what the public was promised as sea ice went into a 'death spiral'; but that's not what they got.

Observations of population numbers

As we have seen, Amstrup and colleagues at the USGS stated in their original supporting document:[118]

> Our modeling suggests that realization of the sea ice future which is cur-
> rently projected would mean loss of $\approx$ 2/3 of the world's current polar
> bear population by mid-century.

But Amstrup's statement was really a summary of the research that underlay
it, which concluded that if future sea ice dropped below a particular threshold,
bears in Seasonal and Divergent ecoregions would disappear. The sum of all
bears residing in those two 'doomed' ecoregions comprise roughly two thirds
of all the polar bears in the world. His summary statement then, is a testable
hypothesis that can be evaluated using two sets of data: once summer sea ice
extent falls to the predicted levels then polar bear population numbers should
fall too. And since sea ice levels for 2007–2016 have already dropped to, and
mostly remained at, that predicted level, the hypothesis is ripe for testing. We
can test whether the global total declined (as per Amstrup's summary statement)
using the global population total but we can also test if either, or both, of the Seasonal and Divergent ecoregions were extirpated as predicted, using population
numbers generated for those regions alone.

A great deal of suitable data is available to allow us to assess whether polar
bear populations in the apparently vulnerable Seasonal and Divergent ecoregions have been extirpated, as predicted by the USGS, or if the global population has declined by as much as 67% (or even less than 67% but by more than
30%, if the more reasonable IUCN prediction is correct).[†] There are, however,
some complications.

Firstly, in 2015 the IUCN reassessed the status of the polar bear. Several new
subpopulation counts were completed as part of this exercise, and several more
in 2016. Thus for the purposes of testing the USGS hypothesis, I will consider
the population counts at 2016 – the most up-to-date ones – correcting, where
necessary, for known flaws. However, I will also mention the IUCN numbers as
reported in 2015 because these are relevant to testing the IUCN hypothesis.

Although new data are not available for all subpopulations, counts have now
been completed for several critical ones that were unsurveyed in 2005. So the
Kara Sea and Chukchi Sea, to which the USGS and IUCN assigned ballpark
estimates of 2,000 bears each in 2005, have now been properly surveyed. The
new estimates are 3,200 for the Kara Sea and 2,937 for the Chukchi Sea.[‡,119]
Note, however, that the latter survey was not completed in time for inclusion in
the 2015 IUCN assessment.

[†] Because the prediction made by the IUCN PBSG calls for a less extreme decline based on
similar sea ice criteria, I first test the USGS hypotheses and note where the IUCN prediction fits
in.

[‡] From 2013 and 2016 surveys respectively.

Similarly, a new estimate for the Barents Sea was completed in 2015, but just too late to be included in the 2015 IUCN assessment. According to a press release issued by the Norwegian Polar Institute, which conducted the survey, the 2015 population in the Svalbard portion of the Barents Sea had increased by 42% (from 685 to 975, an increase of 290) over a similar count conducted in 2004.[120] This was apparently anticipated, despite poor sea ice conditions since 2004, because hunting is still prohibited in the area.[121] This number was confirmed in the 2017 published account of the study, but the increase was said to be not statistically significant.[122]

However, there's another problem with this estimate. 'Svalbard' is not a recognised PBSG subpopulation: the Svalbard archipelago forms part of the Barents Sea subpopulation area. Therefore, the survey is not very useful unless it can be extrapolated to the subpopulation as a whole. However, polar bears have been known to roam widely in the Barents Sea since research on them began,[123] and there is no reason to think that the population changes seen in the Svalbard part of the subpopulation should not also apply to the rest of the subpopulation. So while the authors of the study did not perform such an extrapolation, for my analysis I have assumed that the 42% increase found applies across the entire region.[§] This gives a 2016 estimate for the Barents Sea subpopulation of 3,749, as listed in Table 4.2. This estimate fits well with the comment by Aars and colleagues that in 2004 there were 'about three times' as many bears in the Russian sector as in Svalbard.[126] Using that 2004 Norwegian-to-Russian bear ratio, the Svalbard figure of 975 in 2015 generates an estimate of about 2900 for the entire region, not far off the estimate of 3749 based on an overall 42% increase. The extrapolated Barents Sea figures (based on recent Svalbard data) are especially important since this region is one of only three – Western Hudson Bay and Southern Hudson Bay are the others – for which survey data span the entire 2005–2016 period considered in the hypothesis (although those for Kane Basin and Baffin Bay are almost as long).

The vulnerable ecoregions

The population data for the allegedly vulnerable Seasonal and Divergent ecoregions are shown in Table 4.2. It is clear that neither of the two ecoregions has experienced the predicted extirpation of polar bears. In fact, not a single one of the ten subpopulations within these two ecoregions has been extirpated. The

---

[§]Using the estimate for 2004 of 2,650 derived by Aars and colleagues.[124] Eric Regehr and colleagues performed a similar extrapolation during their analysis of Chukchi Sea survey data that reflected only the US portion of the subpopulation area.[125]

THE POLAR BEAR CATASTROPHE THAT NEVER HAPPENED

Table 4.2: Changes in subpopulation size estimates, 2005 and 2016.

Subpopulation	Estimates 2005	Estimates 2016	Last estimate	Ref.	Comment
W. Hudson Bay*	935	842	2016	[1]	Methods differ between years
S. Hudson Bay*	1,000	780	2016	[2]	
Foxe Basin	2,119	2,580	2010		
Davis Strait	1,650	2,158	2007		
Baffin Bay*	2,074	2,826	2013	[3]	
Seasonal total	7,778	9,196			
S. Beaufort Sea	1,500	907	2010	[4]	Methods differ between years
Chukchi Sea*	2,000	2,937	2016	[5]	
Laptev Sea	1,000	1,000	1993		2005 estimate unchanged since 1993
Kara Sea	2,000	3,200	2013	[6]	2005 estimate was a USGS guess
Barents Sea*	2,997	3,749	2015	[7]	1997 figure used for 2005 estimate
Divergent total	9,497	11,798			
Total	17,275	20,994			

Sources: Except where noted (*), numbers are the same as those used in Aars et al. (2006) or Wiig et al. (2015). See text regarding estimates for WH, BB, BS, KS, CS. Sources: [1] Dyck et al. (2017), [2] Obbard et al. (2018); [3] 2013 estimate from SWG 2016. [4] Regehr et al. (2006), Bromaghin et al. (2015); [5] Regehr et al. (2018) for 2016 estimate; AC SWG (2018) for 2016 estimate; [6] Amstrup et al. (2007); [7] Aars et al. (2006).

36

polar bear population of the Seasonal ecoregion went from about 7,778 in 2005 to approximately 9,196 in 2016 (an 18.2% increase), while that for the Divergent ecoregion rose from 9,497 to 11,798 (a 24% increase). Note, however, that it is likely that due to inherent error ranges in individual estimates, these increases are not statistically significant and may indicate stable rather than increasing populations. Overall, as of 2016, an estimated 20,994 bears lived in the Seasonal and Divergent ecoregions, up 21.5% from the 2005 estimate. Again, this is likely not a statistically significant increase but is nevertheless evidence that a catastrophic decline has not occurred.

Only one of the ten subpopulations predicted to be extirpated – the Southern Beaufort Sea – experienced a statistically significant decline. That assessment was based on an analysis published by Jeff Bromaghin and colleagues in 2015.[127] The paper combined 2001–2006 data for the Alaskan portion of the Southern Beaufort and 2007–2010 data for the entire range, to give a ten-year time series. The conclusion of the study was that a marked drop in bear numbers had occurred over the period 2004–2006 (25–50%), in the middle of the survey period. This statistically significant decline was then blamed – in the paper's conclusions and to the media – on declining summer sea ice. What the authors failed to comment upon, however, was that in the two years immediately prior to the decline, there had been an even more dramatic *increase* in polar bear numbers (see Figure 4.2). In other words, two large fluctuations in population – one up, one down – had occurred during the decade covered by the study but only the decline was mentioned as significant.‖ This suggests that the decline of 2004–2006 may have been a natural and quite temporary fluctuation, and not part of a long-term downward trend caused by lack of summer sea ice. In fact, as Bromaghin and colleagues admit in their paper, by 2007 the survival of bears had started to turn around, and by 2010 numbers were going back up, despite sea ice levels already having reached levels only predicted for mid-century. Moreover, as I explain in more detail in Chapter 5, the Southern Beaufort is a special case due to the unique sea ice conditions there, which cause polar bear numbers to fluctuate in a way not seen in any other Divergent subpopulation.

The Bromaghin study had another problem. There were also known issues with the validity of the estimates for the last few years of the survey. The Southern Beaufort is shared between the US and Canada. As noted above, USGS researchers had surveyed the US portion right through from 2002 to 2010, but the Canadian portion had only been surveyed from 2007 to 2010. This meant that

---

‖ Similarly, back in 2006 when Regehr and colleagues published their population size document on the Southern Beaufort for the ESA decision[128] only data from 2004–2006 was used, even though data from 2001–2003 was also available.

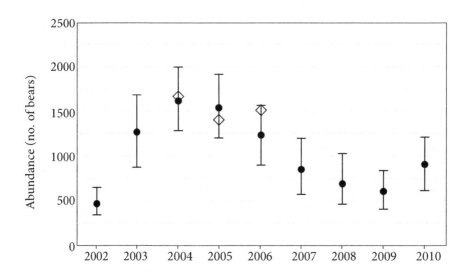

Figure 4.2: Bromaghin's estimates of polar bear numbers in the Southern Beaufort.

Redrawn from Bromaghin *et al.* (2015). Excerpt from original caption: 'Error bars represent 90% bias-corrected confidence intervals based on 100 bootstrap samples. Prior estimates (Regehr *et al.*, 2006) are shown for comparative purposes (open diamonds...)'.

the model they used to estimate the total population size incorporated assumptions about how many bears were missed by not counting Canadian bears in those early years. And the task of estimating the uncounted bears was made even more complex because the methods used by the US and Canadian researchers were different,¶ a point confirmed by the PBSG point in their 2016 meeting report.[129] This may well have skewed results and thus invalidated Bromaghin's conclusion that an overall decline in population size had occurred by 2010.

All things considered, the Southern Beaufort is a special case with respect to population size and should be used with caution when discussing what has happened with polar bears in general.

However, numbers in two other subpopulations – Western and Southern Hudson Bay – did decline over the 2005–2016 period, although both changes were statistically insignificant. For the latest Southern Hudson survey, Martyn Obbard and colleagues used an additional statistical method known as 'Monte

---

¶Such as which bears were captured, and where.

Carlo simulation' to justify their conclusion that the population decline of 17% was probably real, but as far as I could determine, this approach has never been used in the analysis of polar bear survey data before.[130] In Western Hudson, meanwhile, all of the population counts since 2004 have used different methodologies and survey designs. According to Markus Dyck, who conducted the 2016 aerial survey,[131] only two surveys of the subpopulation can be reliably compared: the one from 2011, with an estimate of 949 (range 618–1280) and the one from 2016, with an estimate of 842 (range 562–1121). The apparent 11% decline between the two is not statistically significant. Furthermore, both are likely not statistically distinguishable from the estimate of 935 calculated in 2004. It is noteworthy that an estimate of 1,030 bears (range 754–1,406), generated by an aerial survey of the entire region in 2011, is considered by the PBSG to be the most reliable and representative of the entire region.[132]

In contrast, six subpopulations (Baffin Bay, Barents Sea, Davis Strait, Foxe Basin, Chukchi Sea, Kara Sea) increased between 2005 and 2016, although in most cases not by a statistically significant amount.** The Davis Strait increase of 31% was, however, statistically significant and this is therefore considered the only officially 'increasing' subpopulation.[134] However, only real or imagined differences in methods precluded the 36% increase in Baffin Bay and the 22% increase in Foxe Basin from being statistically significant: both are considered to be 'stable' and healthy subpopulations.[135] Only the large margin of error prevented the 42% increase for the Barents Sea from being statistically significant, and previous estimates for the Chukchi and Kara Seas were not precise enough to calculate significance.

In summary, the population estimates for polar bears residing within Seasonal and Divergent ecoregions have increased or remained stable despite the realization of summer sea ice declines that were predicted to drive population sizes to zero. Although there appears to be a slight increase in overall population, it is probably not statistically significant.

The global population

But do global numbers show the same pattern? In a word, yes. In 2005, when they made their predictions of doom for the polar bear, the global population was approximately 22,500,†† although, as noted above, Amstrup and colleagues at the USGS used a figure of 24,500 for their analysis in 2007. However, by 2015,

---

** Although often denigrated as a 'guess' the CS estimate of 2,000 was nevertheless used in several recent studies that required a population size.[133]

†† Their estimate was 20,000–25,000.

that number had officially increased to about 26,000,[‡‡] according to the IUCN Red List reassessment.[136] And by 2016, the global population was even greater: considering all subpopulations, including those shown in Table 4.2, the total was about 29,500, albeit with a wide margin of error.[137]

So, against all USGS expectations, the growth of the global population has come primarily from real or apparent increases in subpopulations within the allegedly 'vulnerable' Seasonal and Divergent ecoregions: the Chukchi Sea, Kara Sea, Barents Sea, Davis Strait and Foxe Basin subpopulations. These increases more than offset the moderate (and possibly temporary) drop in the Southern Beaufort population and the slight declines recorded for Western and Southern Hudson Bay. Only in the Kane Basin subpopulation, in the Archipelago ecoregion, did a population increase occur that was outside the two ecoregions considered the most vulnerable to decline: a statistically significant 118% increase (from 164 to 357).[138]

Yet remarkably, the 2015 Red List assessment declared the global population trend for polar bears to be 'Unknown', based in part on unevaluated subpopulations and out-of-date surveys.[139] This is unfortunate, when set against the data collected up to 2016, which shows there was a net *increase* between 2005 and 2016 in studied portions of the population worldwide. This newer data yields a conservative global total of about 29,500 bears for 2016 – a 20% increase since 2005.* There is therefore little rationale for supposing unstudied subpopulations have fared differently.

In summary, despite the fact that sea ice coverage since 2007 has repeatedly reached levels not predicted until 2050 or later, not only has the estimated global population size of polar bears not declined by 67% (i.e. to 8100) – or even just over 30% – it has increased by approximately 20% above the estimate used by the USGS analysts who made the predictions.[140] Such 'a modest upward trend' was predicted by critics of the USGS forecasts, based on upward trends in previous decades due to hunting restrictions that are still in place.[141]

Even without a statistical analysis of the estimated data, the USGS hypothesis that global polar bear population numbers would decline by 67% in response to rapid and sustained sea ice coverage of 3–5m km^2 in summer must be rejected, as must the IUCN hypothesis that the decline would be a more modest 30% or more given the same ice conditions. These conclusions are supported by the lack of any major documented decline in subpopulation size worldwide, and the failure of any subpopulation to be extirpated, despite ten full years of

---

[‡‡] A range of 22,000–31,000.

*Moreover, several recent survey results – for Viscount Melville, M'Clintock Channel, and Gulf of Boothia – are still pending, so the total may rise still further.

realised summer sea ice loss to levels below the stated critical threshold.

Chapter 5

What went wrong?

There's no doubt about what's happening to Arctic sea ice ... but their populations aren't declining as was once expected,' said Douglas Clark, a University of Saskatchewan researcher who has worked on human polar bear interaction.

National Post, 2 March 2017[142]

The evidence that polar bear populations did not decline as expected in response to the persistently low sea ice levels seen since 2007 poses an obvious question. Why were the predictions made by the IUCN and USGS biologists in 2006 and 2008 so far off the mark? What went wrong?

In short, recent studies suggest that researchers vastly over-estimated the importance of summer feeding for polar bears. Perversely, they neglected to consider any negative effects of variable environmental conditions for any season except summer. The willingness of polar bear females to abandon traditional denning areas when sea ice conditions deteriorated was vastly underappreciated, as was the ability of bears to operate in sea ice that was less than ideal. Overall, polar bears turned out to be more flexible and resourceful than experts gave them credit for, population sizes were more naturally variable, and ringed and bearded seals turned out to respond much more positively to lower summer ice levels than anyone imagined. In other words, when they made their dramatic predictions, experts simply assumed they knew how polar bears and seals would respond to less summer ice before they had actually observed these animals dealing with less summer ice.

The importance (or otherwise) of summer ice

Polar bear researchers assumed that summer sea ice levels were important because they thought that summer feeding was important. It is now clear that they were wrong: well-fed bears seem able to survive a summer fast of five months, and perhaps more, no matter whether they spend that time on land or on the sea ice. Physiological studies have confirmed that polar bears that spend the summer on the sea ice often consume little or no food,[143] contradicting claims that loss of summer sea ice causes bears to miss essential feeding opportunities.

As noted above,* polar bears feed on ringed, bearded, and harp seal pups and attending adults in the spring, in a period concentrated on a few weeks between March/April and May/June. During this period, two-thirds of the yearly total of calories is consumed. The remainder is consumed in summer and winter but primarily in the late fall. This means that, while persisting ice in the Convergent and Archipelago ecoregions provides continuing feeding opportunities, virtually all polar bears in the Seasonal and Divergent ecoregions effectively fast through the summer, living off their accumulated fat from June or July right through to November, whether they spend this time on land or on the sea ice.[144] One or two successful seal hunts – or foods scavenged or hunted onshore – may decrease slightly the amount of weight lost during the summer fast, but this will make little difference for most bears.[145] A few persistent individuals may consume such abundant local resources as eggs of ground-nesting geese and marine birds or the refuse left after aboriginal whaling, but these appear to be the exception rather than the rule and they seem to get no survival advantage from eating these foods.[146] Similarly, feeding at human garbage dumps was not found to confer any reproductive or survival advantage to polar bears, at least in Western Hudson Bay in the early 1980s.[147]

In the Divergent ecoregion, bears can choose to come ashore over the summer or remain on the ice. For those that come ashore, however, the expected decline in health that was expected to be associated with a longer time spent on land has not materialised. For example, even though the Chukchi and Beaufort Seas have experienced some of the most dramatic declines of summer and early fall sea ice, polar bears in these areas that spent longer ashore seem to have suffered no negative effects. Karyn Rode and colleagues reported that, for 2008–2013, the average time on land for Chukchi Sea bears increased by 30 days (compared to 1986–1995) but there was no concomitant change in body condition or reproductive parameters.[148] Similarly, while USGS researchers working in the Beaufort Sea found that, between 2010 and 2013, three times as many Southern Beaufort bears came ashore as did before 2000 – and that those bears spent an average of 31 more days onshore than they did in the late 1990s – they seemed to experience no negative effects from the increased time on land.[149]

Similarly, on the other side of the Divergent ecoregion, the Svalbard portion of the Barents Sea subpopulation also saw an increase in polar bear numbers between 2004 and 2015 (as discussed in Chapter 4) during a period of pronounced low summer sea ice cover.[150] Throughout this period, there was no associated

*See p. 5.

decline in body condition of adult males, nor any persistent drop in cub production. Ongoing research shows this pattern has continued into 2018.[151]

Therefore, the recent data shows that at least two Divergent ecoregion subpopulations (Chukchi Sea and Barents Sea) – and possibly a third (Kara Sea) – have been stable or increasing alongside the decline in sea ice levels. This is in stark contrast to the situation in the Southern Beaufort Sea, where polar bears have been reportedly declining since the mid-2000s. Unfortunately, however, at the time the ESA decision was being made, the Southern Beaufort was chosen by Amstrup's team to represent the entire Divergent ecoregion:[152] even though Barents Sea bears had been almost as well-studied up to 2005, the USGS was able to commission research dedicated to the US portion of the Southern Beaufort to generate data that fit their model requirements.[†] USGS researchers assumed that the only habitat change capable of negatively affecting polar bears was an increase in the length of the ice-free period in summer, presumably caused by manmade climate change. Therefore, only one seasonal ice variable was used in their predictive models: summer ice extent. The fact that Southern Beaufort was a unique region where spring ice thickness conditions varied naturally was conveniently left out of the model. I discuss this important factor in more detail in Chapter 5.

In contrast to the Divergent ecoregion, when sea ice melts completely in the Seasonal ecoregion, bears are forced ashore, where they largely go without food for the duration. In Western Hudson Bay, where polar bears have been studied longer than anywhere else in the Arctic, the onshore period lengthened suddenly in about 1995, and it was about three weeks longer in 1995–2015 than it was from the late 1960s to 1995.[154] A decline in population size, cub survival, and body condition were initially blamed on this three-week increase,[155] but as I explain in more detail in Chapter 11, there have been no data published since 2004 that support such a conclusion. And in Baffin Bay, Davis Strait, and Foxe Basin, where bears have had to spend up to two months longer onshore than they did in the 1980s, there have been few consequences for their health or survival.[156]

Before moving on, it is interesting to consider how much polar bear scientists' erroneous ideas about the effect of sea ice declines on polar bear survival were driven by the global warming 'meme' and the sharp declines in summer ice (but not winter ice) seen in the years around the time of the predictions. The global warming narrative was certainly prominent at the time, but it was

---

[†]The ESA decision based on Amstrup's model[153] referenced four separate internal USGS reports on the Southern Beaufort Sea: Bergen *et al.* (2007), Regehr *et al.* (2007a), Rode *et al.* (2007) and Hunter *et al.* (2007).

convenient for other reasons. For example, it fitted the basic assumption that Stirling had been taught in the 1960s: that under natural conditions, Arctic sea ice should be a stable habitat that supported stable or growing populations of seals and polar bears.[157] And because human-caused global warming was considered 'unnatural', if ice habitat became 'unstable', polar bear numbers should have declined. Ironically, this concept of dividing the world into stable and unstable habitats and populations had been abandoned by virtually all other biologists by the 1990s.[158] In fact, Stirling himself had collected reams of data from the Southern Beaufort Sea and Western Hudson Bay (and published it!) showing it was simply not true fr polar bears and seals.[159] However, as well as fitting well with Stirling's assumptions, the idea of sea-ice stability also slotted nicely into the meme of human-caused global warming, which also assumed that sea ice was normally unchanging. It is little surprise then that the idea was so enthusiastically embraced that it did not get much skeptical scrutiny.

But even more than important to understanding how scientists got sea ice so wrong is the observation that Stirling and his students were probably facing a limited future in terms of funding and publication opportunities if they could not explain the fluctuations in polar bear cub survival, body condition and population size that were plaguing these, the two most-studied regions of the Arctic. The global warming hypothesis and their error about sea ice therefore probably saved their careers, at least temporarily.

Reduced sea ice has increased, not decreased food availability

Contrary to predictions, recent reductions of summer ice in the Chukchi Sea have been shown to be a huge benefit to ringed seals and bearded seals, which are the principal prey of polar bears.[160] Since ringed and bearded seals feed primarily during the ice-free season, the increase in productivity that came with less summer ice resulted in more healthy seal pups the following spring.[161] Senior seal researcher Lori Quakenbush recently confirmed earlier findings that Chukchi seals have done better in recent years than in the 1970s and 1980s, despite (or because of) less summer ice.[162]

The benefits to polar bears of abundant fat seal prey are pronounced: Rode and colleagues found that, compared to other subpopulations, the body condition of southern Chukchi Sea polar bears in 2008–2011 was second only to bears in Foxe Basin. The individual weights of three adult Chukchi Sea males they captured exceeded 544 kg (1200 lbs), far above the average of about 450 kg (992 lbs).[163] Contrary to expectations, Rode and colleagues also found that reproductive measures (reproductive rate, litter size, and percentage of females with cubs) for 2008–2011 were all better than in 1986–1994, despite the longer period of open water. Consequently, while a Chukchi Sea population count was not undertaken until 2016, comparison with indicators available from other regions, such as Foxe Basin, suggests the population has probably increased or is at least stable.[164] When the 2016 Chukchi Sea population survey was completed, USFWS biologist Eric Regher made the following statement:[165]

> Chukchi bears remain larger and fatter and have not seen downward trends in cub production and survival.

This result led authorities to increase the hunting quota for aboriginal residents from 58 to 85 bears per year.

In Davis Strait, meanwhile, a similar pattern of abundant seals and healthy bears is apparent, despite reduced summer ice. However, this outcome was driven more by the near-total collapse of the hunt for young harp seals in Eastern Canada in 2007–2011.[166] Without the hunt, the population size of harp seals almost doubled, from about 3.7 million in 2006 to 7.4 million in 2014.[167] A population survey completed in 2007 showed a substantial increase in polar bear numbers over previous estimates generated since the late 1970s.[168] With even more seals available after 2007, polar bear specialists have assumed that the number of Davis Strait bears has continued to climb since then. In 2016, this was the only Seasonal ecoregion subpopulation considered to be increasing by the PBSG.[169]

Bears turned out to be flexible and capable

In their attempts to predict how polar bears would respond to changing sea ice forecasted for future decades, polar bear scientists vastly underestimated the innate flexibility of polar bears and their prowess as marine mammals.

For example, polar bear females turn out to be quite willing to shift their preferred denning locations when sea ice conditions deteriorate. Among female bears tagged near Svalbard in the Barents Sea, more than usual have been documented denning on Franz Josef Land, 260 km (160 miles) to the east (in Russia), where sea ice conditions are less variable.[170] This shift in population is much more common now that sea ice conditions have changed, and has been so pronounced that the latest survey of Svalbard in 2015 suggested that perhaps only 200 bears now routinely visit the area.[171] However, this has not been a mass movement beyond the borders of the subpopulation as defined by the PBSG, but a shift within it: Franz Josef Land is well within the Barents Sea subpopulation region, across which polar bears are known to roam freely. In other words, Franz Josef Land and the sea ice around it have simply become more intensively utilised than they were in the 1980s.[172] Compared to 2004, many more bears were found on the pack ice to the east of the archipelago, so that overall there were 42% more bears recorded in the general area of Svalbard. It is not yet clear whether this shift has made possible the increased abundance (a net benefit) or if the increase in numbers would have taken place regardless (no negative effects).

Another unappreciated aspect of polar bears' adaptability is their ability to swim long distances without stopping and to dive for extended periods (>5 minutes) while hunting seals. Polar bears have long been known to be good swimmers,[173] but researchers assumed that large expanses of open water in a warmer world would present serious challenges. However, aside from a single anecdotal account of what was assumed to be four bears that drowned in open water during an early September storm in the Southern Beaufort Sea in 2004, there have been no further reports of polar bear deaths due to drowning during the open-water season.[174] Furthermore, no evidence has been presented to show that long-distance swims are detrimental to the health or survival of the species. Researchers Nicholas Pilfold and colleagues looked at swimming behaviour of Western Hudson Bay and Southern Beaufort Sea bears. They found that from 2007 to 2012, bears in WH made relatively few long-distance swims,[‡] but 60% of those started on pack ice and ended on land during sea ice breakup in July.[175] A larger number of SB bears undertook long-distance swims, but 80% of these took place before the September sea ice minimum, when bears started and ended their swims in the pack ice as the ice edge retreated north.

Another 2008 study recorded a spectacular 9-day, 687-km swim by an adult BS female with a yearling cub, part of an 1800-km trek across ice and water lasting 63-days. She was found to have lost 49 kg and was recaptured without her cub.[176] The authors of the study assumed the cub drowned, but that is just one calamity out of several possible options that could have befallen the youngster. Much has been made of the amount of weight she lost during her journey,[177] and unfortunately, no one knows for sure whether she was able to catch and eat a seal during her trip. However, a comparison shows the 49 kg she lost during her swim and subsequent walk over the ice was slightly less weight than a typical bear sitting on the shore of Western Hudson Bay would have lost over the same number of days, which would have been 54 kg or 119 lbs.[§]

Similarly, a recent paper by Norwegian polar bear specialists documented the swimming and diving capabilities of Svalbard area bears.[178] With large expanses of open water now more common around Svalbard than in the late 20th

---

[‡] More than 50 km.

[§] Derocher and Stirling 1995 determined typical weight loss by WH bears over the summer fast was 0.85 kg per day.

century, the swimming and diving abilities of polar bears are becoming apparent. The authors recorded the movements of one female who regularly (for four years in a row) traveled up the ice-free west cost of Spizbergen (whether she had cubs of the year or not), to feed on newborn harbour seals that had just been weaned:[179]

> The third example polar bear... swam regularly between islands and across fjords, even when accompanied by two [cubs of the year]. She exhibited a set temporal pattern to her space use along the west coast of Spitsbergen, where she moved north from Van Mijenfjorden to Prins Karls Forland and affiliated small islands (PKF), the latter area being the core breeding area for Svalbard's harbour seal population. Her time of arrival at PKF specifically coincided with the end of the harbour seal nursing period, when newly weaned pups were available... in June–July.

In addition, the authors stated that dives of over 5 minutes' duration were common and recorded some that went as deep as 13.9 m:

> Most polar bears seldom dive beyond 3–4 m. However, they are clearly physically and behaviourally capable of diving to greater depths. One individual in the study stood out in this regard, by diving more regularly to greater depths. This individual might be a specialist in aquatic stalking, as she also dove when she was offshore in the drifting sea ice. Alongside swimming below ice floes during aquatic stalking, accessing coastal underwater resources such as cadavers or seaweed are likely reasons for the dives made by polar bears in this study. It is well documented that macroalgae is part of the polar bear diet. [A colleague] reported seeing a female polar bear and her yearling cub diving to a depth of 3–4 m in February to retrieve seaweed, which they consumed. The maximum dive depth reported in this study was 13.9 m. Within this depth range, breath-hold abilities are not likely to limit the depth of dives.

This finding stands in marked contrast to an assertion by polar bear expert Ian Stirling that the three-minute underwater stalk of a bearded seal he and a photographer observed in late August 2014 north of Svalbard must be at the limit of its evolutionary ability to dive underwater:[180]

> ...increased diving ability cannot evolve rapidly enough to compensate for the increasing difficulty of hunting seals because of the rapidly declining availability of sea ice during the open-water period resulting from climate warming.

This under-appreciation of the physical capabilities of polar bears with respect to sea ice and open water is a result of the fact that researchers are only now beginning to see bears perform in all possible sea ice conditions. Back in 2006, it was certainly not possible for polar bear specialists to know how bears would respond to large expanses of open water between ice floes because such conditions had not been common up to that time. This means that polar bear experts like Steven Amstrup and Ian Stirling were guessing when they predicted in 2007 how the bears would respond to the vastly different ice conditions predicted decades into the future. And, as it turns out, their guesses were wrong.

So while it may be true that polar bears *prefer* sea ice of 50% concentration or greater over water less than 300 m deep (in other words, continental shelves), recent data show that this is not a requirement for survival. During the fall in Hudson Bay, for example, most bears leave shore to hunt for seals as soon as sea ice thickness makes it physically possible for them to do so; that is, when the ice concentration is only 5–10%.[181] And in the spring, on Hudson Bay and in the Southern Beaufort, some bears remain on ice that is well below 50% concentration – sometimes over deep water – for weeks on end, rather than go ashore or retreat to more highly concentrated pack ice. And they do this without obvious consequences.[182]

Data that couldn't be mentioned caused problems

As mentioned above, a huge amount of data from the Southern Beaufort Sea and Western Hudson Bay had been published that showed polar bears, ringed seals, and bearded seals did not have stable population sizes or live in stable habitats – even before summer sea ice took a plunge in 2007.[183] One of the reasons that the USGS hypothesis failed so spectacularly is that it ignored or misrepresented previous well-documented evidence of natural fluctuations in population size, body condition, and cub survival that had nothing to do with lack of summer sea ice. The complete focus on summer, when sea ice changes were so pronounced, allowed the evidence of both positive and negative winter and spring effects to be disregarded, in particular in the Southern Beaufort Sea and Western Hudson Bay.

The Southern Beaufort Sea appears to be different to all other Arctic regions. This is because natural fluctuations in winter and spring sea ice thickness periodically have devastating effects on polar bear health and survival. The first well-documented occurrences of thick spring ice were in 1974 and 1975, when multiyear ice from the north was driven onshore, compressing first year and fast ice,[||] causing it to buckle into a thick unbroken swathe.[184] More than a dozen peer-reviewed papers document that ringed seals and bearded seals subsequently left the area because of the lack of open leads and ice that was too thick in most places to maintain breathing holes. And because pregnant seals left before their critical birthing season, polar bears that didn't leave too suffered

---

[||] Fast ice is an unbroken expanse of ice attached to the shore, also known as 'shorefast' ice.

from lack of food. Similar but less severe events also occurred in the early 1960s, the mid-1980s, and early 1990s: about once every ten years.[185]

In the mid-1970s, methods of estimating bear numbers were crude compared to those used nowadays, but according to Ian Stirling and colleagues, the size of the polar bear population in the eastern portion of the Southern Beaufort Sea (then considered a discrete Canadian subpopulation) decreased by 45.6% between 1974 and 1975 (from 1,522 bears in 1974 to 828 in 1975).[186] However, it subsequently rebounded. Moreover, only some of the decline in numbers was due to bears dying of starvation: it was known that some bears left the area and some of these may have returned later.[187] This means that by the end of the 1970s, researchers had a good – and well-documented – understanding of the devastating effect that thick spring ice could have on bear populations.

This understanding becomes important when we look at the situation that developed around the time the USGS was preparing its study in support of the ESA decision. The USGS-led survey of the Southern Beaufort that was conducted in 2001–2006, which was used to support the ESA decision, coincided with a severe thick spring ice episode, which lasted from 2004 to 2006. These ice conditions were later described by Stirling and colleagues as so severe that 'only once, in 1974, did we observe similarly extensive areas of rubble, pressure ridges, and rafted floes'.[188] According to contemporary assessments by a number of seal and bear researchers, this period was as devastating to ringed seals and polar bears as the 1974–1976 episode had been.[189]

But surprisingly, when discussing the eastern half of the Southern Beaufort, the two USGS reports behind the ESA decision barely mention any of this. The pronounced lack of ringed seal pups and the thick ice conditions that their Canadian colleagues had found during the 2004 and 2005 spring field seasons barely warrant a mention. This is particularly surprising because Canadian Ian Stirling was a co-author of both reports.[190]

Instead, a statistically non-significant population decline was reported for the 2001–2006 period,[191] and this was blamed on the effects of reduced summer ice, a 'correlation implies causation' fallacy and an explanation not possible for the 1974–1976 event.[192] Conveniently, official accounts of the devastating years of 2002-2004 in the eastern Beaufort were not published until after the ESA listing process was finalised in early 2008.[193]

In 2015, Jeff Bromaghin's estimate¶ for the ten-year period 2001–2010 – using a newly-developed statistical method – reported that polar bear numbers had dropped by between 25% and 50% in 2004–2006.[194] Oddly, Bromaghin reiterated Stirling's 2008 observation that there had been thick spring ice in the

¶See p. 37.

mid-2000s, similar in scope to the 1974–1976 event. But they then ignored this in drawing their conclusions, presenting the population decline they calculated as a likely result of summer sea ice loss. Why? Because it had already been assumed, back in 2007, that summer ice loss was the only phenomenon that could cause the magnitude of population crash they had documented: a 25–50% decline.[195]

Overall, the failure of 2007 USGS models to take into account the well-documented negative effects of these periodic spring ice phenomena on Southern Beaufort polar bear health and survival means that neither the statistically insignificant population decline recorded by Regehr and colleagues in 2006 nor the 25–50% decline calculated by Bromaghin and colleagues in 2015 can be reliably attributed to effects of reduced summer sea ice.[196] Furthermore, the PBSG has conceded that because the field crews did not sample all regions during the most recent Southern Beaufort survey years (2007–2010), both the survival and abundance estimates in the Bromaghin paper may have been compromised.[197] In other words, the Southern Beaufort population may have recovered more quickly after 2006 than previously assumed, and from a decline that was not caused by loss of summer sea ice anyway.

Given that management of Southern Beaufort Sea polar bears is shared by the USA and Canada, it is pertinent to note the Canadian position on the status of this subpopulation, as well as others within their jurisdiction. In 2008, Canada's Committee on the Status of Endangered Wildlife (COSEWIC) listed the polar bear as a species of 'Special concern' but did not assess subpopulations residing outside, or not shared with, Canada.[198] Based on the same sea ice data as used in the 2006 IUCN Red List assessment, Canadian scientists determined that only two of Canada's thirteen polar bear subpopulations – Southern Beaufort Sea and Western Hudson Bay – had a 'high risk of declining by 30% or more over the next three polar bear generations (36 years)' due to reduced sea ice.[199] Although the models used by USGS researchers to support the ESA decision in 2007 were available to them, the Canadian committee did not use them in their appraisal. Nevertheless, it is apparent that, like USGS biologists and the USFWS, the COSEWIC committee accepted the fallacy that declining body condition and cub survival of Southern Beaufort Sea polar bears was an exclusive effect of summer sea ice loss. The same is true of the latest (2015) IUCN Red List assessment.[200],**

It is not just Southern Beaufort polar bears that have experienced periodic population size fluctuations, changes in body condition, and variations in cub

---

** In 2018, COSEWIC upheld the classification of 'special concern' for polar bears, which will stand for another ten years.

survival that undercut the USGS premise that all such changes must be caused by lack of summer sea ice; Western Hudson Bay bears have as well. The Seasonal ecoregion – of which Western Hudson bay forms a part – was not formally included in the USGS survival model; as noted above,[††] only the Divergent and Convergent ecoregions were assessed. However, evidence from Seasonal subpopulations was used to inform Amstrup's 'expert opinion' input to the predictive model, which is why the USGS document collection submitted to support the ESA decision included an article on the status of Western Hudson Bay,[201,‡‡] and also one about Southern Hudson Bay, also in the Seasonal ecoregion.[202]

As I mentioned in the introduction, although the 1980s and early 1990s were considered 'the good old days' as far as breakup and freeze-up of sea ice in Western Hudson Bay were concerned, polar bears had inexplicably not been doing very well. In the 1980s, weights of Western Hudson Bay females captured declined: the worst year for low spring weights was 1989 (although 1990 and 1991 were not much better), while the worst years for low fall weights were 1985 and 1990. Cub mortality also increased, with a marked increase in the loss of whole litters over what had been documented in the 1960s and 1970s.[203] Birth interval increased from two years to three, as the females who formerly weaned their cubs after their first winter on the ice started to keep their cubs with them for another year. All of these changes happened despite the fact that the population size estimate in 1987 through to 1989,[*] was the highest it had been since surveys had begun.[204]

Until the early 1990s, density-dependent effects (i.e. that the bear population had grown so large it had outstripped the food supply) were seen as the most likely explanation for the 1980s' decline in polar bear health and cub survival in Western Hudson Bay. However, senior Canadian polar bear specialist Ian Stirling was apparently also looking for other explanations: factors like spring sea ice thickness and snow depth over ice. He likely also considered potential changes in primary productivity – the term used to describe the almost microscopic-sized plants (algae) at the bottom of the food chain that get their energy from sunlight and CO_2 and which are subsequently eaten by shrimp-like animals called krill as well as by fish (which are themselves eaten by seals, which

---

[††] See p. 3.

[‡‡] It was actually very odd to have two USGS employees, Eric Regehr and Steven Amstrup, co-author a paper on WH bears with Canadian researchers Ian Stirling and Nick Lunn, and especially odd for Regehr to be lead author. Regehr and Amstrup never worked in WH: it was Stirling's research area. Regehr's WH paper was the only one of the package that had been formally peer-reviewed and published by the time the bundle was turned over to the USFWS. A few, but not all, were peer-reviewed and published after the fact (e.g. Amstrup *et al.* (2008); Durner *et al.* (2009); Hunter *et al.* (2010)).

[*] Best estimate 1,194, range 1,020–1,368.

are finally eaten by polar bears).[205] If primary productivity goes down, there is less to eat for the carnivores higher up in the food chain, such as fish, seals, and bears. Stirling, don't forget, had also been working in the eastern (Canadian) portion of the Southern Beaufort Sea in the 1970s and had seen first-hand the fluctuations in health and survival rates that periodically afflicted bears in that area.[206] One of the things that puzzled him was that the population declines seen in Western Hudson Bay lasted far longer (8–9 years) than declines in the Southern Beaufort (2–3 years).[207]

In an effort to unravel this conundrum, Stirling participated in a small research project on Hudson Bay ringed seals in the early 1990s. This revealed some support for the suggestion that seal numbers were down in 1989.[208] However, similar data from the 1980s showed there should have been lots of seals available between 1979 and 1988.[209] Some of the other possible shifts going on in Hudson Bay that might have affected the abundance of seals or the ability of polar bears to catch them, such as changes to sea ice thickness or the depth of snow over the ice, would have required studies be carried out in the winter and early spring. But doing field work in the winter in the Arctic was not just difficult, it may have been well nigh impossible, at least at that time. Even now, we have very few measurements of winter sea ice thickness or snow cover over the ice for Hudson Bay and the Southern Beaufort – or anywhere else in the Arctic, for that matter. It looked like Stirling was stumped. He was already having problems getting funding for his research: this was not only apparent from marked holes in the data published in the scientific literature, he later admitted as much to journalist Ed Struzik in a 2010 interview.[210]

As far as I can determine, it wasn't really that global warming offered Stirling an answer to his problems, but rather that it gave him something else to focus upon. Instead of trying to get research funds to unravel unsolvable problems of the past, he could instead look for ongoing and future evidence of the effects of global warming on polar bears and ringed seals. The new and very public focus on global warming, and especially the declines in Arctic sea ice that were expected to result from increased global temperatures, must have made Stirling sit up and pay attention. Hudson Bay was considered part of the Arctic because of its dry, continental climate and complete winter sea ice cover. Suddenly, a new focus for research in Western Hudson Bay – sea ice decline blamed on human-caused global warming – must have seemed full of potential. Stirling embraced the idea and by 1993, he and his student, Andrew Derocher, had published a theoretical paper on the topic.[211]

Putting those scientific troubles of the 1970s and 1980s into a metaphorical box and leaving them behind allowed Stirling and his students to move forward. But failing to take those unsettled issues into account meant that by 2006 – when the USGS survival models were being constructed – there was a fatal weak spot in the predictions. Because he hadn't figured out why populations varied naturally, his colleagues overestimated the potential effects of summer sea ice loss.

However, that was all in the future. By the late 1990s, the length of the sea ice season in Western Hudson Bay had indeed declined by about three weeks. However, the correlation with polar bear productivity produced only a weak trend that was not statistically significant.[212] And it did not explain the 1980s' decline in cub survival and body condition, which had happened before the sea ice changes occurred. It was not until the early 2000s that blaming global warming for the sea ice decline and subsequent effects on polar bear health and survival began to look feasible.[213] However, if you look closely at those publications that profess to show a correlation between sea ice cover and polar bear health and survival in Western Hudson Bay, you'll see that virtually all of the inconvenient data from the 1970s – which made the 1980s and early 1990s look alarming by comparison – has been left out. All of a sudden, the 1980s and early 1990s were 'the good old days'. A start date of 1980 was necessary for correlating sea ice observations for the global warming hypothesis because good satellite data only began in 1979, but that start date left out more than ten years of critical polar bear data. In the 2006 paper by Stirling and sea ice expert Claire Parkinson, for example, the polar bear data for Western Hudson Bay starts in 1980, even though data going back to 1965 were available.[214]

Hybridization and cannibalism did not increase

Quite simply, concerns about widespread hybridization and escalating cannibalism were over-hyped. Claims that widespread hybridization of polar bears with grizzlies was underway and might eventually wipe out polar bears were disproven in 2016 and 2017 by DNA testing.[215] A putative hybrid, shot near Arviat in Western Hudson Bay in 2016, turned out to be a blond grizzly, not a hybrid. In addition, all of the hybrids documented in the western Canadian Arctic between 2006 and 2012 turned out to be the progeny of a single polar bear female who mated with two male grizzly bears.

As might be expected of a recovering population, western tundra grizzlies are moving southeast into Manitoba, as far as Western Hudson Bay, and north into the central Canadian Arctic.[216] Polar bear populations in these regions have not contracted: it is the grizzlies that are invading established polar bear territory, which they do primarily in the spring and early summer when sea ice is extensive. The offspring of this single polar bear female with an 'atypical mating preference' do not constitute an escalation in hybridization between polar bears and grizzlies. This phenomenon has been documented occasionally in the

Canadian Arctic since grizzlies were spotted in the region more than 100 years ago.

Cannibalism is another natural phenomenon in polar bears, as it is in all bears.[217] A few incidents recorded between 2004 and 2015 cannot be cited as evidence of an increasing trend in polar bear cannibalism because there have been no comprehensive scientific studies to which they can be compared.[218] Accounts of cannibalism in the literature go back decades, but virtually all are anecdotal accounts that only got recorded because someone was around to witness the event (or the aftermath). Recent anecdotal accounts of polar bear males cannibalizing cubs are no more evidence of climate change than are instances of starving bears,[219] and they are simply not mentioned by researchers any more.

Summary, and who knew what, when

Polar bear specialists emphasised the importance to bears of summer feeding in order to make the case that summer sea ice loss due to global warming was having a deleterious effect. But then it became apparent – especially in the data collected from the Chukchi and Barents Seas, as well as in Davis Strait – that spring was the most critical feeding time, not summer. Polar bears were found to be more flexible in their denning preferences and sea ice concentration choices than experts gave them credit for; the bears were also better at swimming and diving in open water than any of the experts had imagined. Recent evidence of hybridization turned out to involve only one bear, and cannibalism has been abandoned as a claimed consequence of reduced sea ice.

On top of all that, the data no one wanted to acknowledge from the Southern Beaufort Sea in the 1970s and Western Hudson Bay in the 1980s indicated that fluctuations in polar bear population size and survival could occur even when summer ice extent was high. Since those effects are now known, it is clear that spring sea ice conditions (and perhaps winter ice and snow conditions) may be much more important to polar bear health and survival than summer ice extent.

For these reasons, the polar bear catastrophe the public was promised – that two thirds of the world's polar bears would be gone because of global warming – simply never happened. The sea ice dropped precipitously to levels not expected until 2050 but polar bear numbers did not.

Some people may doubt that the public were initially convinced that global warming really meant the end for polar bears, but it is clear the media reaction and feedback from the public to the 2008 ESA decision had USGS biologist Steven Amstrup worried. The public was so sure that a polar bear catastrophe was inevitable that in 2010 Amstrup developed a new model to show that if greenhouse gas emissions were curtailed, all would be well for polar bears. We know this because of a 2010 conservation paper, which discussed Amstrup's experience of publicising the polar bear ESA listing decision in 2007 and 2008.[220] The authors, Ronald Swaisgood and James Sheppard, said that they discussed with Amstrup his 'dawning realization' that the dire warnings of imminent doom for polar bears had been perceived by the media and the public as an inevitable outcome. Amstrup apparently wrote to the authors and said:

> ...I was much chagrinned by the first flurry of reports in the media covering the release of our information. The take home message seemed to be that polar bears are going to disappear and there is nothing we can do about it...I much prefer the concept of presenting the prognosis for polar bears in a way that emphasises that there is hope if we do the right things.' [Steven Amstrup, USGS, Anchorage, personal communication, 9 Sept. 2009]

In other words, the 2007 model devised for the ESA listing decision was so puffed-up it compelled Amstrup and his USGS colleagues to make a new, less alarming model. He knew he'd gone too far and tried to dial it back. Oddly, Amstrup's choice to construct a new model so soon after the first did not cause the ESA decision to be reexamined: it stood as presented. In the end, Amstrup's more hopeful model, designed to encourage the public to act on reducing carbon dioxide emissions, did not do much to change public or media perception, as far as I can tell. Even as recently as February 2019, a newspaper writer at the *Washington Post* trying to make a story about polar bears as alarming as possible cited the 2007 USGS model prediction.[221]

But after more than ten years of listening to the media talk about sea ice death spirals and worse-than-we-thought Arctic scenarios, many people have come to realise that polar bear numbers have not plummetted, as predicted, along with the ice. For a few years now, stories about bears often prompt from readers questions like, 'Wait, weren't all those bears supposed to be dead by now?' Because by 2015, when their revised polar bear assessment was released, it was clear that numbers had not even dropped by the less extreme amount that the IUCN had predicted in 2006.

The ESA decision was virtually rubber-stamped as 'upheld' in 2016;[222,†] However, in contrast, IUCN standards required a complete re-assessment every eight years, which meant a new one was due from the PBSG by 2014. This time, the IUCN had new rules: population numbers for all subpopulations were stipulated for projections that used climate change sea ice predictions, and the

---

† It did not discuss population numbers: like Amstrup and colleagues' 2010 paper, it was vague about actual predicted declines.

Bayesian 'expert opinion' approach used by the USGS was not permitted.[‡] When it was finally released in late 2015, there was a big surprise. Not only was the global population higher than it had been in 2006 (when it was estimated at 26,000 or 22,000–31,000), the assessment *did not* link polar bear survival models to forecasts of Arctic sea ice decline based on atmospheric carbon dioxide levels (as did the 2007 USGS predictions). Rather, polar bear survival was linked to an assumption that sea ice declines already documented would continue in linear fashion over this century.[223] In other words, the PBSG and the IUCN knew the CO_2-driven sea ice models were too flawed to be useful for projecting future polar bear survival. Ultimately, their prognosis was much less alarming than the ESA decision.

It seemed everyone involved knew the USGS model had failed: Amstrup, the PBSG, and the IUCN. But no one said it out loud.

[‡] According to the minutes of the 17th meeting of the PBSG in 2014, http://pbsg.npolar.no/en/meetings/stories/17th_meeting.html. See also Appendix A.

Chapter 6

Defending the model failure

One of the first things that struck me when I began to delve into the scientific literature regarding predictions of polar bear extinction was the fact that I'd never heard about the devastating Southern Beaufort events of 1974–1976: the starving bears, dying cubs and population reduced by half because of exceptionally thick ice in the spring.

Outrage over the obfuscation and misinformation about this phenomenon inspired my first blog post at PolarBearScience in late July, 2012. I began to pay much more attention to what polar bear specialists were, and were not, saying about specific events and research results. It was not until late May 2014 that I got any direct pushback from researchers and it came from my attempts to make some sense of the various population size estimates made over the years by the PBSG. I received a snarky email from PBSG chairman Dag Vongraven that said:

> Dr. Crockford,
>
> Below you'll find a footnote that will accompany a total polar bear population size range in the circumpolar polar bear action plan that we are currently drafting together with the Parties to the 1973 Agreement. This might keep you blogging for a day or two.[*]

After responding to my reply, Vongraven never contacted me again, nor did any of his colleagues. They continued to prefer using the media to defend themselves against my criticisms without mentioning my name.[†] But this changed once I realised that sea ice had already declined to levels not expected until 2050 and made that knowledge public.

In truth, it didn't dawn on me until after the 2015 IUCN polar bear assessment was published that the critical USGS sea ice threshold had already been reached. Before that time, I had focused on what was going on in individual subpopulations. As I reviewed the 2015 IUCN report, I went back to the USGS

---

[*] Part of what he sent read: 'It is important to realise that this [population size, e.g. 20-25,000] range never has been an estimate of total abundance in a scientific sense, but simply a qualified guess given to satisfy public demand.'

[†] http://www.dailymail.co.uk/sciencetech/article-2748995/Is-polar-bear-political-weapon-Arctic-creatures-NOT-threatened-climate-change-says-scientist.html.

papers generated for the ESA decision, and I looked at them with fresh eyes. It also occurred to me at that time that the IUCN's use of all available population estimates for its modelled prediction surely meant anyone else could use those same figures to formally test the original IUCN and USGS hypotheses of future doom. So I went to work in earnest.

I wrote my critique of Amstrup and colleagues' 2007 polar bear survival model up as a formal scientific paper, which was eventually published at an on-line pre-print server.[224,‡] I waited for the polar bear community to respond. But despite a publication format that encouraged comments and review by fellow scientists, the paper was almost entirely ignored in academic circles, despite the attention it was getting online and in the media. Not one polar bear specialist left a review.

I soon found out why: polar bear specialists simply couldn't refute it. In early 2018, I had published the *State of the Polar Bear Report 2017*,[225] a review of the science of polar bear populations.[226] But instead of picking apart that report or my scientific manuscript, biologists Derocher and Amstrup decided to attack an opinion piece I'd written for the Canadian newspaper, the *Financial Post*, which summarized some of my key points. Their critique was published on a website called *Climate Feedback*, run by folks who call themselves 'fact checkers'.

This effort demonstrated that polar bear specialists hadn't commented on my scientific paper because they couldn't refute it in the scholarly manner required by the pre-print journal: all they could do was condemn it with derision, misdirection and strawman arguments. Rather than refute my scientific criticisms, they attempted to regain control of the public narrative. In the process, they exposed their weaknesses. Here is my summary of their point-by-point analysis and my responses to each, presented as the quotes from my op-ed to which Amstrup and Derocher responded in the *Climate Feedback* analysis.[227]

The predicted sea ice decline hasn't led to a fall in polar bear numbers

In my op-ed, I had observed that the predicted falls in sea ice levels hadn't led to the predicted falls in polar bear numbers:

> Although the extent of the summer sea ice after 2006 dropped abruptly to levels not expected until 2050, the predicted 67-per-cent decline in polar bear numbers simply didn't happen. Rather, global polar bear numbers have been stable or slightly improved.

---

‡Later that year, I showed the paper to colleague and friend Dr Valerius Geist (a renowned Canadian wildlife ecologist); he found the argument so compelling he offered to co-author a short summary article with me for a wildlife magazine; see Crockford and Geist (2018).

Amstrup and Derocher both offered up attempted rebuttals of this point. Amstrup's response was to claim that I had got their claim about the timing of the sea ice decline wrong:

> Of course summer ice availability has been reduced from earlier years, but neither observations nor models suggest that what we predicted for mid century has already happened. Here is an image [shown] that may help put this in perspective, and make it clear why our projections focused on mid century and beyond, and that we are not yet in mid-century.

The image Amstrup offered as evidence was a sea ice projection graph (see Figure 6.1), said to be modified from a 2015 USGS technical report,[228] which showed extent approaching zero by 2050 or sooner. In other words, Amstrup was suggesting that levels of sea ice predicted for mid-century *hadn't* in fact been experienced yet. This is clearly a strawman argument: a sea ice projection cre-

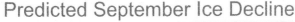

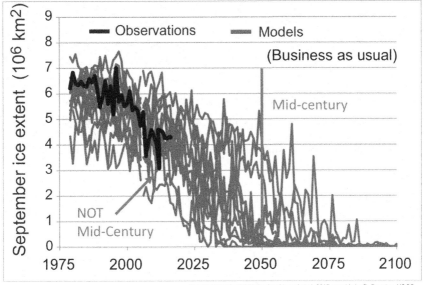

Figure 6.1: The image Amstrup used to suggest I had got his sea ice projections wrong.
  Note that a number of predictions drop to near zero by 2030 and most of them hit zero by 2050. Also, Atwood *et al.* contains only anomaly graphs that are nothing like this figure, which means we really don't know the source of this data.

ated in 2015 is irrelevant to models developed before 2007. The appropriate sea ice image for discussing the 2007 predictions is the one used in the 2007 USGS reports.[229] Figure 6.2 is redrawn from a slightly later version of this graph,[§] and shows that in 2007 sea ice was only expected to approach zero by the end of the 21st century. However, in many of the model runs, levels were predicted to fall below about 5m km^2 by mid-century.

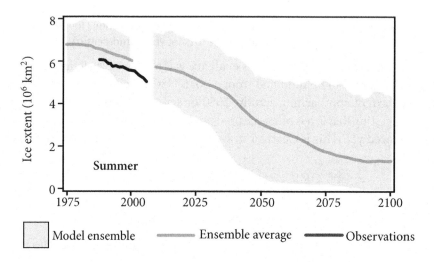

Figure 6.2: The sea ice prediction behind the ESA decision.
This graph is based on the one in Durner *et al.* (2009)[∥], which is the peer-reviewed version of the USGS internal report, Durner *et al.* (2007): the same graph appears in both. Note the extent does not drop to near zero until 2100 or so.

Meanwhile, Derocher offered up two discrete statements, firstly suggesting that their predictions had been based on the length of the ice-free period rather than the ice extent:

This is nonsense. No polar bear scientist has predicted a drop in polar bear abundance based on summer sea ice. We base the assessment of loss on duration of the ice-free period.

It is certainly true that the complex models developed by Amstrup and colleagues in 2007 used multiple aspects of sea ice, which they called 'optimum polar bear habitat', but when it came down to explaining the results, 'summer' was the term used in all the papers. Durner and colleagues stated explicitly that 'summer' was August plus September, and that the average length of this period was not predicted to change over the 21st century, making the average ice extent

---

[§]It appeared in a later peer-reviewed paper by the same group of authors.[230]

for September a critical summer metric.[231] This means that in 2007, it was not the duration of the ice-free period in summer that was described as critical but the threshold of September extent.

In addition, a clear statement in the Executive Summary of the USGS report from 2007, published as a separate document,[232] equates critical levels of optimal polar bear habitat with the season known as 'summer':

> 12. Ultimately, we projected a 42% loss of optimal polar bear habitat during summer in the polar basin by mid century.

The use of 'summer' ice extent (i.e. the September average) as a proxy for critical levels of optimal polar bear habitat is also evident in Figure 6.2, which is clearly labelled 'summer'.[233] Even more telling is the fact that Amstrup and colleagues included a graphic in their 2007 report that showed sea ice extent at 23 August 2007 (near the end of the summer melt season) compared to their sea ice predictions for mid-century (2045–2054) and their comments emphasised that ice coverage had already declined below the level projected for mid-century:[234]

> As of 23 August 2007 declines in Arctic sea ice extent in 2007 have set a new record for the available time series from 1979–2006... Because this new record has occurred 25–83 days before the summer melt season will end in different parts of the polar basin... much more melting and greater sea ice reduction seems likely... But, the sea ice in 2007 already has declined below the level projected for mid century by the 4 most conservative models in our ensemble...

Moreover, the figure included in the 2007 Amstrup report[235] was updated for the book chapter that constituted the peer-reviewed published version that followed.[236] It showed the summer minimum at 16 September 2007, emphasizing that ice coverage at the September minimum (the summer seasonal low) had already declined below the level projected for mid-century by half of the models they used in their analysis[237] (see Figure 3.2).¶

In addition, the description by Durner and colleagues (2007) of this mid-century threshold for summer sea ice is explicit:[238]

> By the mid-21st century, most peripheral seas [of the Arctic Ocean, e.g. Southern Beaufort, Chukchi, Laptev, Barents, and Kara Seas] have very little remaining optimal polar bear habitat during summer.

The 'peripheral seas' referred to by Durner were classified as 'Divergent' sea ice ecoregions by the USGS assessment team and have been ice-free in September (or nearly so) since 2007.[239]

¶See p. 25.

These examples show that average sea ice levels for September – summer – were used by the authors of the USGS reports as a proxy for optimal polar bear habitat at its lowest threshold level, for both the baseline period and the future. Therefore, September ice extent is a valid proxy for evaluating the validity of the prediction that two thirds of the world's polar bears would disappear when sea ice consistently dropped to levels predicted for mid-century.

Derocher's second line of attack was to claim that the *global* polar bear population was not a suitable metric:

> The statement about global polar bear numbers is absolutely unfounded. It is a contrived statement using population estimates provided so that children (or the general public) could give a number of polar bears in the world for school reports and the like.

There are at least three polar bear specialist papers or reports that use global population estimates and/or subpopulation estimates in their assessments of present or modelled polar bear health and survival. The global polar bear estimate is simply the sum of those subpopulation estimates. For example, Amstrup and colleagues used a global population total (24,500), without apologies or excuses, although they also presented ecoregion totals in their model predicting polar bear survival over the 21st century.[240] A supplement to the document supporting the 2015 IUCN Red List assessment included a table of subpopulation estimates (which came to a total of 26,485) with no mention that these were 'contrived'.[241] Similarly, in the 2016 peer-reviewed version of Red List assessment, the authors stated: 'The global population of approximately 26 000 polar bears is divided into 19 subpopulations', with no mention that this number was considered unscientific.[242]

It is clear that polar bear specialists use global and subpopulation estimates when it suits them for modelling purposes, but otherwise claim these are scientifically invalid.

The thick ice in the Southern Beaufort

In my op-ed, I had explained the anomalous situation in the Southern Beaufort:

> …Canadian polar bear biologist Ian Stirling learned in the 1970s that spring sea ice in the southern Beaufort Sea periodically gets so thick that seals depart, depriving local polar bears of their prey and causing their numbers to plummet. But that fact, documented in more than a dozen scientific papers, is not discussed today as part of polar bear ecology.

Amstrup's response was the remarkable claim that periodic thick sea ice was no longer seen in the Southern Beaufort:

> Both Ian Stirling and I have published on the inter-annual and even multi-annual variation in sea ice extent... Ian specifically mentioned in some early publications that there seemed a nearly decadal oscillation in ice thickness, etc... Regardless, as the world has warmed and ice continued to thin, evidence of any such cycle in the Beaufort has disappeared. We did not see a crush of heavier ice in the middle of the first or second decades of the 2000s... Why would researchers spend much time now discussing a pattern in the sea ice that no longer occurs?

Derocher concurred, and suggested that loss of sea ice was now more important for seals and polar bears, citing papers by Bromaghin *et al.*[243] and Hunter *et al.*[244] in his support:

> Heavy sea ice conditions are largely a past issue for ringed seals... It is loss of sea ice habitat as a whole that is negatively affecting ringed seals and thus polar bears.

This is patently untrue, as demonstrated by a review of the scientific literature. Even though Stirling and colleagues argued in their 2008 paper that the thick spring ice conditions in 2004, 2005 and 2006 were caused by storms initiated or intensified by greater amounts of open water in previous summers, they acknowledge that thick ice conditions were indeed present from 2004–2006 and that they were as severe as the conditions of 1974–1975 that had devastating effects on seals and polar bears. This is what Ian Stirling and colleagues had to say about the 2004–2006 event in the eastern half of the Southern Beaufort:[245]

> During our study, sea ice conditions in the southeastern Beaufort Sea showed some major differences from past years... From 2003 through 2006, large areas of the annual landfast ice from northeast of Atkinson Point to the Alaska border... were compressed into high pressure ridges interspersed with extensive areas of rafted floes and rubble (especially in 2005...). In some places, these areas extended offshore from the mainland coast for tens of kilometres. Such heavy ice reduces the availability of low consolidated ridges and refrozen leads with accompanying snowdrifts typically used by ringed seals for birth and haulout lairs... Although we were unable to make a quantified comparison, our subjective impression is that in 12 previous spring field seasons surveying the same area for polar bears (1971–79, 1985–87) only once, in 1974, did we observe similarly extensive areas of rubble, pressure ridges, and rafted floes.

Stirling's observations were corroborated by seal biologists working in the same area at the time.[246]

Since there is evidence that thick ice conditions of varying severity happened roughly every decade from the 1960s to the mid-2000s, we have five decades' worth of data on this phenomenon: certainly enough to deserve comment by biologists *and* to warrant inclusion in future survival models, especially given their previous catastrophic effects on polar bear health and survival.

Derocher's two cited papers[247] are not evidence that less summer ice was the cause of declining polar bear populations in the first decade of the 2000s in the Southern Beaufort. There is *correlation* with less summer ice, to be sure, but that correlation is meaningless: in the springs of those years, there had been thick ice, described as being as severe as the events of the mid-1970s, which had been documented in over a dozen peer-reviewed scientific papers.[248]

Food is unexpectedly abundant

Another of my comments to which Amstrup and Derocher took exception was an observation that food for polar bears appeared to be abundant in the Chukchi Sea, north of the Bering Strait:

> …many scientists were surprised when other researchers subsequently found that ringed and bearded seals (the primary prey of polar bears) north of the Bering Strait especially thrived with a longer open-water season, which is particularly conducive to fishing.

Amstrup argued that the Chukchi Sea was not representative of the wider Arctic:

> The Chukchi Sea is essentially all continental shelf and is probably the most productive of the Arctic Seas. This is in contrast to the Beaufort Sea which, beyond the very narrow continental shelf, is very unproductive. Recent research has shown that this tremendous productivity and the fact that, although ice has significantly retreated, bears there still have fewer ice free days over the shelf than in the Beaufort, can explain why Chukchi Sea polar bears have not yet declined like those in the Beaufort.

However, Derocher argued – rather contradicting his colleague – that there was no scientific evidence that seals were doing well, and again suggested that the Chukchi Sea was an anomaly:

> Both ringed seals and bearded seals are sea ice obligate species: there are significant conservation concerns about both species across the Arctic. The basis of the statement that the seals are thriving is unfounded in the peer-reviewed literature. Both species are listed under the US Endangered Species Act. The polar bears living north of the Bering Strait have not shown the same loss in body condition, survival, and reproduction noted in the neighboring Beaufort Sea because the ecosystems are vastly different in the distribution of continental shelf habitat: huge area in the Chukchi Sea, a narrow band in the Beaufort. Polar bear populations respond to local changes, and with 19 polar bear populations, there will be 19 different scenarios playing out over time. Loss of sea ice in the Chukchi Sea in winter 2017/18 may change the situation there.

It is clear that their arguments were tangential to mine, which was about ringed and bearded seals in the Chukchi Sea responding to a longer ice-free season by *thriving*, contrary to the predicted effects.[249] Amstrup was therefore presenting a strawman argument when he discussed Beaufort Sea seals, as was Derocher in describing Beaufort Sea polar bears. Derocher's comment about ESA 'Threatened' status for ringed and bearded seals is also a strawman. While what he says is true,[250] it is also true that no other Arctic nation or the IUCN is concerned about any Arctic seal species, including ringed and bearded seals: they are all categorised as 'Least concern' on the IUCN Red List.[251]

The causes of thin polar bears

In my op-ed, I had discussed the occasional findings of reduced weight in polar bears:

> …while it's true that studies in some regions show polar bears are lighter in weight than they were in the 1980s, there is no evidence that more individuals are starving to death or becoming too thin to reproduce because of less summer ice.

Amstrup's claim was that declining sea ice was the only plausible explanation:

> We know that polar bears depend on the ice surface to catch their prey. We know that increasing numbers of ice free days have resulted in poorer body condition in some areas (e.g. Southern Beaufort, Western and Southern Hudson Bay), we know that poorer cub survival has followed both declining ice and poorer body condition, and all the evidence suggests these things are linked. Perhaps this is not 'proof' that less available summer ice is the cause (correlation does not necessarily imply causation), but I am not aware of evidence for any other explanation. And I don't think the female polar bears are intentionally having cubs but not feeding them.

Derocher, meanwhile, said that there was evidence that sea-ice declines were the cause:

> There is evidence. Bromaghin *et al.* 2015 and Hunter *et al.* 2010 examine this issue. [Derocher then quoted lengthy passages from both papers describing the models they used to blame sea ice declines for population decline in the Southern Beaufort Sea: for Bromaghin *et al.*, from 2001 to 2010, and for Hunter *et al.*, from 2001 to 2006.]

However, neither one of these responses provide *evidence* that more bears are starving to death or have become too thin to reproduce *due to reduced summer sea ice,* which was the point of my statement. Neither of the references cited by Derocher constituted the evidence he claims: the effects cited from the Southern Beaufort are explained, not by less summer sea ice, but by thick ice in the springs of 2004–2006.[252] Continued poor survival of subadults after 2007 may have been *correlated* with less summer ice but on its own this is not evidence of causation.

Amstrup raised the issue of poor cub survival and reduced weight of females in Western and Southern Hudson Bay. But he should know that these effects can be caused by conditions over the winter and spring that affect prey condition or availability, a subject about which several scientific papers have been written.[253] Previous work by Derocher and Stirling in five separate papers makes clear that weights of bears and cub survival rates declined markedly in the late 1980s and early 1990s in Western Hudson Bay, well before abrupt changes in breakup or freeze-up dates were documented.[254] For example, in one of the papers, they documented worrying declines in body condition of adult females and a marked increase in cub mortality, including the loss of entire litters, stating that:[255]

> The two-fold increase in the number of cubs lost from a litter between spring and autumn during the 1980s represents a substantial increase in cub mortality...From the early to late 1980s, there was a three-fold increase in the proportion of females that lost their whole litter in the spring to autumn period.

In another of the papers, they said:[256]

> Reproduction rates declined in the late 1980s from higher levels in 1966–1984...The proportion of yearlings independent of their mother in autumn dropped from 81% prior to 1980 to 34% in 1980–1992. After 1986, offspring remained with their mothers longer, resulting in the birth interval increasing from 2.1 to 2.9 years. Body mass of most age-classes of females and males declined in the 1980s...Insufficient information was available to determine the cause of declines in reproduction and body mass.

In other words, weight declines and poor cub survival have not been confined to recent years in Western Hudson Bay, as implied. This means these symptoms can have other causes besides a longer-than-usual ice-free season.

The polar bear survival model has failed

Finally, Amstrup and Derocher took aim at my observation that polar bear scientists had failed to develop a predictive model that worked:

> The failure of the 2007 polar bear survival model is a simple fact that explodes the myth that polar bears are on their way to extinction.

Only Amstrup responded, claiming that *many* papers had confirmed the predictions:

> Multiple papers published subsequent to my work in 2007 have corrobo-
> rated the outcomes we projected. However, the accuracy or failure of my
> work to inform the Secretary of Interior cannot be evaluated until mid
> century. And as the figure above shows, we are not there yet.

Remarkably, however, Amstrup only appeared to be able to back this claim by citing one of his own papers, and one, moreover, that was about the development of a predictive model.[257]

The fact remains that summer sea ice hit mid-century-like levels (as defined by 2005/2006 projections) before the ink was dry on the 2007 USGS reports, and has remained at those levels for 10 out of the 12 years since then, 2018 included.[258] Yet polar bear numbers not only failed to decline as predicted, they have increased slightly. Amstrup again tries to use *recent* sea ice and/or polar bear survival model predictions to suggest my critique of his 2007 model is incorrect or premature. However, none of these papers are relevant.

Note that the 2007 USGS model is often considered Amstrup's work (by himself and others) because his opinion alone was used in the Bayesian model to predict how polar bears would respond to various levels of sea ice decline.[259] As a consequence, Amstrup takes any criticism of that model as personal criticism and responds defensively. And as I've shown in previous chapters, some of the assumptions Amstrup made for his 2007 model were simply wrong: he was wrong to ignore the Southern Beaufort thick-spring-ice phenomenon and wrong to assume that ringed and bearded seals would suffer gravely with less summer ice.

That's science for you. But instead of correcting the errors and moving on, Amstrup continues to defend his position. That's a sure sign he is too emotionally invested to view the issue in a scientifically unbiased manner.

In summary

Most of the points made by Derocher and Amstrup in their criticisms of my *Financial Post* op-ed were essential components of my 2017 critique of Amstrup and colleagues' 2007 survival model used to support listing polar bears as 'Threatened' with extinction in the USA.[260,**] These comments by Derocher and Amstrup are the only formal criticisms by polar bear specialists that can be said to have been directed at the premise of my 2017 paper. However, there was little except bluster and misdirection in the comments they made. Insisting that models developed *after* the 2007 USGS reports were published are evidence

---

** The exception was the fourth point, about why some polar bears seemed to be becoming thinner.

69

that my critique is premature is ridiculous. It might fool a few gullible souls, but it won't fool fellow scientists and astute readers. However, now we know why neither Amstrup nor Derocher formally reviewed my 2017 *PeerJ Preprint* paper: they did not have scientifically valid arguments to make. Nothing they said undermines the conclusion of my paper: the assumptions Amstrup made about how the bears would respond to much reduced summer sea ice conditions were wrong.

Chapter 7

Attacking the messenger

'...absolutely the stupidest paper I have ever seen published'

Professor Judith Curry on the *BioScience* paper.

The storm breaks

Eventually, however, polar bear specialists seem to have decided that some kind of response to my criticisms needed to be published in the academic literature. However, the combined efforts of those in the field didn't amount to a response *to my work*, thus confirming my earlier conclusion that they couldn't respond to the science. The first I knew of it was when a journalist contacted me to say that a paper about me was due for imminent publication. It was clear that a media barrage would follow, and with only two or three hours before the press embargo was lifted, there was little I could do about it; I was blindsided.

Their response was first published online in November 2017 in the journal *BioScience*. Entitled 'Internet blogs, polar bears, and climate-change denial by proxy', it is what passes for a formal response to my irrefutable observation that polar bear numbers did not plummet as predicted when mid-century-like sea ice conditions arrived unexpectedly in 2007.[261] This shoddy piece of work, with no fewer than 14 authors, led by biologist Jeff Harvey, will go down in history as a self-inflicted wound for the two polar bear specialists on the roster – Ian Stirling and Steven Amstrup – and an own-goal for its three 'climate warriors': Stephan Lewandowsky, Jeff Harvey, and Michael Mann.

Although nominally a climate scientist, Michael Mann is a political operative, and amongst the most prominent climate scientists – and climate activists – alive today. This is partly because he is among the most criticised scientists alive today, the result of his authorship of the infamous Hockey Stick graph. As a result of this attention, Mann tries to portray himself as a victim, having described in Congressional testimony something he calls the 'Serengeti Strategy':

71

> I coined the term 'Serengeti Strategy'...to describe how industry special interests who feel threatened by scientific findings – be it tobacco and lung cancer, or fossil fuel burning and climate change – single out individual scientists to attack in much the same way lions of the Serengeti single out an individual zebra from the herd. In numbers there is strength, but individuals are far more vulnerable. Science critics will therefore often select a single scientist to ridicule, hector, and intimidate. The presumed purpose is to set an example for other scientists who might consider sticking their neck out by participating in the public discourse over certain matters of policy-relevant science.[262]

However, his status as 'victim' is hardly warranted. He has an extraordinary penchant for derogatory name-calling, and is something of an expert in the 'Serengeti Strategy' himself, having been central to public attacks on a variety of dissenting scientists, including Pat Michaels and William Happer.* The *Bio-Science* attack on me[263] is thus just the latest example of his use of the strategy: intimidation by numbers is the only rational explanation for having 14 co-authors when two could have produced a similar result.

The Harvey *et al.* paper was obviously hostile, and aimed to destroy my public reputation rather than my arguments. A cursory glance revealed that none of the scientific criticisms that I raised on internet blogs and in my papers were addressed. This was not really a response to my work at all: there was no discussion of forecasting methodologies and uncertainties in population counts or anything like that. Instead it was a personal attack, designed to be as damaging as possible to my scientific reputation and to besmirch the status of anyone who had ever reprinted, quoted or cited my polar bear work. It was, in essence, a 'smear job'. In the words of *Financial Post* columnist Terence Corcoran, I was 'climate mauled'.

The authors were the subject of considerable international media attention over the following weeks, and it became clear over the next few days that they had put a tremendous effort into their public relations. No fewer than three – yes three – press releases had been issued prior to publication of the paper by the various institutions at which co-authors were employed.

Innumerable opportunities for co-authors to vent their rage against me via media interviews were thus created. I've copied some examples below.

> Real polar bear researcher [Ian] Stirling, who spent more than four decades studying polar bears and publishing over 150 papers and five books on the

---

*One of his favourite targets is the climate scientist Dr Judith Curry, Emeritus Professor of Earth and Atmospheric Sciences at Georgia Institute of Technology. She was even on the receiving end of one of Mann's attacks in the same Congressional testimony when he introduced the 'Serengeti Strategy' and tried to portray himself as its victim.

topic, says Crockford has 'zero' authority on the subject. [Desmogblog Canada, 30 December 2017]

> You don't have to read far in her [Crockford's] material to see that it is full of unsubstantiated statements and personal attacks on scientists, using names like eco-terrorists, fraudsters, green terrorists and scammers. [Steve Amstrup, quoted by *Motherboard*, 1 December 2017]

When I complained to *Motherboard* that I have never used any of those terms to refer to anyone, let alone a fellow scientist (which a search of my blog will attest), the passage quoted above was changed to this:

> You don't have to read far in her material to see that it is full of unsubstantiated statements and personal attacks on scientists, using names like eco-terrorists, fraudsters, green terrorists and scammers,' Amstrup said. In a follow-up email on Friday, Amstrup clarified that these statements to Motherboard were meant to reflect the climate denier community as a whole, rather than Crockford in particular. In an email to Motherboard, Crockford denied using those terms on her blog.

A few times I was contacted for comment for these sorts of stories but it hardly mattered what I said, the articles that followed were as bad or worse in tone than the paper itself. No journalist seems to have made even a cursory inquiry about the paper's credibility: an article in the *New York Times* by Erica Goode in early April 2018 was a case in point: 'Climate change denialists say polar bears are fine. Scientists are pushing back'.[264] Goode, a former environment editor at the *Times*, simply repeated the claims of the *BioScience* co-authors, as presented in the press releases and in their own words. Amstrup repeated his false claim that his 2007 prediction that two thirds of the world's polar bears would be lost by 2050 used a sea ice model that put the Arctic virtually ice-free by mid-century. This went unchallenged by Goode, even though it was an easy fact to check.

Those who question the global warming narrative struggle to get access to the mainstream media, where environment correspondents are – to a man (or woman) – environmentalists. Supportive voices were therefore few and far between. A rare exception was journalist Donna Laframboise, who called out Goode in an article entitled 'Polar bears and the sleazy *New York Times*',[265] for failing to present readers with an unbiased picture of the polar bear issues raised by the *BioScience* paper:

> People who think polar bears are currently doing well – a separate question from how they might fare in the future – are similarly labeled 'climate denialists' by Goode...Individuals on the other side of the fence, meanwhile, are portrayed as 'real experts' and 'mainstream scientists.'

Later, she concluded:

> Rather than inform its readers in a fair handed manner, the *Times* this week became a mouthpiece for one side in a scientific debate. Erica Goode chose to be prosecutor, judge, jury, and executioner in the case of Susan Crockford.
>
> She sided not with the brave dissident, but with the numerous and the powerful. Crockford wasn't merely assaulted in *BioScience*, her assault was justified and amplified in the pages of the *Times*. By another woman.

Apart from Laframboise, only the *Financial Post* carried a supportive essay. This concluded:[266]

> If this is science, we are all doomed.

The paper's PR blitz suggested that it was a desperate ploy instigated by panic: some very powerful people considered my work to be a very serious threat to the narrative they were selling to the public and the scientific community. These were people who felt that my authority, along with the strong internet influence of other bloggers who were skeptical of certain aspects of global warming alarm, had to be defused. Not challenged, mind you: neutralised.

As discussed in the previous chapter, Amstrup and Derocher – and thus Stirling, who had a close relationship with both – knew they didn't have a valid argument to refute my scientific paper on their failed polar bear survival model. But there is strong evidence that they were concerned about the effect on my arguments on the wider climate debate and wanted to do something about it. A few days after the Harvey *et al. Bioscience* paper was published, a note at the end of a *New York Times* article entitled 'How climate change deniers rise to the top in Google searches,' revealed what may have been an important goal of the paper. Jeff Harvey was quoted as saying that internet search engines should be encouraged to censor blogs and news reports that don't conform to a particular world view on global warming and polar bears.[267]

This surmise is confirmed by the text of the *Bioscience* paper itself, which alludes to the amount of attention I was getting:

> Approximately 80% of the denier blogs cited here referred to one particular denier blog, Polar Bear Science, by Susan Crockford, as their primary source of discussion and debate on the status of polar bears... Prominent among blogs giving Crockford's blog disproportionate attention are [Watts Up With That?] and [Climate Depot], suggesting that her blog reaches a large audience.

Note that Watts Up With That?, run by meteorologist Anthony Watts, currently gets 3–4 million page views per month, while Climate Depot, run by Marc Morano with support from the Committee for a Constructive Tomorrow, gets about the same number per year. Both feature only a small portion of what I write.

The nature of the critique

Outwardly, the paper purported to be an analysis of veracity of polar bear information on the internet. It compared entries on that subject from 45 so-called 'science-based' blogs, to those from 45 so-called 'denier blogs'. The essence of the paper was that the (allegedly correct) information based on their own work was widely cited by science-based outlets, whereas my own (allegedly incorrect) work was only being cited by 'denier blogs'. In other words, my bad influence had spread far and wide amongst the undiscerning 'rubes' who write about polar bears and global warming on the internet.

This was all done in a highly aggressive tone. Ten years ago, questions about the veracity and advisability of giving polar bears 'Threatened' status came primarily through the media, who were then admonished by polar bear scientists for giving 'detractors' a platform. For example, in a revealing article published in the fall of 2007, Stirling and Derocher articulated their frustration with this process of criticisms in a journal article called 'Melting under pressure: the real scoop on climate warming and polar bears'.[268] This contained many very similar arguments as in the *Bioscience* article, but the approach and language were startlingly different. Back in 2007, there was little in the way of solid data to bolster the case, but they used what they had: they addressed as best they could the scientific criticisms to which they objected. A sense of the tone of the article can be derived from the section titles of their paper:

- Assessing the facts
- Signs of decline
- Media mix-ups
- Dire reality.

The word 'contrarians' was used twice to describe the opposition view; 'confuse/confusion' used twice; 'denying' used once. Now compare this to the section headings from the *BioScience* paper:

- Climate-change denial and the Internet
- Climate-change denial by proxy: Using hot topics as 'keystone dominoes'
- Arctic ice extent and polar bears are proxies for AGW denial
- Science-based and -denier blogs take completely different positions on Arctic ice extent and polar bear status
- Overcoming reticence: Scientists as advocates in countering AGW denial.

So ten years on, 'denial' was used five times in the section headings alone, plus once in the title. 'Denier/deniers' 20 times in the text; 'denial' four times in the text (not counting section headings or title); 'deny/denying' nine times in the text (three in the abstract alone); 'confusion' used once; and 'contrarian' was used as a key word only. The difference in tone is remarkable.

Smearing by omission

As noted above, the *Bioscience* paper was an attempt to destroy my professional reputation rather than addressing my arguments. Throughout the paper, the authors therefore referred to me as a 'blogger' as if that were my only credential; they consistently leave out the fact that I have a PhD in zoology, and have worked in the field for four decades. Of course, it is precisely *because* I am so well qualified to critique their work that polar bear scientists feel a need to trash my reputation.

One of the mantras in the paper, repeated by supporters at every opportunity, was a claim that I haven't done field work on polar bears. But you don't need to tag a polar bear to evaluate statements made in published reports. My intimate knowledge of the polar bear literature, which I've studied since the early 1990s, allows me to synthesise decades-old and recent reports while providing critical commentary regarding some of the inconsistencies and sources of bias presented in the material.[269] I use an approach called 'consilience' – a fancy word for a big-picture, interdisciplinary examination of a full range of topics related to an issue, in this case including ecology, life history, genetics, geology, zoogeography, and archaeology. The concept of interdisciplinary study is all but foreign to the one-species, field-research dominated world-views of polar bear specialists.

Another claim made against me in the *BioScience* paper was that I haven't published peer-reviewed papers on polar bears. This ignored the fact that I *have* published peer-reviewed papers on a variety of topics, including Arctic ecology and the evolution of Arctic species, and was untrue to boot, given my *PeerJ* paper. Because of this, the *BioScience* paper had to be changed and a corrigendum issued. Perhaps predictably, a new claim was inserted, this time stating that I hadn't published any peer-reviewed papers '*on the effects of sea ice on the population dynamics of polar bears*'. This still allowed them to ignore my *PeerJ* paper,[270] since although this was about the effects of sea ice on population dynamics it was in an open-review rather than a peer-reviewed journal. Of course, that paper is the one they didn't want the public to see.

Some of the arguments were absurd. For example, the authors stated:

> Crockford vigorously criticizes, without supporting evidence, the findings of several leading researchers who have studied polar bears in the field for decades.

Anyone who reads my blog or has read my recent paper knows this is the opposite of what I do.[271] The fact that I criticise *with* supporting evidence is precisely why these leading researchers feel so threatened. For example, I have published some research work on Pacific walrus, a known prey species of polar bears that in 2011 faced being uplisted by the ESA to 'Threatened' status[272] on the same grounds of predicted sea ice loss that had been used for polar bears. I spent considerable time and effort in 2014 going through the scientific literature on the topic of sea ice cover and walrus haulout behaviour. I wrote a series of blog posts which included not only references to the scientific literature but quotes from those papers. In the end, I wrote four detailed blog posts and a formal report that pulled them all together on the topic.[273] My efforts were ultimately vindicated when the USFWS decided not to list the walrus as 'threatened'.[†] The point is, I approach all of my research this way, including my work on polar bears and it's the way I write my blog. The advantage of an online blog is that you can build on previous work very easily by providing a link to a post that's full of references on a topic rather than repeat them all, which might at first glance look like a post without references.

In the *BioScience* paper, Harvey and colleagues implied there is but one avenue towards expertise in a specialty, which comes through original research and field experience. Moreover, they imply that this definition is not only self-evident but widely accepted, yet offered no references to support such a conclusion. By their definition, Stirling and Amstrup are polar bear experts and I am not. However, researchers into the nature of expertise have concluded that 'interactional expertise' – the ability to *talk about things* because you are familiar with the relevant literature rather than because you are *actively involved in creating it* – is an important level of knowledge.[275] Specialised fields benefit from the work of interactional experts, who review, synthesise, and write commentary that is understandable to colleagues in other fields and to non-scientists. In fact, most specialised field workers embrace their interactional colleagues because they'd rather not spend their time *talking about things*. Scientists write up their original research results to inform peers both within and outside their particular specialty, but few outsiders ever read their papers. Journalists certainly don't, for the most part. However, the huge corpus of specialty reports and academic papers that polar bear biologists have generated over more than five decades of research fairly pleads for review and synthesis by someone who has mastered the literature. If some criticism of the field results from that review process, that's a good thing for everyone, not a tragedy.

[†] In late 2017, the USFWS declared that walrus are not in need of ESA protection because they have shown an ability to adapt to sea ice loss that was 'not foreseen'.[274]

The Rajan and Tol response

However, the many deceits and the aggressive tone of the *Bioscience* paper are only the beginning. There are many other grounds on which it can be criticised. Some of these were set out in a technical comment, written by Anand Rajan and Richard Tol.[‡] Their paper, entitled 'Lipstick on a bear: a comment on internet blogs, polar bears, and climate change denial by proxy'[276] was submitted to *Bio-Science* but was, perhaps unsurprisingly, rejected. The authors published it later on a preprint server.

They pointed out that, among other problems, Harvey and his colleagues had exhibited a general sloppiness that implied a rushed production (spelling errors, nonsensical statements). Moreover, the supplemental data lacked the detail needed to reproduce the results presented in the paper. Rajan and Tol concluded that:

> In sum, Harvey et al. (2017) play a statistical game of smoke and mirrors. They validate their data, collected by an unclear process, by comparing it to data of unknown provenance... They show that there is disagreement on the vulnerability of polar bears to climate change, but offer no new evidence who is right or wrong – apart from a fallacious argument from authority, with a 'majority view' taken from an unrepresentative sample. Once the substandard statistical application to poor data is removed, what remains is a thinly veiled attempt on a colleague's reputation.

I understand that my criticisms make Stirling and Amstrup uncomfortable and even angry. But this is how science works: there should always be someone around to critique your work. It turns out that the real scientific travesty is the fact that no one had effectively done this for polar bear science before I came along.

Censoring opposing views

A lone female scientist without the strong backing of a university must have looked like easy prey to 14 climate-action lions. However, this made the authors so over-confident they got bitten by their own hubris. The only conclusion to arrive at, regardless of which side of the polar bear/global warming issue a reader might fall, is that the paper was a hastily thrown-together attack meant to destroy my professional reputation and make the media leery of quoting me. They

---

[‡] I should point out I did not know either Anand Rajan or Richard Tol before this issue arose: I'd never heard of them. Nor had they heard of me before the *BioScience* paper got worldwide attention. But they came to my defence over this sorry excuse for a science paper.

now have no one to blame but themselves. It will come back to haunt them, this paper of which they were initially so proud.

Ian Stirling is obviously incensed that I have criticised certain aspects of his recent work on my blog and in my various essays and papers;[277] his co-authorship of the *BioScience* paper demonstrates as much. But Stirling stooped even lower. In a disturbing move for an Order of Canada recipient, in early January 2018, only four weeks or so after the *BioScience* paper was published, he telephoned my colleague Val Geist at home, chastised him for having co-authored the Winter 2017/2018 *Range* magazine article with me, told him what an awful person I was, and warned him against any further co-authorship with me lest the association destroy his [Geist's] professional reputation.[278]

Dr. Geist called me a few days afterward to tell me about the incident, which clearly left him shaking his head at the level of desperation it must have taken for Stirling to behave in such an unscientific and unprofessional manner. Note these men are peers in the true sense of the word: in 1999, Stirling won the William Rowan Distinguished Service Award bestowed by the Alberta Chapter of the Wildlife Society, and the next year the same award was won by Geist. Stirling later emailed Geist a copy of the *BioScience* paper to bolster the points he'd made on the phone. Under slightly different circumstances, this behaviour would be called tortious interference.

And people wonder why I don't have papers about polar bears and sea ice published in the peer-reviewed literature! If this is what the most respected polar bear scientist in the world will do to protect an idea he has allowed to define his life's work, imagine what an anonymous reviewer from Stirling's loyal group of less senior researchers would do to keep any critical polar bear paper of mine out of the scientific literature.

I admire Stirling immensely for his field research, especially the reports from the early decades of his career. But warning off a colleague from professional interactions with me was an underhanded abuse of power. It may also be sexist: don't forget that until relatively recently, polar bear research was very much a male-dominated field and Stirling has been the alpha-male of the field since the 1980s. He may be happy to work with women but less amenable to being criticised by them. Stirling and I have a dispute about interpretation of a few pertinent facts: it happens all the time in science. But what Stirling did is not how such issues are resolved and it's simply not how science is done.

Conclusions

The personal attack on me and excessive use of the derogatory slur 'denier' struck many readers – on both sides of the global warming controversy – as blatantly unscientific. Others took issue with the analysis, which even a cursory examination revealed to be contrived.

Ultimately, the authors produced a paper with a fake analysis that could be this century's poster child for what is called the 'reproducibility crisis' in science: the documented phenomenon that about 50% of research results published in the peer-reviewed literature cannot be duplicated by colleagues.[279] As the editor of the *Lancet* has put it:

> The case against science is straightforward: much of the scientific literature, perhaps half, may simply be untrue. Afflicted by studies with small sample sizes, tiny effects, invalid exploratory analyses, and flagrant conflicts of interest, together with an obsession for pursuing fashionable trends of dubious importance, science has taken a turn towards darkness.[280]

But such concerns carry little weight in fields related to climate change. As the Australian physicist Professor Peter Ridd put it in an email to me and several colleagues:§

> Other areas of science are taking on board the Replication Crisis and trying to do something about it. Contrast this with Harvey et al. who do not accept any of their work is wrong and leave a horse's head in Susan Crockford's bed.

---

§Ridd is the latest victim of the climate scientists' 'Serengeti Strategy' and is currently defending himself against being dismissed by James Cook University for the right to criticise the work of colleagues who have been predicting the imminent extinction of the Great Barrier Reef.

Chapter 8

The rise and fall of the polar bear specialist

Why did polar bear scientists become agenda driven?

One of the questions I am asked most often is why polar bear specialists morphed from being honest, objective scientists into agenda-driven activists. How and why did this transformation take place? It is clear that such a transformation happened: I have no doubts that before global warming became a corrupting noble cause, polar bear researchers behaved like proper scientists.

Even though their specialty was rather narrow and emotion-laden – partly because of the dangerous conditions under which they worked, but also because polar bear cubs are so darned cute – these scientists were dedicated, honest, and as unbiased as one could expect, given that most of them were conservationists by definition. Remember, there was very little polar bear research done anywhere before there was concern about the viability of their future, so the field began with a conservation mind-set.

But there was also a political charging of the field brought about by the geographic range of the species. In the late 1960s, at the height of the Cold War, an attempt was made to broker an international treaty between Arctic nations, including the USA and the Soviet Union. Attempting to bring two political opponents together over a conservation goal was admirable, but potentially fraught with tension and problems. How much that contributed to animosity amongst researchers is hard to judge. But I would say there are hints of a condescending attitude on the part of US researchers and a correspondingly defensive attitude on the part of Soviet biologists in some of the early PBSG reports.

Oddly, the US was an underdog in terms of polar bear habitat: it had only one small subpopulation, which it shared with two other countries (the Soviet Union, now Russia, on one side and Canada on the other) – only a short stretch of Alaska coastline was home to American polar bears. The Soviet Union had the largest area of polar bear habitat after Canada, but gave its scientists little financial support for research, publication, or professional travel. The inequality, frustration, and political tension these conditions created was bound to generate strain, particularly when anything had to be decided by the entire PBSG that

81

would later be made public.

Insiders say that Ian Stirling, who joined the group in 1974, played a huge diplomatic role in the early decades of the organisation, especially during the early 1980s. He emerged as a natural leader, and by the late 1990s he was considered the 'father' of polar bear science by his colleagues, the media, and the general public. So later on his views on the role of global warming on polar bear conservation were unsurprisingly hugely influential. I believe that had he not embraced it wholeheartedly when he did, the idea would not have gone anywhere.

Convincing the PBSG that global warming might pose an existential threat to polar bears was not hard work: references to 'climate warming' came up at PBSG meetings as early as 1993, well before the fateful 2005 meeting that resulted in the bears being uplisted back to 'Vulnerable'.[281] But Stirling could only do so much on his own: ultimately, American Stephen Amstrup ended up doing the heavy lifting.

In 2006, Amstrup, who was then lead biologist at the USGS, was put in charge of producing a comprehensive report to support the USFWS position to have the bears listed as 'Threatened.' This leading role in what would be the biggest polar bear conservation fight ever elevated Amstrup to a prominence Stirling likely never imagined was possible. It didn't hurt that Amstrup was not as reticent about media attention as Stirling: he was not shy about telling the world that polar bears were doomed if nothing was done about global warming. In other words, polar bears in the limelight put polar bear researchers there as well: suddenly, leading polar bear specialists had rock-star status with the media.

Polar bear specialists become a clique

The newfound fame and influence and money of the polar bear community made them very unaccepting of dissent. Some years earlier, fellow polar bear specialist D. Mitchell Taylor had simply questioned a few aspects of climate science, a *faux pas* that was enough for him to be consigned to the scientific wilderness by the rest of the polar bear community. Taylor had been a Canadian representative on the PBSG from 1981 to 2008, but at the end of his 28 years of service, he was booted out by chairman Andrew Derocher for expressing (elsewhere) his sceptical views on human-caused global warming. This was remarkable: since its inception in 1965, no one else had ever been 'uninvited' to be a member of the PBSG, for any reason. Here's the text of the original email from Derocher to Taylor explaining why he was not being invited to the 2009 PBSG meeting in Copenhagen:

Hi Mitch,

The world is a political place and for polar bears, more so now than ever before. I have no problem with dissenting views as long as they are supportable by logic, scientific reasoning, and the literature.

I do believe, as do many PBSG members, that for the sake of polar bear conservation, views that run counter to human induced climate change are extremely unhelpful. In this vein, your positions and statements in the Manhattan Declaration, the Frontier Institute, and the Science and Public Policy Institute are inconsistent with positions taken by the PBSG.

I too was not surprised by the members not endorsing an invitation.

Nothing I heard had to do with your science on harvesting or your research on polar bears – it was the positions you've taken on global warming that brought opposition.

Time will tell who is correct but the scientific literature is not on the side of those arguing against human induced climate change.

I look forward to having someone else chair the PBSG.

Best regards, Andy (Derocher)

A few years later, in 2012, the PBSG changed their rules on membership to justify their actions against Taylor. The new rules of membership now included this clause:

It should not be assumed that continued appointment is automatic. For example, members that no longer support the mission and objectives of the PBSG, or those that have been inactive, may not have their membership renewed.

The rules were also changed to allow members to stay on after retirement and to allow full voting membership to biologists employed by activist conservation organizations. These additional changes allowed Stirling to stay on as a voting member after his retirement in 2007 from the Canadian Wildlife Service, even though he has been only minimally active in the profession. It also permitted Amstrup to retain his membership when there were two reasons for him to have been moved out before the rule change: his retirement from the USGS in 2012 and his subsequent employment at Polar Bears International, a non-profit conservation organisation. The new rules also allowed World Wildlife Fund activist Geoff York, who by 2015 was also an employee of Polar Bears International, to become a full voting member.*

In other words, the PBSG is no longer a group of government-appointed scientists with a mandate to generate plausible global population estimates and

---

*York has an undergraduate degree in English and a general Masters degree in Biology without a thesis. Usually, you are required to have an undergraduate degree in Biology (or Science) to do a Masters degree in Biology. It appears York's M.Sc. gave him academic credentials for his prodigious field work: however, he is still an activist rather than a scientist.[282]

coordinate polar bear research on behalf of the citizens of Arctic nations, but an autonomous conservation organization with a rigid mission to promote human-caused global warming as an existential threat to polar bears.

So the polar bear specialists had quashed all dissent, and they had money and power and influence. But unfortunately, they had yet to convince the public. As I discussed in Chapter 5, Amstrup soon realised he'd gone too far in suggesting that polar bears were doomed to extinction. The rhetoric had been so effective that the public assumed it was already too late to save the bears. Appeals for action on global warming appeared to be falling on deaf ears.

The realization that he'd pulled the rug out from under himself prompted Amstrup to muster his colleagues to produce a follow-up paper designed to give the public hope.[283] The new paper, which garnered lots of media attention, showed that if greenhouse gas emissions were curtailed, polar bears could be saved.

By that time, Amstrup and colleagues in the US had a Democratic President who seemed willing to back them up. But when the massive social changes Amstrup expected from Obama did not materialise – after all the hard work he'd put into making the case for polar bears – by his own admission, he became disillusioned with government work. He retired from the USGS to take a paid position as an activist for Polar Bears International, not to do science but to inspire action on global warming:[284]

> The lack of action on climate led Amstrup to retire from his government job in 2010 to become chief scientist at Polar Bears International.

> 'I left the USGS not because I'd lost my interest in research, but because I knew that inspiring action to halt global warming was the only way to save polar bears,' he said.

Leaving the government made Amstrup eligible for accolades he would likely not have received otherwise. He was awarded the Indianapolis Prize in September 2012 at a gala event and pocketed a cash award of $100,000 for his part in having polar bears declared 'Threatened' under the ESA. He got the genuine red-carpet treatment at the annual BAMBI awards in Germany a couple of months later, where he was a real oddity amongst the fashion icons, rock legends, and film stars who are the usual recipients of these prizes: Lady Gaga, Rock Hudson, Sophia Loren, and U2 have all been winners in the past.

So to say that Amstrup has a vested interest in seeing polar bears remain listed as 'Threatened' under the ESA is an understatement. He considers it his legacy work and is determined not to have it made redundant. And he has the financial backing of a non-profit organization to back him up.

The IUCN reassesses in 2015

Unfortunately for Amstrup, the IUCN listing on which his prominence rested soon began to look very shaky. As early as 2012, the IUCN standards committee apparently realised that the PBSG's 2005 recommendation to uplist the bears to 'Vulnerable' status based on future threats was embarrassingly devoid of science. IUCN modelling specialists looked carefully at the US justification for listing polar bears as 'Threatened' and they were not impressed. They saw glaring scientific shortcomings. We know this in part because of emails obtained via FOIA requests to the USGS and the USFWS.[†] The emails, which can be seen in Appendix A, confirm that about the same time that Amstrup was accepting high-profile prizes for his work, the IUCN was picking it apart. They also show that H. Resit Akakaya, a modelling expert and chair of the IUCN Red List Standards and Petitions Subcommittee, which develops guidelines for threatened and endangered species assessments and evaluates petitions against the red-listing of these species, was in contact with PBSG member Øystein Wiig ahead of the new polar bear survival assessment that was due in 2014.

As a follow-up to these email discussions, the IUCN sent representatives to the next PBSG meeting to reiterate their position. According to the minutes,[‡] Dena Cator and Simon Stuart from the IUCN informed the group of the strict new guidelines that were now in place, adherence to which was mandatory for the new polar bear assessment. Most importantly, they told the PBSG that Amstrup's Bayesian network approach would be unacceptable and that any new computer model had to include population size estimates for all subpopulations.

Ultimately, what the PBSG came up with for their 2015 assessment –which conveniently upheld the 2006 status of 'Vulnerable' – was a model that used out-of-date and 'substandard' population estimates (because that is all they had for most regions). And as I mentioned in Chapter 5, they also did not use ice models based on projected levels of carbon dioxide in the atmosphere; they simply assumed sea ice would continue to decline at the same rate in the future as it has since 1979. Yet the result was a probabilistic prediction that was far from frightening: they suggested that by 2050, there was a 70% chance that a 30% decline in global population size *might* occur and that extinction was virtually

---

[†] These emails were obtained by the Energy and Environment Legal Institute, E&E Legal, and the Free Market Environmental Law Clinic and were sent to me by lawyer Chris Horner in 2014, unsolicited.

[‡] 17th meeting of the PBSG held in June 2014 in Fort Collins, Colorado (published online at the PBSG website) http://pbsg.npolar.no/en/meetings/stories/17th_meeting.html.

impossible, even if sea ice virtually disappeared in the summer.[285,§]

It's easy to see why Amstrup is so unhappy with me calling out the failure of his model: it was bad enough that the IUCN Red List expert modelers implied it was poor science, without an upstart from outside the specialty also showing it was wrong.

Conclusion

I cannot emphasise too strenuously how detrimental to science has been this takeover of the PBSG and its individual members by noble-cause advocacy. The high-profile status of polar bear conservation made polar bear research an exemplar for science as a whole, but the advocacy on display by participants in the field has contributed strongly to the growing disdain with which unbiased scientists and the public now view it. The PBSG is no longer a scientific organization, and I'm not the only one who thinks so. Mitch Taylor is also concerned about the decay of science on display in polar bear research. He emailed me and others with his thoughtful response to the *New York Times* article that appeared 10 April 2018 regarding the *BioScience* paper. I have reprinted an excerpt below.

Excerpt from 'Accountability in polar bear science'
by Dr Mitch Taylor

It has become a lot more difficult to talk about polar bears since they became an icon for climate change as a cause. The information has become secondary to the mission for a number of people who were formerly chiefly concerned with research and management of polar bears. The mission is nothing less than saving the planet by saving the polar bears. Ironically the biggest obstacle to this initiative has been the polar bears themselves.

The real story has been the extent to which polar bears have managed to mitigate the demographic effects of sea ice loss so far. In retrospect this is perhaps not so surprising because polar bears have been around since the Pliocene which means they have persisted through not only glacial cycles, but also through all the natural climate cycles during the glacial periods and interglacial periods.

Did Susan misrepresent the predictions from Amstrup's 'Belief Network' [Amstrup *et al.* (2007)]? Has she misunderstood the population estimates provided by the various technical committees and specialists groups? That is easy to check, because these papers are published. They are part of the record. I have

---

[§] As far as I am aware, Amstrup has never made reference to either of the IUCN/PBSG assessments in any of his recent interviews or essays, even though he is a coauthor on both reports.

been active in polar bears since 1978. I didn't recognise 12 of the 14 names on the paper written criticizing Susan for publishing an article about polar bears because she does not have any direct experience in polar bear research or management. Does anyone need to point out how hypocritical this is? Since when does anyone need to tag a polar bear to compare what was predicted to what has happened, based on published information?...

There are two ways to get a scientific consensus. One is to present the data and the analysis in a manner that is so persuasive that everyone is convinced. The other way is to exclude or marginalise anyone who does not agree. This occurs so commonly now that it has become an accepted practice. The practice of science has become secondary to governments, NGOs, journals, and scientists who feel that the ends justify the means.

The response to Susan's work is politically motivated, not an argument against her conclusions. The journal's response to this article and to her complaint was also political. Sadly, *BioScience* is not a credible scientific journal anymore. We have fake news and fake science.

Is it really so difficult to see what the Amstrup predictions were indexed to, to see if that index has changed, and see if the demographic data are consistent with Amstrup's predictions or not? Susan has already done the work to show that the polar bear demographic data and sea ice data (all collected and reported by others) do not support the Amstrup et al. (2007) predictions...

To me the loss of credible information is the real harm that has resulted from turning scientific inquiry into an agenda driven exercise... even for a good cause. Some may see parallels within climate science world to the polar bear experience.

Chapter 9

Climate science gutted by lost icon

As I've already shown, since the start of this century, the polar bear has been the favoured icon of those who promote the idea of human-caused global warming. It has been routinely featured in media essays about the effects of global warming, even in articles about the Arctic or climate change that were not about bears at all. Polar bear images have always been a blatant appeal to the emotions of readers.[286] For a while, the approach worked in getting the public on-side: people were all for 'action' on climate change if it meant that polar bears would be protected from going extinct. But people today are generally better informed about the current status of polar bears. Most know the bears have not been dying in droves as they were predicted to do, and they mostly know that starvation is a natural cause of death for polar bears. Increasingly, climate activists are realising that polar bear images and Arctic doomsday messages no longer generate the immense public support they once did.

Moreover, a number of recent reports, such as the Arctic section of the 2017 US Climate Science Special Report,[287] have failed to mention polar bears in their coverage of Arctic sea ice decline. NOAA's annual Arctic Report Card has not mentioned them since 2014, despite covering bears every year between 2008 and 2014. Even Al Gore seems to have forsaken the icon: after playing a starring role in his 2007 documentary, *An Inconvenient Truth*, polar bears didn't even get a mention in the follow-up, *An Inconvenient Sequel: Truth to Power*. After more than a decade of campaigners and researchers proclaiming that polar bear populations were in terminal decline, the first 'canary in the coal mine' of climate change is losing its utility.

Starving bears: the last throw of the dice

Although readers are still subjected to the occasional irony of images of fat, healthy polar bears gracing stories about bears starving to death due to sea ice loss,[288] climate change stories in the media feature polar bears less often than they used to. I don't think that's an accident. I believe it is largely a deliberate response to the fact that several calculated instances of starving polar bear images used to manipulate public sentiment on behalf of climate change campaigns have backfired in a big way.

This animal tragedy porn, as I call it, has been used for many years. It began with a vengeance in the summer of 2013, when it was becoming clear that population numbers had not declined as predicted in response to the ultra-low summer ice levels of 2012. By that time, Stirling had retired and was a celebrity tour guide and lecturer for a group of wealthy ecotourists on a summer cruise around Svalbard. The group happened upon the carcass of an emaciated polar bear on the north end of western Spitsbergen, at a place called Texas Bar. A professional global warming activist (and photographer) named Ashley Cooper was part of the tour group and took a number of photos. These soon hit the international media, where they were augmented by some damning quotes from Stirling. A photo essay about the dead polar bear carried by *The Guardian* on the 6 August was blunt in its assessment:[289]

> *The polar bear who died of climate change – big picture.*
>
> A lack of sea ice, caused by global warming, meant the bear was unable to hunt seals and starved, according to an expert who had been monitoring the animal in Svalbard, Norway.

An accompanying article by the same authors carried this headline:[290]

> *Starved polar bear perished due to record sea-ice melt, says expert*
>
> Climate change has reduced ice in the Arctic to record lows in the past year, forcing animals to range further in search of food.

Stirling was quoted in this article as saying:

> This 16-year-old male polar bear died of starvation resulting from the lack of ice on which to hunt seals.

In the days that followed, the international press picked up the story and ran with it. The following headlines are just a sample of the media storm:

> 'Norwegian polar bear found starved to death'.[291]
>
> 'Starved polar bear in Norway may be a victim of climate change'.[292]
>
> 'A victim of climate change? Polar bear found starved to death looked 'like a rug'.[293]
>
> 'Is this starved polar bear which died as 'skin and bones' the 'categorical proof' that climate change is wiping out the species?'[294]
>
> 'Was this polar bear a victim of climate change?'[295]
>
> 'Starved polar bear proof climate change deadly'[296]

The dead Svalbard bear that Stirling and his group found had a faded '87' spray-painted on his rump from an encounter with Norwegian researchers who captured him far to the south in April, when he was recorded as being a healthy weight. But a truly healthy bear does not go from fat to starvation in less than four months. Well-fed bears in several regions routinely fast for this length of time without starving to death.[297] Whether it was old age that set off the starvation or the ravages of an illness, the bear clearly did not die because he could not get enough food: he died because he could not retain his body fat.

Backlash from the public on social media and in the comments of online news reports was swift and heavy. One mild version said simply: 'Maybe it just died, it does happen you know.'

The criticisms were severe enough that Stirling undertook damage control via Polar Bears International on the 8 August, with a claim he had been misrepresented by the media:[298]

> I was very clear throughout my discussions with the passengers about this bear that although starvation appeared to me to be the likely cause of death, in the absence of reliable information from a proper necropsy, this conclusion cannot be stated with absolute certainty. That is a very important scientific distinction. Thus, I was a bit disappointed, though not that surprised, that I have been quoted as saying it is certain the bear died of starvation in some news outlets. That simply isn't correct.

> Something to still reflect upon though is that although we cannot say unequivocally that the bear in northern Svalbard died as a result of climate warming, such an event is entirely consistent with the predictions for polar bears as a result of climate warming. And, if climate warming continues unabated, with associated loss of sea ice at critical periods for feeding, polar bear scientists predict an increase in such sad events.

> In some other parts of the archipelago, we saw and heard of bears that were thin, and one large, skinny male was behaving threateningly near a settlement. But some of the bears appeared to be doing fine. However, when we went north into the pack ice to look for bears, all of those we had a good look at were in excellent physical condition. Clearly, bears that are able to remain with annual ice over the relatively shallow waters of the continental shelf appear to still be doing fine.

However, there is no evidence that Stirling contacted any of the media outlets directly to complain about the misrepresentation he claims occurred: complaints of being misquoted are generally taken seriously and amended quickly. And despite the widespread hand-wringing about climate change perils for polar bears that August, the next month at least one newspaper wrote about how the bears were thriving, suggesting the message of Stirling's bear that died of climate change had faded quickly.[299]

Apparently, memories of the communication failure faded just as quickly. Only two years later, another activist photographer, Kerstin Langenberger, made a similar attempt to use an image of another painfully thin Svalbard polar bear as a victim of climate change. She posted the photo and her heartfelt story about polar bears dying of climate change on Facebook in late August 2015. It soon migrated to other social media sites and spread in viral fashion across the Internet. However, her amateur PR attempt also backfired when it became apparent the animal had been injured and was photographed in the process of dying a natural death. This time, a number of polar bear researchers (including Stirling) were willing to point out the true context of the image and refused to support Langenberger's emotional conclusion. A larger number of media outlets than in 2013 took a jaundiced view of the story.[300]

Finally, a similar, but professionally-orchestrated incident in late 2017 failed spectacularly when *National Geographic* magazine was forced to apologise for implying that a video of an emaciated Canadian polar bear it had posted on its website was 'what climate change looks like'.[301] In this case, the video and still photographs of the bear that went viral were taken by activist photographer Paul Nicklen,* who had long-standing ties to *National Geographic*. Details revealed by Nicklen's colleague Cristina Mittermeier suggest that he left the emaciated bear to suffer for days while he arranged to get his photographic equipment flown in to the remote site on Somerset Island in Nunavut, Canada. After the filming was complete, the crew let the bear swim away and told no one about its pitiful condition.

These actions were grossly unprofessional. A quick phone call by Nicklen to a local conservation officer would likely have resulted in the bear being put out of its misery and locals kept safe. But it would also have spoiled the story if news of the emaciated bear got out before he was ready to publicise it, so Nicklen chose to preserve his exclusive rather than do the ethical thing.[302] Moreover, Nicklen was putting other visitors to the area, especially local Inuit and their families, at risk of attack. Hungry bears can take desperate actions: the following summer, an emaciated bear ambushed an armed guard from a tourist ship in Svalbard, and only quick action by his companions prevented the attack from being fatal.

There is a white lie being perpetuated by a few vocal polar bear scientists, which is that loss of body condition in polar bears is the first symptom of climate change associated with loss of sea ice. But loss of body condition (getting thinner) is also usually the first indication of impending death for all polar bears: starvation is the leading cause of death for this species. But you can't tell the difference between polar bears made thin by man-made climate change and those that are thin due to natural causes. Even a necropsy will not be conclusive: there are so many natural reasons for a bear to lose weight – and even starve to death – thats it's virtually impossible to say that any particular thin bear is emaciated

---

*Nicklen works with the NGO, SeaLegacy.

due to a lack of sea ice on which to hunt for food.

By my calculations, there are at least eleven natural causes[303] of polar bears becoming thinner and/or emaciated to the point of death, all of which must be ruled out before starvation can be blamed on lack of sea ice:

1. Lack of experience hunting (for young bears, 2–5 yrs)

2. Competition from older, bigger bears (for young bears, 2–5 yrs)

3. Competition from younger, stronger bears (for old bears, >20 yrs)

4. Poor judgment

5. Broken or rotting teeth (especially in old bears)

6. Injuries from fighting (especially to the jaws)

7. Injuries from hunting or falls (especially to the jaws)

8. Illnesses (including cancers that cause muscle wasting)

9. Thick ice in spring (fewer seals to hunt)

10. Thick snow over ice in spring (making seals hard to find)

11. Less food for seals in summer (means less food for bears next spring).

The first four causes in the list would not be discernable from a necropsy. Similarly, the last three (9–11) reflect conditions in winter and spring that can affect survival and body condition later in the year and would also not be obvious from a necropsy. These last three causes of poor body condition are more likely to be obvious if more than one bear is affected in a local area.

For example, thick ice in spring was the reason given for many bears starving in the spring of 1974 in the Southern Beaufort. Similarly, thick snow over ice was the likely reason that many bears that came ashore in less-than-good condition near Churchill in the 1980s, and perhaps for the lower cub survival that was documented at the time. And less food for seals in summer explains why the condition of virtually all bears in the Chukchi Sea improved after 2006 when there was less summer ice compared to the 1980s: less summer ice meant more time for seals to feed and therefore more fat seal pups for polar bears to eat the following spring.

It is possible that one of the last three listed causes was responsible for the apparent low survival rate (about 3%) of yearling bears that were born in 2010 and 2015 in Western and Southern Hudson Bay, although the researchers involved offered no explanation for their unusual finding.[304] They did admit, however, that although the ice-free season was unusually long in 2010, even by recent standards, that was not the case for 2015.[305] In other words, survival of yearling cubs was low in two recent years in two adjacent regions but there was a possible correlation with reduced sea ice for only one of those years.

The reason that a close examination of a thin bear is required to at least attempt to determine the precise cause of its condition is apparent in the description below of an emaciated bear, encountered during routine field work in the Southern Beaufort Sea well before climate change became a survival issue:[306]

> I captured an emaciated but very large male polar bear one autumn when he should have been near his maximum weight. His weight was less than half that of similar-size males at that time. He seemed to be fit and his teeth were in excellent shape. On examination, however, we discovered that his maxilla [upper jaw] was broken through and there was a pronounced gap in his palate. The front portion of his upper jaw was attached only by the skin and musculature of his lips. His ability to bite and hold large prey was seriously compromised. How this injury was sustained is not clear. He has not been recaptured, and given the bear's lean state just before the harshest season of the year, I suspect he did not survive the winter.

The failure of appeals to emotion

In short, it is apparent that the repeated use of polar bear tragedy porn to inspire 'action' on climate change over the last five years has backfired in a big way, culminating in the 2018 *National Geographic* apology. A recent paper by psychologists Stephan Lewandowsky – one of the *Bioscience* authors – and Lorraine Whitmarsh described the problem of using inappropriate anecdotal accounts and images to advocate political action of global warming and called starving bear images prime examples of 'illegitimate emotional triggers'.[307] In this regard, these authors not only concurred with my stance on these incidents but documented for the academic record what was essentially an Internet phenomenon.[308]

The use of polar bear images to advocate for action on climate change encourages people to *feel* rather than think about global warming. It is deliberately manipulative. Now that there is so much more information available about polar bears and their current survival status, the public backlash regarding the *National Geographic* video can be seen as evidence that many people have had enough of being tricked and are perhaps offended by the implication that they are unthinking puppets.

In fact, the images most likely to be seen in recent years are photos of fat, healthy polar bears, even from regions like Hudson Bay, and the Barents and Beaufort Seas, where bears were once said to be most at risk due to sea ice loss. A swarm of hundreds of already-fat bears descending on the beached carcass of a giant whale on Wrangel Island in the Chukchi Sea, including at least two sets of quadruplet litters, was given international media attention in September 2017.[309,†]

Similarly, reports in early 2019 of an 'invasion' of more than 50 polar bears, which put a small town on the island of Novaya Zemlya (which separates the Barents and Kara Seas) under seige, were accompanied by photos and video of very fat bears: even the young cubs were fat.[311,‡] This put to rest the notion that these bears were in distress due to sea ice loss. While the decline in summer ice loss had happened, the predicted catastrophic repercussions to polar bear health and survival had not.

The continued health of polar bears worldwide, despite sharp loss of sea ice coverage, has made this species extremely unhelpful to climate change campaigners. It was hoped that stories about polar bear suffering might encourage public sympathy for global warming policies. But instead, the animal has come to symbolise the irrational bias imposed on biology by climate politics. Predictably, this situation led some to wonder: could another Arctic species take its place?

For a time, it looked like the Pacific walrus might be a candidate, as it too was slated to be listed as 'Threatened' under the ESA after a petition was filed in 2008 by the Center for Biological Diversity, the same activist organisation that had helped to kick-start the polar bear status change back in 2006. Driven by press releases issued by the USFWS between 2010 and 2014, several widely-publicised stories about tens of thousands of Chukchi Sea Pacific walrus hauled out on ice-free Alaskan beaches in 2014 suggested this species might replace the polar bear as icon of the Arctic.[312] But after my comprehensive report on the history of walrus gatherings and sea ice was published online a few months later, accompanied by a widely-viewed video called *The Walrus Fuss*, that notion seems to have disappeared.[313] Although press releases and news stories about walrus haulouts appeared as late as the summer of 2017, they simply never got the international traction with the media as earlier ones.[314] And by the fall of 2017, the possibility of making Pacific walrus into a climate change icon disappeared in a puff of ESA smoke when the USFWS announced it would not list the walrus as 'Threatened' because it had proven more resilient to sea ice changes than previously thought.[315,§]

[†] Official reports have since been published that confirm Chukchi Sea polar bears are not only thriving, but are one of the largest subpopulations in the Arctic.[310]

[‡] Even more ironically, most bears at this time of year are at their lowest weight of the year.

[§] A lawsuit challenging that determination, filed by the Center for Biological Diversity in March 2018, was to be heard by an Alaska court, but as of December 2018, that has not yet happened.

Public trust has been lost

The polar bear as an icon for climate change is virtually dead because the distorted predictions made by polar bear specialists and their advocacy since has caused the public to lose the trust they once had in their expert opinions. Two journalists have recently explored this topic with essays entitled 'How the narrative on polar bears has become a problem for Arctic environmental groups' and 'Why fake news is harming the Arctic'.[316]

Unfortunately, the public seems to have lost trust in *all* scientists involved in the global warming endeavour, not just polar bear researchers. Support for action on climate change has lost traction: concern about human-caused global warming has declined virtually everywhere.[317] Over 2018, the media has spent an inordinate amount of time promoting so-called 'extreme weather' events (hurricanes, heat waves, freezing weather, blizzards) as emotional triggers to sell the catastrophic global warming message.[318] But is the public mentally exhausted from the relentless barrage of doomsday messages that don't materialise? Despite heavy media coverage of the pessimistic 'Summary for Policy Makers' issued by the IPCC in early October 2018, the response from the public was lacklustre. As Rex Murphy at Canada's *National Post* has written, the IPCC has cried wolf too often.[319] But I'd add that outcome was hurried along by polar bear specialists saying 'the bears are dying' when they were not.

In closing, I note that one of the conclusions of the *BioScience* paper was that 'deniers' have deliberately used polar bears as a kind of 'wedge' strategy to debunk global warming, similar to the approach used by US creationists to block the teaching of evolution.[320] The *BioScience* authors chose the term 'keystone domino' to describe the way that the failure of polar bears to die off as predicted has been used to disparage the tenets of manmade global warming and seed doubt that global warming would cause an apocalypse. Hence, the 'climate-change denial by proxy' clause in their title, and this statement in their abstract:

> By denying the impacts of AGW on polar bears, bloggers aim to cast doubt on other established ecological consequences of [manmade global warming], aggravating the consensus gap.

Apparently, pointing out the evidence – provided by polar bear researchers and published in peer reviewed, scientific journals – that polar bears have not responded as predicted to an abrupt, decade-long loss of summer sea ice, is 'denying the impacts of AGW on polar bears.' According to those *BioScience* authors, it is only 'denier bloggers' who have noticed that as the polar bear has fallen from its vaulted position as flagship species of the AGW movement, it may foreshadow other problems with global warming evidence.

As I've shown, it was the media and activists – backed by scientists – who elevated the polar bear to its iconic status in the first place. The public were told that polar bears were sensitive indicators of human-caused global warming. They were assured it was a *fact* that the bears were extremely vulnerable to even small changes in summer sea ice coverage and were veritable 'canaries in a coal mine' for increasing global temperatures. However, recently published evidence showed that polar bears were much less vulnerable to changing conditions than the public were told, and many of their survival strategies were flexible rather than rigid. When evidence presented as fact turned out to be false, the public lost trust. And because it was the media, activists and scientists who misrepresented the facts, the public have lost trust in all of them: not just polar bear scientists but *all scientists* involved in promoting a pessimistic agenda on global climate.

That loss of trust is not the fault of 'denier bloggers', it's the fault of the scientists who sold assumptions as if they were facts. Steven Amstrup at the USGS did not know, back in 2005–2007, specifically how polar bears would react to reduced summer sea ice conditions. He could not possibly have known because those conditions had never existed in modern times. Amstrup made some assumptions about how polar bears might respond, but he was guessing. As it turned out, he guessed wrong. But it was the selling of his assumptions as facts that has turned the public against him and his colleagues.

If Amstrup had admitted he was only guessing, he wouldn't be in this position. But if he'd admitted he was only guessing, he wouldn't have gotten polar bears listed as 'Threatened' under the ESA. There was so much at stake for Amstrup that he oversold his case, and unfortunately he got caught. And now the climate change movement is suffering the consequences. It seems to me that the fall of the polar bear as principal icon for global warming has at least exacerbated, if not caused, the downfall of global warming concern amongst large swathes of the general public, including Nunavut Inuit.[321]

Chapter 10

On population estimates, then and now

As part of past status reports, the PBSG has traditionally estimated a range for the total number of polar bears in the circumpolar Arctic. Since 2005, this range has been 20–25,000. It is important to realise that this range never has been an estimate of total abundance in a scientific sense, but simply a qualified guess given to satisfy public demand.

Proposed footnote to the PBSG Circumpolar Action Plan, 30 May 2014. Dag Vongraven in an email to me.

The difficulty of counting polar bears

For animals that are hunted, it's particularly important to understand the size of the total population, as well as of all the subpopulations, so that hunting can be managed in a sustainable manner.[322] For populations at risk of decline for other reasons, it's important to know if programs put in place to reduce the risks have been effective.

Counting any population of wild animals is problematic. It requires either counting the animals you see in a small area and somehow extrapolating that figure to a much larger area, or counting all the animals you see over a large area (usually by air) and then trying to figure out how many animals were actually there that you did not see. How many were hiding or otherwise invisible, or that you simply missed (or counted twice)? A population count is *always* an approximation and usually comes with a mathematical 'error range' (such as '±100'). The error range is an estimate of how much the count estimate may be wrong, with a high degree of certainty.

The method that biologists prefer to use for population estimates is called 'mark-recapture' or 'capture-recapture'. Researchers capture bears in a particular area, mark them with a satellite collar or an ear tag, and release them. A year later, they return and do the same thing again to see how many of the bears marked the previous year were recaptured. After this field work has been done, computer models are used to determine an estimate of bear numbers for the entire region. However, to make the models work, the researcher must make a number of assumptions: he or she must choose how the model crunches the numbers to arrive at an answer.

Jim Steele is a Californian ecologist who has experience with these kinds of studies. He devoted an entire chapter of his 2013 book, *Landscapes and Cycles*, to explaining some of the problems associated with counting polar bears in Alaska. In an essay he adapted from that chapter,[*] he provided some fascinating insights into how differences in just one assumption can vary the final estimate. In this case, he explained how the concepts of 'apparent survival' and 'biological survival' varied population estimate results:[†]

> In mark and recapture studies, the estimate of population abundance is skewed by the estimate of survival. For example, acknowledging the great uncertainty in his calculations of survival, in his earlier studies polar bear expert Steven Amstrup reported three different population estimates for bears along the South Beaufort Sea. If he assumed the adult bears had an 82% chance of surviving into the next year, the models calculated there were 1,301 bears. If survivorship was 88%, the abundance climbed to 1,776 bears. If he estimated survivorship at a more robust 94%, then polar bear abundance climbed to 2,490. [Amstrup *et al.* 1986] Thus depending on estimated survival rates, a mark-and-recapture study may conclude that the population has doubled, or that it has suddenly crashed.
>
> ...
>
> Amstrup diligently followed up his earlier study on the apparent survival of South Beaufort bears using radio-collared bears over a 12-year period. It turned out that his high-end apparent survival estimate of 94% was still too low. If only natural deaths were used, polar bears had a 99.6% biological survival rate. [Amstrup and Durner 1995] Most bears died at the hands of hunters. If death at the hands of hunters was also considered, then biological survival was still higher than apparent survival, but fell to 96.9%. In 2001 Amstrup concluded that the South Beaufort Sea population was increasing and the current hunting quotas insured a growing population.[Amstrup *et al.* 2001]

The whole thing is worth a read because Steele explains very clearly, in layman's terms and with useful diagrams, not only how such studies are typically done but how they can go wrong. His comments take into account many of the points about Southern Beaufort bears found in Chapter 5.

---

[*]The original chapter is called 'Inuit and illusions in the time of the most polar bear';[323] the essay is 'How "science" counts bears', 3 July 2013, http://wattsupwiththat.com/2013/07/03/how-science-counts-bears/.

[†]In one case, the researcher assumes why bears captured one year were not captured the next (they left or they died), in the other, a detailed study is done that shows, in fact, whether bears left or died.

Even though they are fraught with such logistical issues, mark-recapture studies are still considered ideal. However, zoologists work in the real world, and sometimes they are forced to use less precise methods of arriving at an estimate; perhaps when resources are scarce, or the region is large and/or inaccessible. For example, analyses of hunting information or counts of the dens of females at places where they congregate in high densities have both been used as starting points for polar bear population estimates.[324]

For decades, biologists (including polar bear specialists) have tried various methods of improving the accuracy and/or efficiency of population estimates, but in the end it's the only way to get some understanding of 'how many'. Unfortunately for polar bears, such improvements and other changes made to methods of counting mean that virtually no two estimates from any one region are truly comparable over time.[325] This is particularly true for the Southern Beaufort and Western Hudson Bay, the two best-studied polar bear subpopulations in the Arctic, which are so often presented as the strongest examples of the impact of changing summer sea ice over time.[326]

The polar bear paradox

For the many birds and mammals that have faced conservation risks over the last few centuries, getting a handle on a starting population size – a benchmark figure – is almost always attempted, even if the estimate is known to be less accurate than scientists might like. For example, due to decades of over-hunting, the gray whale[‡] was said to have declined to approximately 200–300 individuals by 1938,[327] the sea otter[§] to less than 2000 individuals by 1911,[328] the northern elephant seal[||] to approximately 20–100 individuals by 1900,[329] and the humpback whale[¶] to less than 5,000 individuals by 1966.[330]

Were all of these numbers the result of comprehensive, scientific population surveys undertaken at the time? No: they were preliminary estimates based on various combinations of hunting records (i.e. harvest data), reports by hunters of increased effort needed to find remaining individuals, and results of limited field surveys. They were not guesses, but early attempts to provide the best estimate possible given huge areas of geography, limited funds, and low densities of animals.

Were the authors of the studies publicly ridiculed for using those numbers in their publications, or for referring to those numbers in magazine articles or

---

[‡] *Eschrichtius robustus.*

[§] *Enhydra lutris.*

[||] *Mirounga angustirostris.*

[¶] *Megaptera novaeangliae.*

media interviews because these estimates are not scientific enough? Not that I have seen. And as far as I know, neither the USFWS nor the Sea Otter Recovery Team has been reviled for suggesting that only about 2000 sea otters remained in 1911, even though there is no evidence that this estimate is a scientifically accurate number. In fact, I have never seen the authors of any paper, book, or essay who have cited a benchmark population estimate for any other species, later criticised or ridiculed by their colleagues for doing so, except when the topic is polar bears.

Polar bear specialists stand out in this regard: they deride anyone who cites a benchmark figure for polar bears in the 1950s or 1960s, insisting that no one knows how many polar bears there were in the past, and that all of those early estimates were simply 'guesses'.

In 2018, Derocher and a student of his, Stephen Hamilton, teamed up to challenge prevailing polar bear population-size estimates.[331] In the process, they provided a new global population estimate, but afterwards their study became very strange, because it cited the *BioScience* paper discussed earlier in this book in order to dismiss the use of global polar bear estimates in any scientific discussion about declines or increases over time (which would include my critique of the 2007 polar bear survival predictions – my 2017 paper – although they do not say so):[332]

> The global estimate, however, was acknowledged for its lack of precision and accuracy, and was not used for population assessment. Because of widespread interest in polar bears, the global estimate was sometimes referenced to satisfy public curiosity. Nonetheless, these estimates were misapplied by some to create doubt on the effects of anthropogenic climate change on polar bears.[333]

Their paper is a formal statement of a paradox that seems to exist only in polar bear conservation. This is that while the global estimate of polar bear numbers has been used in several predictive models of future survival, researchers insist those numbers cannot be used to assess the accuracy of those models.[334] And as their colleagues have done for years, they simply insist that there is no plausible estimate for the 1950s or 1960s that can be used as a reference point for conservation measures.

They also refuse to honestly portray the context of those early estimates. For example, Amstrup, writing on the website of the conservation organization Polar Bears International, where he now works, said of estimates of polar bear numbers in the 1960s (emphasis in original):[335]

> One of the most frequent myths we hear about polar bears is that their numbers are increasing and have, in fact, more than doubled over the past 30 years. Tales about how many polar bears there used to be (with

claims as low as 5,000 in the 1960s) are undocumented, but cited over and over again. *Yet no one I know can come up with a legitimate source for these numbers.* One Russian extrapolation presented in 1956 suggested a number of 5,000 to 8,000, but that figure was never accepted by scientists. The fact is that in the 1960s we had no idea how many polar bears there were.'

That 'one Russian extrapolation' mentioned by Amstrup was made by his fellow polar bear biologist and long-standing member of the PBSG, Savva Uspenski,[336,**] and the results were published in a Russian scientific paper at the time. Moreover, Uspenski was not alone in attempting to estimate the number of bears living in the 1950s and 1960s, when the mind-boggling numbers of animals killed by hunters worldwide started to raise conservation concerns.[337] None of these early estimates – including Uspenski's –were guesses, but rather were reasoned attempts by scientists to arrive at a plausible approximation of total abundance. In other words, these early polar bear experts were using the best available science of the day, and their estimates ranged from a low of 5,000–8,000 to a high of 17,000–19,000.[338] For example, the number of maternity dens in eastern Svalbard was noted to have declined when number of bears killed by sporthunters skyrocketed.[339] Uspenski's global estimate of about 5000–8000 individuals in the mid-1950s was based on the number of dens counted on Wrangel Island extrapolated across other major Arctic islands of Russia and North America, and adjusted for the proportion of pregnant females (20%) observed in Franz Josef Land.[340] Canadian biologist Richard Harington (1965) used a combination of methods: results of aerial surveys in Western Hudson Bay, his own knowledge of Arctic Canada, plus variations of the methods used by other researchers (including Uspenski), to arrive at an estimate of 'well over 10,000'. Norwegian biologist Thor Larsen's estimate was the highest of them all. He had reviewed earlier estimates and made a logical attempt to arrive at an informed census at 1970. However, he appears to have over-estimated the number of bears in the Svalbard area ('about 3,000' seems way too high for a population that had been particularly ravaged by over-hunting), and misrepresented Uspenski's global estimate as a Russian total:[341]

> Probably the best figure is obtained by summarizing the estimates made within limited regions of the Arctic. They are as follows: Alaska, 1959: 2,500; Canada, 1968: 6,000; USSR, 1968: 5,000–7,000…A careful and preliminary estimate suggests about 3,000 bears in the Svalbard area. The harvest data from Greenland suggest a population of at least 1,000 bears in that region. Totalling all the figures, we arrive at an estimated overall world population of between 17, 500 and 19, 500 polar bears. It is reason-

---

**See p. 8.

able therefore to suggest that the world population of polar bears is close to 20,000 animals.

Based on all of these accounts, in order to assess the effectiveness of polar bear conservation measures put in place in the early 1970s, I have used a range of 5,000–15,000 as a benchmark figure (average 10,000) for the 1960s. I consider this figure both plausible and reasonable. Polar bear specialist Markus Dyck used this same figure in a 2013 interview about the status of Canadian bears.[342] Is it comparable in accuracy to modern population estimates? No, it's not. But that's true for virtually all benchmark estimates for animal populations that suffered precipitous declines due to over-hunting in the late 19th and early 20th centuries. However, most polar bear specialists today do not accept this figure, or indeed any other figure. This is a standpoint that is virtually unheard of elsewhere in the wildlife conservation field.

In the media

Any mention of early estimates of polar bear numbers is now routinely disparaged. Numerous examples of this behaviour exist, beyond the statement by Amstrup quoted above. For example, NASA climate scientist Joseph Romm derided a review of Bjørn Lomborg's newly-released book, *Cool It*, written by scientist-author Michael Crichton[††] because Crichton said that 'polar bear populations have actually increased five-fold since the 1960s.' Romm turned to polar bear specialist Andrew Derocher, who at the time was chair of the PBSG, to provide a 'scientific' rebuttal of that statement (my emphasis):[343]

> The bottom line here is that it is an apples and oranges issue. The early estimates of polar bear abundance are a guess – *there is no data at all for the 1950-60s. Nothing but guesses.* We are sure the populations were being negatively affected by excess harvest (e.g., aircraft hunting, ship hunting, self-killing guns, traps, and no harvest limits). The harvest levels were huge and growing. The resulting low numbers of bears were due only to excess harvest but, again, it was simply a guess as to the number of bears.

Similarly, Peter Dykstra, writing for the Society of Environmental Journalists' magazine in 2008, noted at least a dozen instances of writers citing or implying a particular polar bear population size number in the 1960s or 1970s. He scoffed at them all. It didn't matter what the number was (those listed varied from 'about 5,000' to '12,000 or less'), the derision was the same: 'polar bear researchers say those old estimates were no better than guesses.' Dykstra then quoted four polar bear specialists (Steven Amstrup, Andrew Derocher, Thor

---

[††] Whom Romm refers to as a 'confused global warming denier'

Larsen, and Ian Stirling) for their opinions on these early estimates, just to drive the point home.[344] Amstrup was quoted as saying:

> How many bears were around then, we don't really know because the only studies of bears at that time were in their very early stages – people were just beginning to figure out how we might study animals scattered over the whole Arctic in difficult logistical situations. Some estimated that world population might have been as small as 5000 bears, but this was nothing more than a ['wild ass guess']. The scientific ability to estimate the sizes of polar bear populations has increased dramatically in recent years.

Derocher's response was this:

> I have seen the figure of 5,000 in the 1960/70s but it is impossible to give it any scientific credibility. No estimation of any population was attempted until the early 1970s and even then, this was done very crudely for perhaps 10% of the global population and the estimates were highly questionable.

Norwegian biologist Thor Larsen, who was doing polar bear research in the 1970s, told Dykstra this:

> Most data on numbers from the late 1960s and early 1970s were indeed anecdotal, simply because proper research was lacking. As far as I can remember, we did stick to a world-wide 'guestimate' of 20–25,000 bears in these years.

While in 2008 Larsen might have recalled that an estimate of 20–25,000 was what he and colleagues used in the 1970s, as I've noted above, the published literature shows the estimate he gave in 1972 was actually 'between 17,500 and 19,500' or 'close to 20,000',[‡‡] and included at least one major error. His paper on the subject also showed that those early estimates were not 'anecdotal' but the best science available at the time. Subsequent documents also show the estimate he gave in 1972 was far from accepted by his colleagues at the time. But in 2008, he knew it was important to support his colleagues on this issue.

It is apparent that none of these polar bear specialists expected anyone to check the literature to see if what they claimed was true. In 2008, they were already used to their word being accepted as gospel by the press, the general public and even colleagues in other biological fields. Their chosen field of work was exotic, dangerous, and low paid: who else would choose a career that was more like a vocation except men (and they were virtually all men at that time, Environment Canada's Wendy Calvert being one notable exception) of unusual dedication, bravery and honesty? Over the years, they had grown accustomed to being treated with unbridled awe and respect for the work they did with polar

---

[‡‡]See quote on p. 103.

bears. But by the turn of the century, the global warming issue caused a few of them, especially Stirling, Amstrup, and Derocher, to play fast and loose with facts on occasion, and their colleagues, including Thor Larsen, knew better than to contradict them in public. Well, most of them did.[*]

Is the global total actually higher?

That the global population size for the 1960s was never agreed upon by polar bear specialists isn't the only problem: recent population size estimates have also been low-balled. This makes it look like little has changed since international protection was given to polar bears across the Arctic in the early 1970s. But the notion that there has been no recovery of population sizes since then is simply not plausible. As I mentioned in Chapter 2, it was clear as early as the late 1980s that numbers had rebounded substantially due to conservation efforts. Most studied populations had doubled in size.[345] In his 1988 book about polar bears, Stirling suggested that by the late 1980s:[346]

> ...the total population might be as large as 40,000 animals because of incomplete or inaccurate survey data.

What he meant by this comment is that global estimates presented by polar bear specialists assume the number of bears in several large regions of the Arctic is zero, or that they have otherwise inadequate data. As a consequence, he felt the upper end of the range of an estimate that included those regions would have been close to 40,000 in 1986.

For example, in 2009 the global population estimate offered by the PBSG was 20,000–25,000, a range which was unchanged since 2005.[347] The figures were the sum of all subpopulations that had any kind of an estimate, rounded up or down.[†] However, they didn't include three large regions that were home to substantial numbers of bears: the Chukchi Sea, East Greenland, and the Kara Sea. In addition, the estimate used for the Laptev Sea was long out-of-date and almost certainly far too low.

Altogether, the lack of any kind of reasonable estimate for these four subpopulations probably led to the midpoint of the range given by the PBSG in 2009 being an underestimate by at least 10,000 bears, and the total range being understated by more than 20,000. Moreover, using plausible methods to revise all out-of-date subpopulation estimates, as explained in the next section, would

---

[*] As discussed in Chapter 8, PBSG member Mitch Taylor suffered mightily for expressing in public his disdain of global warming fearmongering.

[†] The actual totals were 19,608–25,162, with a mid-point of about 22,500.

put the current global average higher than Stirling's highest estimate for the late 1980s.

The global estimate for polar bear numbers should simply be the sum of all the subpopulation estimates, however they are defined. Officially, in 2015, the IUCN and PBSG put the global total at about 26,000 (22,000–31,000), figures that included all of the subpopulation estimates. But many of these were decades out of date, with little hope of being revised, while others have been updated since then (Table 4.2).

I've taken the liberty of proposing a new estimate that resolves these issues and brings those figures up to date. I suggest that the sea ice ecoregion concept is useful for revising these estimates, as long as the Southern Beaufort Sea subpopulation is left out (because of its unique sea ice conditions).

I suggest that the out-of-date Laptev Sea subpopulation estimate of 1000 is unaccountably far below others in the Divergent ecoregion (Table 10.1). Covering roughly 2.5 million square kilometres in area (both land and sea), the Laptev Sea is considerably larger than both the Chukchi and Kara Seas, which cover only about 1.7m km^2 each, yet is similarly dominated by the continental shelf habitat that's considered ideal for polar bears.[348] It has both mainland and offshore island habitats suitable for denning, including the eastern half of the Severnaya Zemlya archipelago and all of the New Siberian Islands. There is therefore no reason that it should not contain many more bears than have been estimated for the Chukchi or Kara Seas – in other words, more than 3,000. Therefore, a more plausible current estimate for the Laptev Sea is about 4,000 bears, with a range of 2,022–6,444 (using a similar ratio for the range as given for the 2016 estimate for the Chukchi Sea, discussed in detail below).

Table 10.1: Population numbers in the Divergent ice ecoregion compared to Foxe Basin.

Subpopulation	Population estimate	Year of estimate	Area (km^2) land, water	Area over shelf (%)
Foxe Basin	2585 (2096–3189)	2010	1,181,019	96
Kara Sea	3200 (2700–3500)	2013	1,763,680	87
Chukchi Sea	2937 (1522–5944)	2016	1,789,692	98
Laptev Sea	≈1000 (800–1200)	1993	2,459,282	85

2016 population sizes from Table 4.2; other figures from Hamilton and Derocher (2018).

As I've mentioned in Chapter 4, a similar extrapolation to the one I calculated for the Barents Sea (Table 4.2) based on survey results for the Svalbard half of the region, was used by USGS researcher Eric Regehr and colleagues[349] for the Chukchi Sea: they used data from a small area within US territory to extrapolate to the entire Chukchi region. In addition, based on their 2016 estimate for the Chukchi Sea, they further extrapolated so as to derive an estimate for the entire Chukchi/Southern Beaufort region shared by the US and Russia. This method generated an estimate of 4,437, although with a wide uncertainty range of 2,283–9,527. Subtracting the estimate for the Chukchi alone would put the 2016 estimate for the US/Russian portion of the Southern Beaufort at about 1,500 (761–3,583), also with 'significant uncertainty'.[‡] That's rather more than the estimate of 907 (548–1,270) calculated in 2010 for the entire Southern Beaufort (including the Russian/US portion and the Canadian portion). This is the first hint from specialists that the Southern Beaufort population has recovered from the 2004–2006 thick spring ice event, as it did from a similar 1974–1976 decline.[350]

Details of my approach to estimating populations in some of the other subpopulations can be found in Appendix B.

The final projected mid-point estimate for the global population is 39,226 (range 26,142 to 57,727), shown in Table 10.2. I contend this overall increase of about 56% over PBSG's 1993 estimate of about 25,000 (range 21,500–28,500)[351] is not only scientifically plausible, but it's about the kind of increase we'd expect more than three decades after Ian Stirling suggested that an upper limit of about 40,000 polar bears may have existed in 1986. Keep in mind that, using my benchmark figure of 10,000 for the late 1960s, the 1993 estimate of 25,000 was a 150% increase, or more than double. The lower end of my projected range is about the same as the 2015 IUCN PBSG mid-point estimate of 26,000 and the upper end is what Inuit and other Arctic residents are afraid might be true.[§] The 56% increase projected for 2018 might be just barely statistically significant but, most importantly, it paints a more realistic picture of polar bear abundance at the present time than does the IUCN assessment (Figure 10.1).

In contrast to the above exercise, Derocher and Hamilton's paper further low-balls already data-deficient polar bear subpopulation estimates.[353] Their revised estimates were based on an untested prey diversity index that they correlated with bear density. Table 10.3 shows the numbers they generated. Their revised global average total using these adjusted figures comes in at 23,315 (with a range of 15,972–31,212), lower even than the 24,500 figure used by USGS bi-

---

[‡] For the purposes of this exercise, I conservatively use the estimate of 1,500 to apply to the entire S. Beaufort, including the Canadian portion.

[§] It also means that, based on subpopulation size, only about 50% of the world's polar bears live in Canada, in contrast to the oft-quoted figure of 'two thirds', which is based on the fact that 13 out of 19 subpopulation regions are within Canada.

Table 10.2: Projected and accepted polar bear subpopulation size estimates at 2018.

Sub-population	Estimate at 2015 (Projected to 2018)	Year of estimate	Ref.
Baffin Bay	2826 (2059–3593)*	2013 up 36%	[1]
Davis Strait	3237 (2750–3813)	2018 up 50%	[2]
Foxe Basin	3612 (2934–4465)	2018 up 40%	[2]
W. Hudson Bay	1339 (980–1828)	2018 up 30%	[2]
S. Hudson Bay	943 (658–1350)	2011 stable*	[3]
Barents Sea	3763 (2698–5112)*	2015 up 42%	[4]
Kara Sea	3200 (2700–3500)*	2013	[5]
Laptev Sea	4000 (2022–6444)	2018 projected	[2]
Chukchi Sea	2937 (1522–5944)*	2016	[6]
S. Beaufort Sea	1500 (761–3583)*	2016	[7]
East Greenland	3000 (1522–5944)	2018 projected	[2]
N. Beaufort Sea	1300 (750–1800)	2018 projected	[8]
Kane Basin	357 (221–493)*	2013 up 118%	[1]
M'Clintock Channel	625 (365–884)	2018 up 120%	[2]
Viscount Melville	354 (266–442)	2018 up 120%	[2]
Gulf of Boothia	2229 (1218–3240)	2018 up 40%	[2]
Lancaster Sound	3557 (2463–4652)	2018 up 40%	[2]
Norwegian Bay	447 (253–640)	2018 up 120%	[2]
Official total 2015	26,000 (22,000–31,000)		[9]
Estimated total 1986	'as many as 40,000'		[10]
Projected total 2018	39,226		[2]
Projected range 2018	26,142–57,727		[2]

*indicates actual recorded increases. [1] SWG (2016); [2] Crockford this table; [3] Obbard *et al.* (2015); [4] Crockford (2017d); [5] Matishov *et al.* (2014); [6] Regehr *et al.* (2018); [7] AC SWG (2018); [8] Stirling *et al.* (2011); [9] Wiig *et al.* (2015); [10] Stirling (1988).

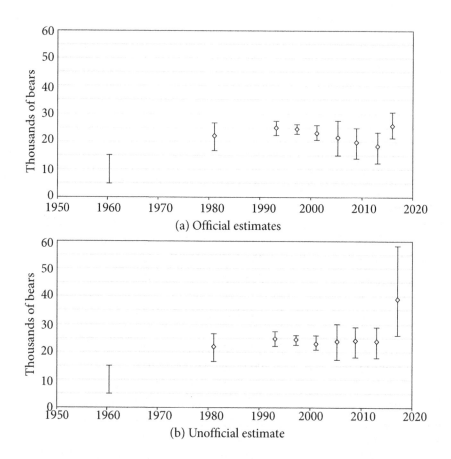

Figure 10.1: Official and unofficial estimates of polar bear numbers.
Upper graph uses totals reported in PBSG status tables (to 2013), with min/max;
lower graph uses the same figures, but adds back in the so-called 'inaccurate'
estimates dropped between 2005 and 2013 (in 2014, the PBSG finally did the
same).[352] The 1960 figure is a ballpark estimate.

ologists in 2007,[354] and about 3,000 lower than the figure used by the IUCN in 2015.

Despite being described as poor habitat for polar bears, the Hamilton and Derocher estimate for the Arctic Basin is more than twice the size of any estimate previously provided for that region (formerly called 'Queen Elizabeth'), which was about 200 bears.[355] In contrast, their East Greenland and Chukchi Sea estimates are less than half the values used by the IUCN in 2015, and the Kara Sea estimate is one third the size of the estimate published by Russian researchers.[356] The Laptev Sea estimate they used is even lower than the 1993 estimate, which is now more than two decades out of date. The warning from the authors that 'our proposed relationship between prey diversity and polar bear density should be used with caution' might be the understatement of the year.[357] They also warn that '... our [global] estimate should not be used to compare with previous estimates as an indication of growth or decline in the global popular bear population.'[358] So why, I wonder, did they bother to publish it?

Table 10.3: Modelled estimates of data-deficient polar bear subpopulation size.

Subpopulation	Estimate	Range
Arctic Basin	489	248–725
Chukchi Sea	823	416–1220
East Greenland	991	501–1469
Kara Sea	989	500–1466
Laptev Sea	812	411–1203
Total of above modelled estimates	4104	2076–6083
Excluding Arctic Basin		
From above	3615	1828–5358
Per IUCN 2015	8200	

From Hamilton and Derocher (2018).

It seems to me that unless the approach for achieving it is changed, a 'scientifically accurate' global estimate for polar bears may never be realised: the area is too vast, the expense involved is too high, and the interests of stakeholders are too varied. Using the present IUCN/PBSG approach, there will always be some subpopulations that will have out-of-date estimates and a few where the estimates will be based on less-than-ideal methods. Even within the same subpopulation, surveys have been done using such inconsistent methods in different years that it is doubtful if the results are truly comparable – the Southern Beaufort Sea and Western Hudson Bay are two examples of this problem.[359] Politics are getting in the way for some of these estimates and that may never be resolved: Russia may never truly cooperate with the objectives of western nations regarding population surveys, perhaps partly because the funds required are so high.

It's been almost 50 years since the IUCN PBSG was formed, with a primary mandate of generating a sound global estimate:

Top on the list of research priorities is the urgent need for more precise knowledge about the size of the world's polar bear population, the regional distribution, and the dynamics of reproduction.[360]

On its website,[||] the PBSG describes their global population estimate this way:

> …it simply expresses a reasonable range in numbers, based on a combination of the best available information and understandings of polar bear habitat.

The fact that the PBSG now dismiss the worthy scientific goal of discovering the size of the world's polar bear population tells us that embracing human-caused global warming as the greatest risk to polar bear health and survival has corrupted the science of polar bear conservation. Polar bear scientists took themselves too seriously from the beginning, something which was obvious from their refusal, even in the 1980s, to agree on a benchmark population figure. No matter how 'unscientific' they thought it was, they should have agreed on a number, as other biologists who study depleted species have done.

This 'no benchmark' stance became truly problematic when global warming replaced over-hunting as the existential threat to polar bears because that's when the PBSG deemed the global estimate 'unscientific.' But how can anyone judge the effectiveness of conservation measures – or modern predictive computer models – when there is no agreed-upon start figure and no trustworthy global estimates to compare over time?

Given this state of affairs, perhaps what we need are near-simultaneous aerial surveys of the world's polar bear populations, say within 2–3 years of each other. Aerial surveys are much less expensive, time-intensive, and invasive for generating population estimates than traditional mark-recapture methods, and consistency across all subpopulations worldwide would mitigate somewhat the disadvantage of higher margins of error. The PBSG could have organised the science and funding for such a study years ago, including making appeals to wealthy philanthropists and non-profit conservation organizations. But now, I'm not sure they can be trusted to do so without their advocacy for global warming biasing the results.

Ultimately, insisting that global population estimates are worthless and that no credible benchmark population size exists makes polar bear specialists look foolish. If they are intent on salvaging their careers, it is not too late for them to re-embrace the goal of gathering a global estimate and to back away from the failed hypothesis that a bit less summer sea ice is an existential threat to polar bear survival.

[||] As at 11 July 2014 [accessed 18 February 2019], http://pbsg.npolar.no/en/status/pb-global -estimate.html.

Chapter 11

Concerns ahead for polar bears

There are a number of concerns worth voicing regarding the future of polar bears and polar bear research. It doesn't matter that the polar bear icon of the campaign against human-caused global warming is dead, and may have taken support for action on climate change with it: there are still issues left to be resolved and attitudes to be adjusted as the realities of thriving polar bear populations sink in.

What will future polar bear research be like?

Will traditional mark-recapture studies be abandoned across the Arctic? In Canada, where most of the world's polar bears live, concerns of aboriginal Arctic people (Inuit) about mark-recapture studies have already changed the shape of polar bear research. Such studies require chasing a polar bear at very close range with a helicopter – almost always a female, often accompanied by young cubs – until she can be shot with a tranquilizing dart. When the bear is immobilised, standard measurements and tissue samples are taken. Satellite radio collars are put around the necks of females to monitor their future movements, while all bears (including males and young bears that are captured) have identification and (sometimes) radio-frequency ear tags attached.* In addition, while she is powerless to stop it, the mother's defenseless cubs are often passed around so the researchers and field crew can take photos of each other with the adorable young bears. Virtually all polar bear specialists have at least one photo of themselves with tiny polar bear cubs posted online, as if it was a trophy or critical rite of passage. The tranquilizing drugs eventually wear off enough for the bear to rouse itself and stagger off but it may take weeks for residues of the drugs to clear the animal's system.

A newspaper article published in May 2008 describes many of the issues surrounding these types of studies, which came to a head after survey efforts

---

*Collars cannot be used on adult males because their necks are bigger around than their heads, so collars fall off; young bears are still growing, so a collar tight enough to stay on when captured would later choke them.

in Davis Strait had ended and a new survey of Foxe Basin bears had begun.[361] It described the concerns of Inuit hunters regarding a plan to tranquilise about 300 bears for research purposes in 2008: even though hunters are compensated for killing bears they cannot use for food, the number still seemed excessive.[†] However, Inuit were also upset about the potential effects of the colllars on living bears:

> Hunters have almost always opposed the use of such techniques, especially satellite collars, saying they threaten the animal's health.
>
> [Paul Quassa, the mayor] said hunters fear that the collars will cause bears to get their heads stuck through breathing holes in the ice while hunting seals.
>
> And hunters in Repulse Bay have complained that researchers attach the collars at a time of year when the bears are thin. They say that later in the year, when bears get fat, the tight collar chokes them.

Elizabeth Peacock, a polar bear biologist for the Government of Nunavut at the time, dismissed these worries:

> We're professional. We know what we're doing. People have been putting collars on bears for years. We go to the [Hunter and Trapper Organization] meetings. We understand their concerns but we have a job to do.

However, in the end, Canadian Inuit objected so strenuously to routine use of mark-recapture that the Foxe Basin population study in 2008 was abandoned; an aerial survey was done the following year instead. Later, mark-recapture studies were essentially banned throughout Nunavut, the Northwest Territories (in the western Canadian Arctic) and northern Quebec because aboriginal government agencies refused to issue the necessary permits for such work.

Polar bear specialists refer to this conflict as a 'control of research' issue.[362] It has meant that polar bear researchers who cannot make their research methods mesh with Inuit concerns are effectively out of work in most of Canada. The big exception is Western Hudson Bay, most of which is in Manitoba, and therefore outside Inuit government control. Mark-recapture studies are done in the Manitoba portion of the subpopulation but not in the Nunavut portion, which may skew the validity of some recent results.[363] Elsewhere in Canada, however, we may have seen the end of mark-recapture studies, except in special circumstances. For example, aerial surveys have become the new standard for population estimates in Nunavut and elsewhere in the Arctic, although mark-recapture work is still done in Alaska.[364]

[†] Health Canada guidelines ban the consumption of meat from an animal killed within a year of being tranquilised and hunters are given $300 for every bear they kill that is therefore unfit to eat.

The need for accountability in research and publication

Some polar bear researchers insist that capturing polar bears is essential for them to do their work properly: that the kind of information they gather from a sedated bear is invaluable even before a satellite collar or ear tag is installed to track its movements.[365] As a consequence, certain data have been standard for decades:[366] sex, estimated age of cubs, weight to the nearest kilogram, and body length. Also, to determine age, one of the bear's smallest premolar teeth is pulled out for later analysis and blood samples are taken. However, it seems that while this information is always collected, it is not always reported in the scientific literature.

The fact that the province of Manitoba is not subject to the rejection of mark-recapture studies means putting collars on females with cubs has continued unabated throughout most of Western Hudson Bay. However, none of the detailed information said to be critical for determining accurate population estimates and effects of sea ice loss (especially the body weights of adult females) has been published. Stirling and his colleagues have continued to tell the media that there is recent evidence of reduced body condition and cub survival due to reduced sea ice in Western Hudson Bay, even though they are surely aware that this data has not been made public.[367]

In fact, almost a dozen papers on various aspects of Western Hudson Bay polar bear health and life history, based on capture/recapture data, have been published since 2004, much of it student work supervised by Derocher.[368] Yet none of these papers have reported female body condition or cub survival data. Since recording body mass and age of cubs is part of the standard morphometric data collected by biologists during mark-recapture studies, this means the data almost certainly exists but has not been published.[369]

But why has the data not been published if it indeed supports the connection between sea ice loss and declining body condition and cub survival? The obvious answer is that the data in fact *do not* support the narrative. And if the data do not support it, then the related claim – that the population is declining in size because of impacts on health and survival due to the longer ice-free season – is also not supported by evidence. And that means the Inuit may be right: there has not been a population decline in Western Hudson Bay. It also means that polar bear specialists cannot be trusted to reveal data that does not support their claims that polar bears are suffering due to sea ice decline.

Another concern is the accuracy of population estimates. As noted above, the popularity of aerial surveys for determining population size is growing, not only within Nunavut but throughout the Arctic region (including the Barents and Chukchi Seas). The downside of this method is that margins of error are so large that it is impossible to determine if a potentially catastrophic decline in numbers – or a mind-boggling recovery – has taken place.

For example, the 2015 aerial survey of the Svalbard portion of the Barents Sea generated an estimate that was a 42% increase over a similar study done in 2004. However, that 42% increase was deemed statistically insignificant.[370] Keep in mind that the IUCN Red List uses a threshold of a 30% decline in population numbers to designate species vulnerable to extinction. However, it would likely take a 50% decline in polar bear population numbers to be statistically significant. In other words, if only a 50% decline or greater is statistically significant, that makes the Red List criteria for designating a vulnerable population scientifically invalid for polar bears.

Polar bear specialists rarely mention this issue in public because it means virtually all their population survey efforts are scientifically pointless, at least as far as determining conservation status is concerned. They simply ignore the issue of statistical significance entirely if a decline in numbers is registered and emphasise it when an increase occurs. For example, when a recent survey of Western Hudson Bay polar bears showed an 11% decline, the media was encouraged to report that a documented drop in numbers had occurred, even though it was statistically insignificant.[371] It's a different story when the numbers go the other way, such as the 42% increase in the Barents Sea noted above. On that occasion, the PBSG made sure to mention the increase was not statistically significant in their summary of the Svalbard survey,[372] and chose not to extrapolate the survey results to the entire Barents Sea region.

In short, documented increases are dismissed as mathematically irrelevant while declines – no matter how statistically insignificant – get headlines. This practice reveals that polar bear specialists have an agenda to present population numbers as declining, even if that position is not scientifically supported. Again, it indicates that an erosion of trust in these researchers is justified.

The need to acknowledge natural cycles of Arctic climate

Since the late 1990s, polar bear specialists have largely refused to acknowledge that climate (and thus sea ice conditions) in the Arctic is known to be naturally cyclical. This is especially disturbing since this information is prominent in their earlier published papers and reports. For example, writing in a special report for the Canadian Wildlife Service on their polar bear research in southeastern Baffin Island (i.e. southern Davis Strait) from 1974–1979, Ian Stirling and colleagues included the following statement in their background information:[373]

From the 1880s to the 1940s the Eastern Canadian Arctic experienced a general climatic warming trend...Since 1960, however, a definite cooling trend has developed. This trend is characterised by a marked decrease in the mean daily summer temperatures (June-August), a marked increase in winter precipitation and in the mean daily winter temperatures (September–May). Consequently, snow accumulation is greater than ablation, and permanent snowbanks are expanding.

Similarly, researcher Jack Lentfer told the 1972 PBSG meeting:[374]

Long term warming and cooling trends occur in the Arctic and probably affect polar bear distribution and numbers. Climatic trends should be considered when assessing bear distributions and population data on a long term basis.

East Greenland has also had documented periods of cyclical sea ice, with lots of ice some decades and less ice in others. Most of this evidence comes from the historic period, derived from the records of indigenous hunters and explorers to the region.[375] Polar bear researchers are aware of this, as shown by the same report by Jack Lentfer, who said of the changing climate and sea ice cover in East Greenland:[376]

Changes in ocean currents and climate affect sea ice. Vibe (1967) ... distinguishes three different climatic periods, each about 50 years long, between 1810 and 1960, reflecting three stages of penetration of East Greenland ice into Davis Strait. He believes that conditions of 1810–1860 are now repeating themselves. He designates this as a drift ice stagnation stage where...Greenland ice does not penetrate far north into Davis Strait. The climate is cold, dry, and stable.

Several authors have presented data indicating that sections of the Arctic have experienced warming trends prior to about 1950 and have experienced cooling trends since that time. Zubov's (1943) data show a warming of the Arctic for approximately 100 years prior to publication in 1943. He shows that Arctic glaciers have receded and the southern boundary of Siberian permafrost has moved northward. Zubov also present [sic] comparative data obtained during the drift of the 'FRAM' [1894] and the drift of the 'SEDOV'[1937], 43 years later, over similar tracks in the Eurasian sector of the Arctic Ocean. The mean ice thickness was one-third less and the mean air temperature 4°C higher in 1937–40 than in 1893–96. Dorf (1960) quotes Willett (1950) who states that in Spitsbergen mean winter temperatures have risen ~8[sic] between 1910 and 1950. ...Mitchell (1965) states that world climate during the past century has been characterised by a warming trend from the 1880s to the 1940s. Thereafter, the warming trend appears to have given way to a cooling trend that has continued to at least 1960 with some evidence that it was continuing to 1965.

Past cyclical sea ice regimes have also been documented in Newfoundland and Labrador[377] and have been acknowledged by polar bear researchers, at least in earlier reports.[378] Although some polar bear specialists today have claimed that polar bears were once common in Newfoundland and Labrador, there is no evidence to support such an assertion.[379] While there was plentiful ice during the late 1800s in the region, perhaps enough for females to den in northern Labrador and for a few bears to venture south as far as the Gulf of St. Lawrence in the spring, actual sightings were few.[380] This was almost certainly because the Davis Strait subpopulation had been so decimated by the first waves of commercial whalers that by the late 1800s, there would have been few bears remaining, despite the abundance of harp seals for them to eat.[381] Further back in time, archaeological evidence from northwestern Newfoundland, at L'Anse aux Meadows, indicates that a climate warmer than today existed about 1000 years ago: too warm to have supported the ice necessary for females to den, even in northern Labrador, and perhaps too warm to have brought ice and bears to Newfoundland even in the spring.[382]

In addition, as just one example of many across the Arctic, both Greenland and Svalbard seem to have had cyclical climates on millennial time scales, and this would have had the potential to affect polar bear health and survival. New evidence from a study on clams and mussels with temperature-sensitive-habitat requirements provides evidence that the western Barents Sea around Svalbard experienced much warmer temperatures and less sea ice than today during two early Holocene periods, including the so-called 'Holocene Thermal Maximum' that stretched from about 10.2 to 9.2 thousand years ago.[383]

Barents Sea polar bears clearly survived that previous low-ice period (and others), probably as they are doing today: by staying close to the Franz Josef Land archipelago in the eastern half of the region where sea ice is more persistent.[384] Evidence of prior warm periods in Svalbard and the obvious survival of polar bears through those times challenges the notion that recent warming has been (or will be) too rapid for polar bears to survive without huge changes in their present distribution.[385] Although it must be frustrating for Norwegian researchers and their colleagues to see 'their' bears abandoning Svalbard for Franz Josef Land because of recent low ice levels, they are not witnessing a biological catastrophe.[386]

To put the warmth of the Holocene Thermal Maximum into historical context relevant for polar bears, understand that there was a very cold, ice-age-like period just before. This period, the Younger Dryas, began about 12.9 thousand years ago and lasted about 1200 years. At that time, Barents Sea polar bear females likely made dens as far south as Denmark, because their skeletal remains are found in numerous locations along the south coasts of Sweden and

Norway.[387] However, the transition from the Younger Dryas cold period to the Holocene Thermal Maximum warm period took place very rapidly according to records from nearby Greenland. Warming took place in 'steps' of about five years each over a period of about 40 years.[388] As a consequence, after more than a thousand years of utilising denning habitat on the edges of the Baltic and North Seas, Barents Sea polar bears had to adjust very rapidly to denning only in Franz Josef Land.

But it is not only long-term Arctic sea ice cycles that are rarely, if ever, mentioned in recent papers: shorter-term cycles that are well known to polar bear researchers are glossed over as well. Recent papers and press releases tend not to mention the devastating effects on polar bears of recurring incidents of thick sea ice in winter and spring in the Southern Beaufort, as well as similar incidents in Western Hudson Bay (see Chapter 5). If the incidents are mentioned at all, the effects are blamed on lack of summer sea ice.[389]

This reticence on the part of polar bear specialists to acknowledge the cyclical nature of Arctic climate has negatively impacted their credibility. Arctic climate changes naturally, as does sea ice: polar bears have evolved the biological mechanisms to deal with those changes over scores of millennia.[390] Even if humans are somewhat to blame for recent declines in sea ice, there is nothing that has happened so far (or has been predicted to happen in the future) that polar bears, as a species, have not lived through before. This blind spot for historical context appears to be the consequence of not expecting polar bear biologists, with their educational and vocational focus on conservation and wildlife management, to have more than a cursory knowledge of evolution and geology.

Does Arctic eco-tourism impact polar bear survival?

In August 2011, a 17-year-old English high school student from Eton College named Horatio Chapple was mauled to death, and four others were injured, during an early-morning attack by a polar bear on their camp while on an adventure expedition to Spitsbergen. Seven years later, an armed guard from a tourist ship was ambushed and mauled by an emaciated bear on a remote island north of Svalbard in late July 2018: the guard was part of a four-member team sent ashore to make sure the area was safe for tourists to observe the tundra landscape up close.[391] In both cases, the bear was shot dead, but while the world was horrified by the first incident, it was outraged by the second, because affluent tourists were seen as selfishly endangering the lives of polar bears simply by visiting the Arctic.[392]

It appeared that the same animal rights activists who for decades pushed hard for well-heeled adventurers to 'shoot with a lens' rather than a gun had turned with a vengeance on eco-tourism. It remains to be seen if this kind of over-reaction to the death of a single bear that was near death himself will resurface the next time something like this happens, or if it was simply a reflection of how things can get blown out of proportion on the Internet. Yet there has been reasoned concern that because more people now travel to the Arctic than was the case in the 1960s, polar bears have been put at more risk of being shot in self-defence.[393]

However, there is no evidence that tourist companies and their charges are being willfully negligent in their treatment of Arctic wildlife, environments, and local residents. Quite the contrary: most of these organizations seem to zealously embrace the concept of 'low impact' tourism.[394] The facts of the 2018 incident say more about the formidable danger that polar bears present than it does about negative impacts of tourism: an armed guard almost died because a polar bear was successfully able to ambush him – when he and three other armed guards were there *specifically* to look for bears – and the emaciated bear had an intent to kill.

What will happen to zoo bears?

As the public comes to reject the notion of resilient polar bears as icons of global warming, what will happen to bears held in captivity to be 'ambassadors' for the climate change movement? It is inevitable that the zoo-going public will come to realise that polar bears are not currently in any danger of extinction and that captive polar bears are simply revenue generators. While zoos present themselves as part of a global solution to save the bears from extinction because they are educating the public about the perils of global warming, they may experience the same kind of public backlash levied against *National Geographic* for misrepresenting an emaciated polar bear image.

Here is one example. A polar bear cub named 'Knut' was born in late 2006 at the Berlin Zoo and was hand-raised by zookeepers after being abandoned by his mother. He was the first captive-born bear in more than 30 years to survive infancy at that facility. The cub quickly became a massive visitor attraction, and generated such high revenues that he has been estimated as the 'biggest cash-grossing animal of all time'.[395] Knut was not only a revenue generator for the zoo but was also exploited as an icon of global warming by Germany's environment minister. Despite protests from environmentalists that hand-raising Knut was unethical (although they seemingly saw nothing wrong with keeping Knut's mother and others in captivity), the zoo held firm and reaped the financial benefits of their celebrity inmate until his death in 2011 from a viral infection of the brain.

Other than that brief flurry of protest in Berlin, polar bears kept in captivity around the world in the last few decades seem to be immune to the kind of protests that plagued zoos in the 1970s. Animal rights protestors were so persistent then, with the backing of public sentiment, that many zoos were driven to give up holding polar bears for display. All of that changed when polar bears became an icon for global warming: suddenly, it was OK with everyone for zoos to keep polar bears and to breed them in captivity. Even the UK activist organization Freedom for Animals has been pretty much silent on the recent practice of keeping polar bears in captivity.

Part of the reason this new zoo agenda is working is that in 2012, Steven Amstrup – having just won several high-profile awards for his part in getting polar bears listed as 'Vulnerable' in the USA – made a special plea via his new position at Polar Bears International to the Association of Zoos and Aquariums.[396] He encouraged the organization to use polar bears as a living icon to 'engage' the public and inform them about the perils of 'climate disruption'.

> Four years after polar bears were declared 'threatened', there has been no official call for GHG mitigation. Inaction among our leaders means the public must take initiative to alter our path, and zoos can lead that call to action. The more people who have opportunity to see polar bears and understand their plight, the more likely we are to alter our warming path in time to save them. Although few have opportunity to see polar bears in the wild, millions see them in zoos. The St. Louis Zoo alone, the focus of a recent series of news stories about polar bears and zoos, annually has opportunity to inspire 3 million visitors.

Zoos are not breeding polar bears in captivity so that eventually, there may be polar bears to release into the wild (as was done with bison in the USA many years ago): polar bears born in captivity cannot ever be released into the wild because they have not learned from their mothers how to hunt and survive in the Arctic. Even Amstrup acknowledges that this is true.[397] Breeding programs occasionally produce adorable cubs, which draw huge audiences to the lucky facilities, but of the few cubs that are born, many simply don't survive. Many zoos in the USA are now PBI-accredited 'Arctic Ambassador Centers'.‡ But what are zoos going to do when the public turns against their teaching moments, boycotts their polar bear displays, and lobbies against breeding programs? What happens to the captive bears then?

---

‡ See AZA.org.

Resolving conservation status confusion

One issue that continues to affect the public's perception of polar bear conservation efforts is confusing terminology: in particular, what the term 'Threatened' with extinction implies about population size for polar bears.

As we know, both the 2006 IUCN Red List assessment and 2008 ESA decision were based on purported future threats, ultimately based on climate model predictions. However, the public and the media often assumed that polar bear numbers must have been very low and still declining because they were listed as 'Threatened' or 'Vulnerable'; this would be true for most other species classified as such by the IUCN and the ESA.[§] I have spoken to a number of reporters and elementary school teachers, for example, who were convinced that only a few hundred to a few thousand polar bears must currently exist worldwide, based on the ESA status of 'Threatened.' Others have apparently misunderstood the ESA classification system entirely and assume that being placed on the Endangered Species List automatically means polar bears are already near extinction. This confusion is understandable but was entirely avoidable.

Both the IUCN and the US Environmental Protection Agency (which oversees the ESA, via the Department of the Interior) have done a grave disservice to the public by using classification terms that for decades have meant one thing but now can mean two entirely different things. Much of the confusion would have been avoided if polar bears had been given an entirely new status term. 'Future threatened'. This would have distinguished the *potential risk* to polar bears or other species sometime in the future, from species that currently have been reduced to low numbers and are already at risk of extinction. Even better would have been something entirely different, like 'hypothetical risk'.

In short, the peculiar way in which polar bear conservation status has been defined is too confusing to be viable. It is entirely correct to state that polar bears are currently thriving: such a statement is not at odds with a conservation status based on possible future declines in population size that have not yet materialised (and which may never do so). This state of affairs needs to be fixed by conservation organisations before it permanently undermines the public's trust in their assessments. At present, both the IUCN and the ESA have become a laughing stock over their determination that the polar bear is 'Threatened' or 'Vulnerable' to extinction because of summer sea ice loss when the scientific data show that it is much more resilient to changing ice conditions than previously thought.

[§]However, some species are classified as 'Threatened' or 'Vulnerable' because of ongoing reductions in available habitat or disruptions in their range due to human land use, rather than currently reduced population size.

Understanding why polar bear numbers can grow quickly

As I touched upon in the Introduction, there is evidence that polar bear populations have the ability to recover rapidly from a temporary decline or to expand in size quickly when conditions are favourable. This was evident in the large number of bears that were still available for sport hunting after a six year hiatus during World War II, even though a truly astonishing number of bears had been removed from the Barents Sea region in the 40 years before 1930. It is also evident in the documented recovery of Southern Beaufort Sea polar bear numbers after the spectacular decline due to thick spring ice events in the early 1970s.

In contrast to the situation in the 1970s, when triplet litters were considered rare, one female with robust one-year-old triplets was photographed by researchers in the Chukchi Sea in 2010 and at least two quadruplet litters were noted on Wrangel Island in September 2017. This is yet another indication that reproductive conditions have improved with less summer sea ice in this region. It also shows how populations can grow quickly: not only had the female noted in 2010 given birth to three cubs, she had accomplished a rare achievement: all three youngsters had survived into their second year and were in good condition.[398]

This suggests that the high incidence of triplet litters and bears weaned at one and a half years that was documented in the 1970s in Western Hudson Bay was evidence of a biological mechanism for spectacular population increases in areas where prey abundance is high. Western Hudson Bay bear numbers had been markedly reduced by over-hunting until the 1960s, but afterwards they began to increase rapidly. This period of population increases coincided with the start of polar bear research in the region, during which unusually high proportions of triplet litters were documented. In addition, most females before 1985 weaned their cubs at one and a half years rather than two and a half years, as in most other populations, even though they had similar rates of mortality.[399] All of this went on in Western Hudson Bay while the bears undertook one of the longest summer fasts (at least four months) in the Arctic: only Southern Hudson Bay bears fasted for so long, even in the 1970s and early 1980s.

The following statement made by Ian Stirling and co-author Nick Lunn[400] sums up the issue rather succinctly:

> In the early to mid-1980s, the natality [cub production] of female polar bears in Western Hudson Bay was the highest recorded anywhere in polar bear range, and nowhere else did females successfully wean cubs at 1.5 years of age instead of at the normal age of 2.5 years. Subsequently, a long-term decline in condition of adult female polar bears and survival of their cubs was documented from the 1970s through the late 1980s...,

as reflected by a significant decline in condition indices.

This decline did not constitute a threat to the population because even when natality was at its lowest in the late 1980s, the rates were still higher than the upper range of values for bears elsewhere in the Arctic...

...the more important (but unanswered) question is probably not why natality declined from the early 1980s but how could natality have been sustained at a level so much higher than other polar bear populations in the first place, what facilitated the successful weaning of yearlings there but nowhere else in their range, and how could females manage these physiological feats in a habitat where pregnant females must also fast for 8 months or more?'

Those questions, presented by Stirling and Lunn back in 1997, are still unanswered because, shortly after they were posed, the focus of polar bear research in Western Hudson Bay shifted to documenting population responses to reduced sea ice.[401] No one seemed to care about the biological mechanism for rapid population growth when the worry was that polar bears could not survive if Arctic sea ice disappeared in the summer.

Surprisingly, the minutes of the 2016 PBSG meeting show that Eric Regehr, lead author of the 2015 IUCN assessment and of many Chukchi Sea studies, had this to say:[402]

...we tend to think of polar bears as a long-lived K-selected[||] species that are slow to recover, but from demographic modelling [i.e. population size estimates over time] there are some surprisingly high population growth rates... This relates back to the potential that we may be underestimating the resilience of polar bear subpopulations.

Preparing for increases in human-polar bear conflicts

Increases in polar bear numbers across the Arctic are fuelling concerns about increased human-polar bear conflicts, although these are still being blamed on sea ice loss due to global warming.[403] While actual attacks on people remain relatively few, close calls seem to be increasing in many areas, and the potential for more serious injuries and fatalities is very real; often, both people and bears die. Bears can also destroy property while searching for food, and they often kill dogs, which cash-strapped residents may be unable to replace. Many polar bears that live in areas where they are not hunted may have completely lost their fear

---

[||] 'K-selected' animals, according to the theory, are long-lived, with long gestation, few offspring, extended parental care and requiring a long time to reach sexual maturity. The theory says that stable environments, like Arctic sea ice, should support large population sizes of 'K-selected' species (like polar bears and seals) without marked fluctuations in population size due to habitat variation. See Crockford (2015a).

of humans, a problem that has perhaps been exacerbated by tourist operations that vie to bring bears and people into very close contact on a regular basis (as they do around Churchill, Manitoba).

In Canada, Inuit residents have expressed concerns about growing numbers of bear sightings around their communities in recent years, even while scientists insist that numbers are declining.[404] This is especially true in Western Hudson Bay since 2007 or so. Part of this controversy stems from the fact that 30 or 40 years ago, native hunters and their families living along the northwest shore of Hudson Bay rarely encountered polar bears when they were out and about in the spring and summer. But the situation is significantly different now, and polar bears are encountered onshore in all seasons, including winter – when the bears should be out on the ice.[405]

In recent years, it is apparent that some Western Hudson Bay bears have left the sea ice much further north than they used to do (and also earlier in the season) and have caused problems in and around communities north of Churchill, including Arviat, Rankin Inlet, and Whale Cove. It is possible that some of these bears once caused problems in Churchill or are the offspring of such individuals: problem bears – so-called 'green dot bears', a reference to the mark placed on them before release – that have been flown north for decades as part of Churchill's Polar Bear Alert Program.[406]

In other words, air-lifting problem bears out of Churchill and releasing them further north may have simply taught bears with little fear of humans that both natural and human-associated food resources also exist further north: some bears may now aim for the Arviat region (and north as far as Rankin Inlet) when they come off the ice. In addition, the documented presence of mothers with newborn cubs at Arviat indicates that some of these Western Hudson Bay bears are now giving birth outside of all known denning areas south of Churchill. Is this a new phenomenon? It appears so, but we cannot really say for sure because scientists have apparently never looked for polar bear dens north of Churchill on the west coast of Hudson Bay, although parts of Foxe Basin have been surveyed.[407]

Two fatal attacks in the northern portion of Hudson Bay during the summer of 2018 (one of which involved multiple bears) highlighted these concerns. One attack occurred on Sentry Island, which sits several kilometers from the community of Arviat (population about 2500), on 3 July.[408] Since sea ice receded away from that area of the north coast earlier than it did further south, it seems the bear involved must have come off the ice by the third week of May or perhaps earlier. This is about two months earlier than bears came ashore around Churchill, Manitoba the same year: according to reports published online by the Churchill Polar Bear Alert Progam, there were only a few bears around in

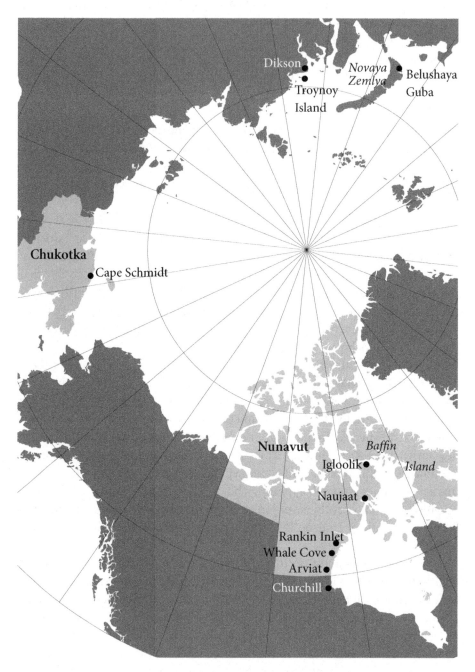

Figure 11.1: Places mentioned in the text.

the week of 9–15 July, but many more by the next week.

In other words, the bear involved in the fatal attack outside Arviat in early July, as well as about a dozen others observed in the area around the same time (according to local informant Gordy Kidlapik), appear to have left the ice before it was actually necessary, and came ashore much further north than most bears in the Western Hudson Bay region.¶ This is in contrast to the pattern in the 1980s, when all bears came ashore near Churchill or points south, and migrated north over the course of the summer, then, in the fall, intercepting newly-forming sea ice near Churchill and points north.[410]

The fact that the fatal attack in July took place on an island used by local Inuit to collect eggs laid by ground-nesting Arctic terns was a clue that naturally-occurring attractants rather than human-associated attractants (like community refuse and tethered dogs) may have lured bears ashore before sea ice conditions made it strictly necessary. In addition to the Arctic tern rookery on Sentry Island off Arviat, there is a huge migratory bird sanctuary just a few miles south, on the McConnell River delta, where a variety of ducks and geese congregate to nest in early summer (and near where other bears were seen in early July). The population sizes of most of these nesting waterfowl species are many times higher now than they were in the 1980s, because hunting restrictions have been put in place.[411] In fact, for some species, such as the snow goose, there are now so many millions of birds that they create ecological problems everywhere they go,[412] as a CBC news report explained:

> In the 1970s and '80s, there were between two million and three million snow geese in central North America. Now there are about 15 million.[413]

The presence in the area around Arviat of natural attractants that may not have existed in the 1980s (or which may have been much smaller then) undermines the suggestion that attractants within Inuit communities are primarily what draw polar bears to the region.

About eight weeks later in the 2018 season, on the 23 August, a second fatal attack occurred. This time it was in the Foxe Basin polar bear region, along the northern coast of Hudson Bay. The story goes like this: Darryl Kaunak, Leo Ijjangiaq and Laurent Jr. Uttak, three young but experienced hunters from the community of Naujaat (formerly Repulse Bay), were headed out on a two-day hunting trip when they had to land on White Island (about 100 km offshore) due to mechanical problems with their boat. While attempting repairs, sea ice blew ashore and prevented them from leaving. Darryl Kaunak was killed and his

---

¶In the weeks following the early July fatal attack, a bear that repeatedly approached a group of Arviat residents staying at summer cabins outside the community was shot and reported as a defence kill. By the end of July, four others that were deemed a threat had also been shot.[409]

two companions were injured when a female polar bear accompanied by a cub attacked while they were having morning tea. A warning shot by Ijjangiaq did not deter the approaching adult bear. She first grabbed Uttak, but then chased down Kaunak when he ran. She fatally mauled him. One shot at the bear failed when the gun jammed but the bear was finally killed when Ijjangiaq located another rifle. The bear's cub was killed afterward.

Still held captive by ice, four more bears were attracted to the scene of the attack over the next few days and two of them were shot by the survivors as they waited for help to arrive. Rescuers located the camp a few days after the attack, but because of heavy ice they had to wait for the assistance of a Coast-guard icebreaker to reach the camp. In all, the survivors had to wait five days before their ordeal was over: four bears were killed (not five as first reported) and one young man lost his life.[414] Conservation officials later reported that all of the bears involved in this attack were in good condition (Rogers 2018b). Since attacks by adult female polar bears with cubs are rare, this incident is even more troubling: most polar bear attacks involve young males between two and five years of age[415] A claim by one journalist that the hunters got between the female and her cub is not supported by the survivors' statements.[416] As was true for the July attack, this one occurred well outside the community. And since the men had not yet been hunting, there were virtually no attractants aside from the hunters themselves. The bear that attacked Kaunak was in good condition, not thin, and there was so much ice that she may have walked off the ice onto the beach in order to attack him.

Lastly, an astonishing third (but foiled) attack in the same region a few days after the White Island incident (on 25 August) got less media attention because tragedy was averted.[417] The tide was out, and a young Inuk fisherman named Jon Powell was pulling in the nets he had set in Rankin Inlet. What he did not realise was that a young female bear (about two years old) was stalking him from the water. The bear waited until he'd turned his back, then burst out of water after him. Alerted by others nearby, he was able to shoot the bear before she reached him. Apparently, the bear had been stealing fish in the area for several days. But this time, she was after the fisherman, not his fish (since she could easily have taken the fish from his net).

Although it seems more likely than not that Nunavut residents in northern Hudson Bay are correct that polar bear numbers have increased in recent years, two facts about that summer's attacks are irrefutable. None of the incidents in-volved bears that had been on land for longer than is usual in the area (in fact, they had been on shore for two months or less), and all but one of the bears involved was in good condition, not starving from lack of seals to eat. These facts do not support the claims by Stirling and Derocher that reduced sea ice coverage was to blame for these attacks.[418]

Nor do the facts support the statement made by Derocher that 'you can't equate seeing more bears with there being more bears'.[419] History says otherwise. In November 1983 there was a fatal attack in Churchill and another person was mauled: in August the next year (1984), a man was severely mauled by a big healthy male just north of Churchill while on a fishing trip. According to Stephen Kearney of the Manitoba Wildlife Branch, '…this was the final evidence required by many Churchill residents to conclude that polar bears were becoming more numerous and aggressive'.[420] As I've noted previously, by 1987, polar bear numbers in Western Hudson Bay were at an all-time high: the mid-point estimate was almost 1,200 bears, with a range from 1,020–1,368.[421] As a consequence of the 1983 and 1984 attacks, new procedures to deal with Churchill's problems bears were put in place, including the practice of flying some bears about 50 km north of town.[422] Apparently, the town of Churchill equated the appearance of more bears causing problems and more bears attacking people with there being more bears, so then they did something about it.

Has the number of polar bears in Western Hudson Bay increased over the last decade or so? It is not only entirely possible, but probable. The ice-free season in Western Hudson Bay has been about the same since 1995, when a sudden step-change added about three weeks to the summer fast endured by Western Hudson Bay polar bears, although year-to-year variation has been large.[423] In other words, sea ice conditions are no worse now than they were in 1998. It appears, however, that the population has adusted to this shift, perhaps because those bears with only average fat-storage physiology (who were previously barely able to survive a typical four-month fast) have been eliminated from the population. Strong evidence suggests that the young seals that are easiest for polar bears in the area to catch have left the ice by mid-May[424] and this means that early breakup dates cannot have impacted polar bear health and survival, because they have not come as early as mid-May.

However, late freeze-up dates in the fall, especially after a challenging winter (as occurred in 1983) have had devastating effects.[425] Consequently, the female bears that survived the sudden, extended fast brought on by a much later-than-average freeze-up in 1983 would have been individuals with the best fat storage metabolism in the population; their superior genes would have spread through the population over the following generations.

Late freeze-up eliminates the bears with the weakest survival abilities, making the population as a whole a lot more resilient to future years with similarly late freeze-up. Quite simply, the fact that some individuals did not survive the late freeze-up years of 1983 and 1998 would have been beneficial for Western Hudson Bay polar bears living today, even if the population temporarily declined.[426] Ongoing natural selection means that most individuals in the current Western Hudson Bay population have better fat-storage physiology and are able to survive an onshore fast of at least five months.

This means it is entirely possible for there to be as many bears now as there were in the late 1980s (1,194, range 1,020–1,368), or even more, as I discussed in Chapter 10.[427] However, as noted earlier it is also possible that, compared to even 10 years ago, a much larger proportion of the population now comes ashore north of Churchill and that some pregnant females stay there over the winter to have their cubs.

More importantly, it is not just northern Hudson Bay that is seeing more polar bears. Evidence of increased numbers of bears is everywhere, and not just in summer when bears are forced ashore by receding ice. Newfoundland and southern Labrador, which see polar bears from the Davis Strait subpopulation occasionally visiting in spring when ice on the Labrador Sea extends far to the south, had a record number of sightings and problem incidents in 2017, with 2018 not far behind. Some of these sightings happened in late winter, when sea ice levels were near their seasonal maximum and before bears had begun their intensive feeding on newborn seals.[428] On land in winter, bears are attracted by caches of frozen meat, cemeteries, the smell of cooking food, food fed to dogs (and the dogs themselves), stored food, garbage, sewage, petroleum products (such as oils, lubricants, antifreeze, and insulation) as well as plastic-coated cables and vinyl seats.[429] It's hard to fathom how the presence of many bears ashore from late January to March could be blamed on reduced amounts of sea ice, since polar bears cannot reach Newfoundland and southern Labrador without a prodigious amount of ice being present, but some polar bear specialists have tried.[430]

On the other side of the Arctic, where Russia meets Alaska, there have also been more problems with polar bears in the last decade. Chukotka, on the Russian mainland of the Chukchi Sea, has had numerous problems in summer with bears in recent years (especially in the community of Ryrkaypiy), including a fatal attack in 2011 at the village of Cape Schmidt.[431] Further west, Dikson (a small port community on the Kara Sea), is said to have been 'under seige' by at least a half dozen polar bears in mid-October 2018,[432] although the problem went away by early November when sea ice formed as usual and the bears returned to the ice. A similar story in September 2016 emerged about a weather station on Troynoy Island, further to the east (but also on the Kara Sea), when the five scientists manning the station had their dog eaten and were trapped for weeks inside their cabins when ten adult polar bears and two cubs surrounded the encampment.[433]

Winter problems with bears also seem to be on the increase worldwide, although good records from the past with which to compare recent ones are hard to come by, with reports from Arviat in Western Hudson Bay, East Greenland, Newfoundland and Labrador, northern Quebec, Svalbard, and Chukotka.[434] There are few natural foods available over the winter for polar bears. Seals are hard to catch and hunts are often unsuccessful,[435] which is why most bears are at their lowest weight at the end of winter. It also means competition amongst bears for the limited good winter foraging areas has always been high, but with increased numbers of bears competition must be even fiercer. Bears that come ashore in winter are looking for an easy meal: more problem bears and winter attacks than previously almost certainly indicates more bears. Recent winter attacks by healthy polar bears in southern Greenland have been blamed by locals on abundant prey: in other words, there are more bears than there used to be because there is plenty for them to eat.[436] The same has been said for recent problems with polar bears in Labrador: more bears because of abundant harp seals.[437] Keep in mind that often we are only aware of incidents via the media. The 'close-calls' that residents experience, on a regular basis, seldom make the news.[438]

The most recent and spectacular winter incident is one reported in early February 2019. More than 50 fat, healthy bears had apparently been causing problems in the small Russian miliary town of Belushaya Guba on the southwest coast of Novaya Zemlya, which separates the Barents and Kara Seas.[439] The bears had been terrorizing the residents since early December: entering buildings, confronting people, and prowling the streets day and night. Residents said they had tried all kinds of methods to drive the animals away but had been unsuccessful; shooting the bears was not an option because of their protected status. Eventually, by 9 February, a state of emergency had been declared and the Russian military was sent in to help.

These animals on Novaya Zemlya were almost certainly Kara Sea bears who had walked across the island from the east coast, where sea ice is seasonally plentiful (the island is not very wide).** The sheer number of animals drawn to the area by abundant attractants, including the town dump, made for a good story. But media attempts to make the bears seem desperate for food seemed ludicrous seen against the photos of dozens of corpulent bears, including fat cubs.[440] And the sea ice history of the area exposed the falsehood that this phenomenon had been caused by a lack of sea ice.[441] Ice charts showed the bears could have left the island in late November when sea ice descended on the southeast coast but

---

** The sea ice history of the area shows there has not been any ice on the west coast of Novaya Zemlya in December since the early 1980s, and since the 2000s has been ice-free all winter, as has the west coast of Svalbard.

they chose not to do so. The bears chose to spend the winter on shore where they knew there was food to be found around human settlements.

However, within a few days, the emergency was resolved by very determined harassment of the bears, which forced them onto the ice, which by that time was positioned just off shore. The follow-up report by the Russian news agency TASS (18 February 2019) did not actually state that no bears were killed in the process but it seems likely that some might have been.[††] Whether these bears will cause similar problems in the future because of their habituation to human presence remains to be seen.

Compare these recent examples of problems with bears in winter with the experiences of Dutch explorer William Barents and his crew, who were forced to spend the winter of 1596–1597 on the northern tip of Novaya Zemlya in the Kara Sea (latitude 76N, see Figure 1), when their ship became trapped in the sea ice in September. Crew member Gerrit De Veer (1609) kept a journal account of the long, horrifying winter they spent on shore, in a shelter they built with materials salvaged from the ship. They called their winter home *Behouden Huys* ('the saved house').

This part of Novaya Zemlya is close to the major polar bear denning region of Franz Josef Land, although denning also occurs on Novaya Zemlya itself. If polar bear numbers in the region were as high in the late 1500s as suggested for the early 1800s (Andersen and Aars 2016) – in the neighbourhood of 10,000 bears – the persistent problems with polar bears that Barents' crew documented were almost certainly due to there being a large number of bears present, not low sea ice levels.

An English translation of De Veer's journal is now available online and it offers a fascinating glimpse of what it meant to live through that year trapped onshore under almost-constant fear of attack by polar bears and of losing their stored caches of food to the bears.[442] The Dutchmen were plagued by polar bears almost the entire time they were on Novaya Zemlya, except for the period of intense Arctic darkness that ran from early November through early February. Bears stalked the crew almost continuously from mid-September 1596 until the day before they left on 13 June the following year, including during the spring period when bears should have been out on the ice hunting seals (April–May). One bear they killed on the 12 February was so fat it yielded 'at least one hundred pounds of fat' - eerily reminiscent of the fat bears that invaded Belushaya Guba in 2019. The amount of effort it took one small group of people to stay alive with abundant polar bears on the prowl is astonishing.

Yet, small bands of Inuit had inhabited Arctic Canada and Greenland for

---

[††] http://tass.com/economy/1045282.

centuries at the same time William Barents was on Novaya Zemlya. They were in essentially the same precarious position as Barents and his crew but without the guns. How did they protect their food caches and dogs from marauding bears – or themselves while they slept at night? It boggles the mind to think about but we will probably never know. After the great slaughter of late 1800s, a large number of those bears disappeared, which means modern Inuit and people living along the Arctic coast of Russia have lived for more than a century with many fewer bears than their ancestors did. But the pendulum is rapidly swinging back. Every day of the year, many residents of the Arctic now live with the same polar bear threat that Barents' crew faced. Claims that this increased risk of polar bear attack is the fault of human-caused global warming just don't hold up. In virtually all recent cases, the cause can be seen to be more bears, not a lack of sea ice. How are communities going to cope with this new risk?

More people now live in the Arctic than they did 50 years ago and the communities they inhabit are larger too. Although the solution devised by the town of Churchill is held up as an example of how best to deal with large influxes of bears without high bear fatalities, it is not a solution that can be deployed everywhere.[443] The costs of securing stored food and personal garbage, incinerating community garbage, employing numerous bear patrol officers, housing problem bears in a central holding facility, and relocating bears via helicopter may be prohibitive for many small hamlets.

However, many communities have been doing their best with limited resources out of sheer necessity. Community refuse dumps and privately stored food are common problems: they not only attract bears but provide a food reward. A dump with a fence around it still attracts bears, providing only a partial solution. In Nunavut, the town of Arviat has had a polar bear patrol program for several years and also has a fenced dump.[444] Bears found within Arviat that refuse to leave have been successfully captured and relocated a few kilometres away by truck without too much cost. Dedicated officers that seek out loitering bears and scare them off are also used in Arviat, as they are in a few communities in Alaska and Greenland.[445]

But bear patrols are only usually employed during a few months in the autumn when bears are most likely to be a problem. And seasonal patrols offer little real security to communities where polar bears can appear at virtually any time of year: a female bear and her cub entered the town of Igloolik in Foxe Basin in early January 2019 and were killed by a cautious resident.[446] Community patrols also provide no security for individuals who leave town at any time of year to visit, hunt, fish, pick berries, collect eggs, or just enjoy the outdoors, as one Arviat family discovered in early July of 2018.[447] In short, rising bear numbers mean everyone in the Arctic needs to be prepared to meet a bear at any time of year, including times when bears should be on the ice.

Most people, including those who live and work in the Arctic, want polar bears to exist as a species: they want to continue to see polar bear fill their role as apex predator of the sea ice ecosystem.[448] But as is true elsewhere in regions where dangerous animal predators live, co-existing with humans can be problematic when numbers exceed a threshhold.

In the 21st century, the biggest conservation challenge may be helping Arctic communities cope with increasing numbers of potentially deadly and destructive polar bears without having to kill too many bears. This is the reality that lies ahead, because the polar bear catastrophe that was promised back in 2007 failed to materialise. And despite decades of handwringing, polar bear numbers are not only higher than 50 years ago, but may be much higher than leading polar bear specialists are willing to entertain, perhaps as high as 39,000 (range 26,000–58,000). While it is true that too many bears is not the future polar bear specialists envisioned, it is the real-life consequence of the fact that the polar bear is a species fully adapted to living in ever-changing Arctic conditions. Almost overnight, the conservation success story has morphed into an evolving saga of tenuous co-existence between flourishing polar bears and terrified Arctic residents.

Chapter 12

Why I do what I do

I'm a professional scientist with a PhD, who also writes an internet blog about polar bears. I am, in modern parlance, a science communicator: in addition to my scientific books and papers, I have written books, magazine articles, opinion pieces and videos for the general public. I have been interviewed on film about my research for a *Nature* documentary. I continue to give public lectures and provide news commentary to journalists and science writers. I am a scientist who shares and teaches outside of a classroom.

My PhD signifies the achievement of an accepted level of scientific instruction, innovative research and professional presentation of results. I know what a rational, scientific approach to research looks like (and how to do it) because that's how I was trained. I was taught to back up my assertions with evidence and to be sceptical of extraordinary claims.

Polar bears being classified as 'Threatened' with extinction based *only* on what some scientists thought might happen to them in the future, *was* an extraordinary claim. It had never been done for any other animal before it was done for polar bears. When I looked into the scientific basis for that assertion, I found flawed assumptions, over-confidence, and failure to address evidence that was well covered in the literature. Further probing revealed failed predictions.

When it became clear that the 'Threatened' status didn't hold up to scrutiny, it disturbed me to see polar bears being used to promote particular political policies regarding claims of human-caused global warming. I write about polar bear ecology and related conservation issues that come up in the literature and the media because I think the public needs to understand all sides of a scientific issue before they decide if they want to support proposed political policies based on that science.

There is a huge body of polar bear literature: very few people outside the field ever read it, let alone read it critically. That's how I learned so much about the Arctic and polar bears: I read carefully, compared papers, and listened to a range of knowledgeable people talk about Arctic issues. This is, by the way, how one learns about a new topic at the university level (and in the real world). No one teaches you: you teach yourself. I became an expert on polar bears by reading virtually everything that's been written about them and related Arctic topics. The fact that I've never put a collar on a polar bear is no hindrance to this knowledge.

I have written more than 30 papers for peer-reviewed journals or book chapters on a variety of topics, including evolution, paleoecology, genetics, endocrinology, and zoogeography. I have a firm foundation in zoology and have read widely across related disciplines, although evolution and evolutionary theory are my primary intellectual interests. I take my cue from the geneticist Theodosius Dobzhansky, who in 1937 wrote a book called 'Genetics and the Origin of Species', which was an early attempt to understand the genetics of evolutionary change over time. Dobzhansky later famously stated that 'nothing in biology makes sense except in the light of evolution' and in that I quite agree.[449]

I have always been a general-interest zoologist and this approach allowed me to build a successful career outside academia. I turned a serendipitous opportunity at the Royal British Columbian Museum in 1975 – to learn how to identify animal bones found in archaeological sites – into a career skill that's supported me financially to this day. I am now an expert – recognised as such across the world – in the identification of ancient animal remains, especially fish bones from the eastern North Pacific.

However, several of my most significant scientific papers were inspired by my interest in how ancient bones inform our knowledge about how and why the global distribution of some species has changed over time (a specialty called 'zoogeography'). Sometimes, changes like this can be an indicator of past climate change. For example, when my colleagues and I identified bones of enormous bluefin tuna from a number of archaeological sites on western Vancouver Island, we were astonished, because such huge fish are not found there today. So I pursued the topic until I had a paper published in the respected scientific journal, *Fishery Bulletin*. In this case, it turned out that climate change was an unlikely explanation for the change in distribution, but I would not have known that without a thorough investigation.[450] Since then, I have authored or co-authored similar papers on other species (including northern fur seals, ringed seals, shorttailed albatross, and mountain goats) whose distributions have changed over time.[451]

I also became interested in the origin of aboriginal domestic dogs, whose remains are ubiquitous in ancient North American archaeological sites. Historical records kept by early explorers suggested that aboriginal dogs on the south coast of British Columbia were different from dogs in other areas. Whereas most dogs elsewhere were relatively large, short-haired animals that resembled a dingo, some dogs on the south coast (in Salish and Makah tribal territories) were long-haired and resembled a modern Samoyed. My attempts to confirm or refute these historical accounts led to a Master's degree program in biology, where I pursued what are now called 'ancient DNA' studies. Leaders in the field of ancient DNA, which was fairly new at the time, were developing innovative techniques in molecular biochemistry to explore the genetic makeup of prehistoric animals and species from material extracted from ancient bones. [452]

Those ancient DNA investigations eventually led to my ground-breaking work on evolution, where I used two species pairs (domestic dog/wolf and polar bear/brown bear) to explore the biological basis of how and why new species are generated. I asked a simple but difficult question: how, in strictly biological terms, did a wolf turn into a dog – or a brown bear transform into a polar bear? I developed a testable hypothesis to explain the origin of dogs and polar bears as well as all other vertebrate species, which became the topic of my 2004 PhD thesis and a later paper. [453] For this investigation, I not only had to learn minute details about the complex biological arenas where hormones, genetics, and foetal development collide, but to understand how it all began, I had to study the role of iodine and other molecules in the atmosphere. As far as I'm concerned, this work was my greatest scientific achievement.

I went on to write a book for non-scientists on the role of thyroid hormone in evolution. Entitled 'Rhythms of Life: Thyroid Hormone and the Origin of Species,' it was published in 2006. You may have seen me talking about dog evolution in the 2007 Nature documentary called 'Dogs That Changed the World' or heard me talking about dog origins on Canadian or American national public radio programs, like CBC's Quirks and Quarks and NPR's Science Friday. Those positive experiences in science communication laid the foundation for writing blog posts about polar bear ecology and evolution for internet audiences a few years later.

However, before I developed an interest in blogging, I did some work with colleagues on a fascinating archaeological site in the eastern Aleutians (near Dutch Harbour, Unalaska) that revived my childhood interest in the Arctic. Contrary to our assumptions going into the project, it became clear when we began examining the animal bones that the site had had an Arctic climate when it was occupied by ancient Aleut people 2500–3500 years ago. Abundant discarded remains of very young ringed and bearded seal were recovered, as well as some bones of walrus and polar bears, all attesting to the presence of much more sea ice than is found there today. Quite unexpectedly, we had found evidence of past climate change that had not been revealed by any other studies: our work provided incontrovertible evidence that Dutch Harbour had consolidated sea ice in spring and early summer between about 4000 and 2500 years ago. In addition, follow-up analysis suggested that people of the Thule Eskimo culture – who eventually expanded across the Arctic into Greenland with their highly-diagnostic tool kit of stone lamps, whaling gear, and carved ivory – must have came from Unalaska originally.[454]

As a consequence, the petition to have polar bears listed as 'Threatened' under the ESA in 2007 came at a time when I had been entrenched for years in the scientific literature on climate change and sea ice ecology of the far north, as well as the history of human occupation of the Arctic. My long-standing interest in polar bear evolution was piqued by this new conservation concern. In early 2007, I was asked to suggest changes to a draft version of a document that was meant to inform US Congress about polar bears in advance of the final ESA ruling: virtually all of my suggestions were incorporated into the final document.[455] This experience showed me that a niche existed for my big-picture knowledge and suggested that I could make a useful scientific contribution to the field.

By late July 2012, I began writing blog posts for Polar Bear Science. By the end of 2018, the blog had more than 1.5 million views and I had published a scientific paper on my polar bear research.[456] In addition, I had published a number of scientific reports, videos, and opinion pieces about polar bears and walrus, a science book for children, and my very first novel, a polar bear attack thriller.[457]

That science-based novel was my attempt to convey some nuggets of Arctic ecology to readers who would never pick up a science book. I enjoyed writing it much more than I thought I would, even though I gave myself nightmares imagining a walk through a town where hungry polar bears lurk behind every bush and down every alley! Feedback from readers, as well as healthy book sales, convinced me that the goal I'd set had been achieved: I had written a story that people enjoyed reading and that also taught them a bit of science.

This journey of mine, from fish bones to polar bears, produced an eclectic but immensely enjoyable and productive career. It was not the usual route to success for a scientist, but I made it work. It required a mix of self-discipline, skepticism, scientific curiosity, and entrepreneurial drive, plus the courage to do without the financial security that comes with being an employee. An academic career would not have been the right place for me, of that I am sure.

Ian Stirling, whose work I've discussed throughout this volume because he is perhaps the most respected senior polar bear researcher alive today, did his undergraduate degree in zoology at the same university that I did – the University of British Columbia in Vancouver – albeit a few years earlier. In other words, Stirling and I have the same educational foundation, but we took different paths, and at different times, when it came to our professional careers. Stirling followed a standard path: after completing his PhD in New Zealand on Antarctic Weddell seals, he got an opportunity to go to the Arctic to study polar bears with the Canadian Wildlife Service* in 1970. He held this government job for his entire career, until his retirement in 2007, although at some point he added the role of adjunct professor at the University of Alberta.

Figure 12.1: Polar bears at the Stanley Park Zoo in the mid-1970s.
Photo by the author.

In contrast, I got my career-defining opportunity to learn the identification of animal bones the summer before I'd finished my undergraduate degree. I went straight from university to a job in a speciality I never knew existed but for which I was eminently qualified. It was a surprising path to be on, but it felt right. However, I believe that the many hours I spent during my time at UBC in the mid-70s watching the polar bears at the Stanley Park Zoo (see Figure 12.1) really cemented my childhood interest in evolution. In the years that followed, the nagging questions of how and why the polar bear came to be a unique species were never very far from my thoughts. Much later, in the early 2000s, I had an opportunity to earn my PhD and attempt to answer those very questions. Eventually, as Stirling did, I added the role of adjunct professor to my list of accomplishments.

---

*Now called 'Environment and Climate Change Canada'.

Throughout my long career, I have taken on many jobs that required the support of non-government organizations. On and off since the 1970s, private archaeological consulting companies have paid me to identify the bone remains from archaeological sites. Today, the field of archaeozoology could not function without relationships like this. Very little archaeological work today is done by government or university departments: virtually all of it is done by private companies who take on the financial burden of fieldwork plus the analysis of all material excavated from the ground. In addition, much of the work I do for biologists, including the identification of fish bone recovered from the stomach contents and faeces of marine mammals, is funded by government departments on a contract-by-contract basis. Working on contract, for private companies as well as government or university departments, is something I've done my entire career: both as an individual and as a member of the private contracting company, Pacific Identifications, which I own with two colleagues.

It therefore amuses me greatly to see that some people consider a small contract I held with The Heartland Institute a few years ago to be evidence of scientific malfeasance. The claims that I am on the 'payroll' of The Heartland Institute, am 'supported' by them, or even that I am paid by them to write my blog, keep making the Internet rounds. But they are absolutely groundless. From 2011 to 2013, I was paid $750 a month on a contract (the equivalent of one day's income for me) to make summaries of published papers relating to the ecology of vertebrate animals (my avowed specialty) that I thought might not be covered by the forthcoming report of the Intergovernmental Panel on Climate Change (IPCC AR5 2014).

These summaries were to be included in an upcoming Nongovernmental International Panel on Climate Change report[458] that was intended to ensure that a balanced perspective of the literature was available to the public. The report was published by The Heartland Institute, although Heartland had no input on what papers I looked at or what I wrote. The monthly payments ended (as did the contract) when my work on the NIPCC report was finished in early 2014. I have not received any money from Heartland since, except for travel expenses to their 2017 conference when I was invited to give a short lecture. The irony is that I have worked on contracts for most of my 40-plus-year career but no one has ever accused me of funding bias before I took a contract from The Heartland Institute. I write what I write – in my blog posts, scientific papers, reports, videos, and opinion pieces – based on my own scientific assessment of the data. That has been true for my entire career.

The controversy that exists in polar bear science is not a dispute over facts (the data that has been collected) but rather, the interpretation of those facts and their historical and scientific context. If a paper discusses polar bear cub survival, for example, and presents figures that indicate survival was low in 2016 compared to thirty years before, a critical reader must ask, what about forty or fifty years ago? If there are similar data from forty years ago, why have they been left out of the analysis? If correlations are made in the paper between cub survival and length of the ice-free season, a discerning reader must then ask themselves, what do the data on sea ice conditions thirty *and* forty years ago look like? One must also consider these additional questions: has cub survival and sea ice coverage always been calculated using the same method and what does cub survival look like in other regions that have different or similar ice conditions?

When I write about polar bears on my blog, I try to make sure that I clearly explain the relevant historical background and context for a paper or topic. I also provide maps. Maps are not a trivial component: few readers outside the Arctic are familiar with Arctic geography, so providing location information is essential. I provide references for claims and statements that I make and quote the literature extensively so that readers can see the original words of the researchers involved as well as my interpretation. I provide copies of those references where that does not violate copyright law but where that is not possible, I try to include links to the location where published material can be found. I remind readers that I may share a copy of certain papers with them if they write to me and ask for it, even if I may not be able to post it online. In other words, I encourage people who really care about a particular issue or topic to read the original literature.

I believe in the sanctity of science, where no one's work is above clearly expressed, rational criticism – my own included. I am always prepared to be wrong: it's hard to do but absolutely necessary. I should point out here that the *BioScience* paper, which I've discussed extensively in this volume, was nothing of the kind: it did not explain why the authors disagreed with me on any particular issue, with specific quotes or references. They did not defend their scientific stance on issues where their views clashed with mine: they merely took it as given that their opinions were right. Such a blanket condemnation of critics is not how science advances and it is not how it is supposed to be done. Every single co-author of that *BioScience* paper, as well as the editors and publishers of the journal, violated that basic tenet of science, including Ian Stirling, Steven Amstrup, Michael Mann, Jeff Harvey, Eric Post, and Stephan Lewandowsky.

The scientific paper that makes up the core of this book was submitted to the scientific journal *Arctic Science* for review, although in a draft form different from the final version now available online. One reviewer chosen by the journal, a mountain goat researcher, who willingly signed his name to his comments, objected to the length of the paper (fair comment – it was too long) but suggested I rewrite the manuscript with a focus on the failed polar bear survival prediction section because he considered it the most interesting issue of those I had presented. In contrast, the anonymous polar bear researcher who reviewed the paper ripped through most of it with comments like 'wrong,' 'false,' and 'not true' – except for the section on the failed survival prediction, which garnered not a single comment. He/she also accused me of lying when I declared I had received no funding for the submitted paper:

> Given that the author has written several articles or 'briefings' for the Global Warming Policy Foundation and that the GWPF actively recruits such briefings it seems unlikely that funding was not provided to convert the cited briefing (Crockford 2015) into a draft manuscript for possible publication in the scientific literature.

In fact, the cited briefing paper, 'The Arctic Fallacy: Sea Ice Stability and the Polar Bear,' was not 'recruited' by the GWPF.[459] I wrote it and asked them if they would like to publish it. They agreed and provided their usual compensation, as would be the case if I'd submitted an article to a magazine. The GWPF did not know I was writing the scientific paper that I eventually submitted for publication to *Arctic Science* and they provided no funds either, before or after its submission. I sent an email to the editors of the journal, objecting to the libelous accusation made by the second reviewer and suggested it revealed an unacceptable, pre-existing bias. Given the positive remarks from the first reviewer (and the lack of negative comments by the second), I suggested that I rework the failed survival prediction section and resubmit the revised manuscript for a new review. The editors refused. Was I denied the option of rewriting and resubmitting because that reviewer accused me of lying about funding? I'll never know.

However, I revised the manuscript anyway, sent it to several biology colleagues for review, and after further revisions, resubmitted to another journal. The second journal also rejected the paper, because the editors insisted that the only way to properly assess the 2007 USGS prediction would be to collaborate with Steven Amstrup and USGS scientists to rerun their original model with the old sea ice projections plus the new polar bear survival data (that showed bears in several areas were not dying in droves as expected). However, since Amstrup and colleagues had just published new survival predictions based on a new model with new sea ice projections (not the 2005 ones), that option was really not possible.[460]

Instead, I chose to publish the manuscript at *PeerJ Preprints*, which made the paper freely available, searchable online, and allowed extensive comments to be made by anyone, negative and positive. In other words, it offered both open access *and* open review. Almost two years after it was published online, not a single polar bear or sea ice specialist has made a comment on the manuscript. New data published after the initial submission and a few changes suggested by colleagues that reviewed the paper were easy to incorporate, which is clearly marked as Version 3. That paper forms the core of this volume because the information it contains provides critical context to the current controversy over polar bear conservation.

There is no political motivation in anything that I do. Politics hold little interest for me, religion even less. I have worked in science for my entire career and plan to do so until I die. Writing about polar bear science is what I do for recreation because science is not just what I do, it is who I am. Science grounds me and guides me through my life: that's been true since I was in my teens.

More than ten years ago, my then 20-something year old daughter found the poem by William Stafford called 'The Thread'. She used the poem to introduce a photo album of my life she'd put together as a gift for my 50th birthday. 'Yes, that's it,' I thought when I saw it. Science is my *thread*. My daughter's thread is art rather than science, but she understands that having a thread leads to a meaningful life.

I have children I love and grandchildren I adore. I share my love of science with them whenever I can and hope I am able to provide the means for my grandchildren to see polar bears in the wild someday, something I was never able to do for my children or even for myself. I have no doubt there will be polar bears for them to see when the time comes.

The Thread

There's a thread you follow. It goes among things
that change. But it doesn't change.

People wonder about what you are pursuing.
You have to explain about the thread.

But it is hard for others to see. While you hold it
you can't get lost.

Tragedies happen; people get hurt or die; and
you suffer and get old.

Nothing you do can stop time's unfolding. You
don't ever let go of the thread.

William Stafford

Acknowledgments

I thank M. Cronin and several anonymous reviewers of previous drafts of my original scientific paper, which improved the scientific argument presented in this volume. My sister, a professional historian, as well as several colleagues, also gave editorial advice on the book. Andrew Montford was immensely helpful in helping to structure the work for publication, for which I am most grateful.

Appendix: Emails obtained under FOI

The emails below, circulated among members of the Harvey *et al.* author team, were obtained under a Freedom of Information request.

```
From:  Ian Stirling [mailto:  ]
Sent:  31 March 2017 16:12
To:  Harvey, Jeff; Steven Amstrup; Stephan Lewandowsky
Subject:  Re:  Submitted!
```

Well done Jeff. Good luck with the submission,

Ian

```
From:  Harvey, Jeff
Sent:  Friday, March 31, 2017 7:00 AM
To:  Steven Amstrup; Stephan Lewandowsky
Reply To:  Harvey, Jeff
Subject:  RE: Submitted!
```

Dear co-authors,

The paper was submitted by me this morning! The files attached are what I sent. Again, you are all deeply thanked for this, and lets hope we get it in. The message is vitally important so I think that we have a great chance. And your efforts were Herculean! I'll keep you all informed!

Very best for the weekend,

Jeff

```
From:  Eric Stephen Post
Sent:  Monday, April 3, 2017 9:16 AM
To:  Stephan Lewandowsky
```

145

Subject: Re: Submitted!

In agreement with everything thats been said here - thanks much, Jeff, for pulling together such a nice piece of work!

Best wishes,
Eric
Eric Post
Professor, climate change ecology
Department of Wildlife, Fish, Conservation Biology
University of California, Davis

On Apr 1, 2017, at 5:44 AM, Stephan Lewandowsky wrote:
Well done indeed, and thanks for letting me be part of it. I am impressed by how the paper has evolved and I really hope that will recognize its importance.
Regards steve

Professor Stephan Lewandowsky
University of Bristol

From: Ian Stirling
To: Harvey,Jeff; Peter Roessingh; Eric Stephen Post; Ellers,J
Subject: Re: Bioscience
Date: Friday, July 14, 2017 3:13:23 PM

Hi Jeff, this very good news.

Any guestimate on when it might come out? I think BioScience is a very widely circulated and read publication. Bottom line though will be the take-up/response from the press, public, other scientists. Might be worth getting embargoed copies of gallies to a few good journalists ahead of time to maximize initial impact.

Thanks for all your work and leadership on this,

Ian

From: Harvey, Jeff
Sent: Friday, September 8, 2017 06:30

To: Stephan Lewandowsky; samstrup; Ian Stirling; Ellers,
J.; Michael Mann; post@ucdavis.edu
Reply To: Harvey, Jeff
Subject: FW: BioScience - Decision on Manuscript ID 170167

Dear co-authors,

Now some good news finally! But what you think? I am
sure that Bioscience want this article, [redacted passage]

I can easily revise this and resubmit it. Or do you think
we need to start again with Earth's Future? Either way
this will be open access as we will pay for it here.

I opt to revise for Bioscience.

Best,
Jeff

On Wed, Nov 8, 2017 at 2:25 AM, Harvey, Jeff wrote:

Dear [redacted],

Here are the proofs of our article Hope you enjoy it; we
feel that this will go big over at least the social media.
Our main messages are that climate change denying blogs
do not use the peer-reviewed science to base their arguments
and also choose a few 'sexy' topics to try and debunk,
using them like strategically placed dominoes placed in
front of thousands of others, each representing a separate
line of evidence for AGW.

Hence the title 'proxy'. I am sure that we hit denier blogs
pretty hard here, especially with figure two. We have
pushed back the embargo period to 29 November to avoid
US Thanksgiving...

Jeff

From: Eric Stephen Post <post@ucdavis.edu>
Date: Friday, October 13, 2017 at 4:32 PM
To: Katherine E Kerlin <kekerlin@ucdavis.edu> [media relations at UC Davis]
Subject: paper forthcoming on confronting climate change denial

Hi Kat,

I thought I would let you know that an international group of colleagues and I just had a paper accepted in BioScience on 'Internet blogs, polar bears, and climate change denial by proxy'.

We're anticipating it's going to make quite a splash. I would be grateful if you would consider writing up a brief press release on it.

If that sounds appealing to you, I'll ask the lead author for a copy of the final, accepted version, as well as embargo information.

Best wishes,
Eric

Eric Post Professor, climate change ecology
Department of Wildlife, Fish, & Conservation Biology
University of California, Davis

From: Eric Stephen Post
Sent: Wednesday, November 8, 2017 1:18 PM
To: Katherine E Kerlin [media relations at UCDavis]
Subject: Re: paper forthcoming on confronting climate change denial

Hi Kat,

Thanks so much for your interest in this piece, and the approach you've outlined below sounds great. Please do reach out to Jeff and their media person.

Ill see what I can do about getting you the list of blogs. One of the other co-authors compiled it, but I'm sure they'd be willing to pass it along.

Thanks again and best wishes,
Eric

Eric Post
Fellow, John Muir Institute
Professor, climate change ecology
Department of Wildlife, Fish, & Conservation Biology
University of California, Davis

On Tue, Nov 7, 2017 at 2:05 AM, Harvey, Jeff wrote:

Dear [redacted, but is likely Dana Nuccitelli],

As someone who writes great pieces for the Guardian and
Skeptical Science on climate change, I wanted to give you
the heads-up on a paper that is coming out very soon in
Bioscience in which I am the lead author.

I have arranged for the embargo period to clear on November
22 at 1200 eastern standard time in the United States,
after which time many of my co-authors and I will make
press releases.

Other prominent authors on the paper are are [sic] Michael
Mann, Stephan Lewandowsky, Steven Amstrup, Ian Stirling
and Eric Post.

Our paper focuses on how internet blogs and online sources
either report or distort the science on Arctic ice extent
and loss, polar bear demographics and how these are linked
with climate change.

We all think that it is a pretty powerful paper that we
are hoping will generate a lot of discussion in both the
social and mainstream media.

There is a good chance that we will get the cover article,
which will add to the impact. I can send you the proofs
if you like;

It would be great to hear from you and I would appreciate
any advice from you on how we can ensure that this paper

gets widespread coverage. We are making sure that it is
open access, and I am looking to write to other journalists
and scientists to get maximum attention for it.

By the way, in case you don't know me, I was one of those
scientists who countered distortions from [redacted, but
clearly is Bjorn Lomborg] for years and I co-wrote a very
critical review of his book The Skeptical Environmentalist
for Nature in 2001.

I am a senior scientist at the Netherlands Institute of
Ecology and a professor at the VU University in Amsterdam,
where I study both multitrophic interactions and teach
courses in science and advocacy.

Very best regards,

Jeff

_____

Appendix B: Additional notes on population estimates

The Arctic Basin is a bit of a black hole population-wise, since its unclear if any bears actually live there year round or if those spotted in the area simply use it as a spring feeding area and/or summer refuge, so I'm happy to leave my estimate for this area as zero. But recent surveys put the Chukchi number at about 2,937 (1,522–5,944) and the Kara Sea at 3,200 (2,700–3,500).[461]

The estimate of 2,000 for East Greenland used for the IUCN Red List assessment in 2015[462] was the low end of an estimate of 2,000–4,000 proposed in 1993.[463] That estimate was reduced officially to 'unknown' by 1997, even though it was noted that a minimum population size of about 2,000 (and perhaps as large as 2,500) would be required to support the intensity of harvest that occurred in the 1990s.[464] I suggest a quite plausible estimate for East Greenland in 2018 is 3,000 bears (range 1,522–5,955, the same as the Chukchi estimate range).

The Northern Beaufort Sea subpopulation is currently likely to be the higher of two estimates calculated by biologists in 2006;[465] while the lower estimate has been used since then (980; 825–1,135), I suggest the higher one (1,300; 750–1,800) is more appropriate now, given recent documented increases in most other subpopulation regions like Svalbard, Baffin Bay and Kane Basin, which grew by 42%, 36% and 118%, respectively, over previous estimates.[†]

Given the 118% increase in the Kane Basin, I have accordingly increased the estimates of the other small regions in the Canadian Archipelago sea ice ecoregion with out-dated figures by a similar amount, 120% (M'Clintock Channel, Viscount Melville and Norwegian Bay). I have projected that large regions like Foxe Basin, Gulf of Bothia, and Lancaster Sound have likely increased by 40%, as did the Svalbard area population. I used a somewhat greater increase (50%) for Davis Strait because of its abundant prey base, while Western Hudson Bay was increased by a more modest 30%. Southern Hudson Bay was left without

---

[†] Note the 2013 Kane Basin estimate of 357 (range 221–493) was stated to be a 59% increase over the 1997 estimate of 224,[466] but 224 was a recalculated figure, not the original 164 (range 94–234) generated by Taylor et al. (2008) and used in the 2015 Red List assessment.

an increase, given that it is the most southern region within the entire range and numbers have consistently remained quite stable since the 1980s.[467]

Notes

Chapter 1 Introduction

1. Linden (2000), p. 53.
2. Amstrup (2003).
3. Stirling and Parkinson (2006), Figure 3.
4. Castro de la Guardia *et al.* (2017); Cherry *et al.* (2013); Lunn *et al.* (2016); Obbard *et al.* (2016); Scott and Marshall (2010); Stirling and Parkinson (2006); Stirling *et al.* (1999, 2004).
5. Castro de la Guardia *et al.* (2017); Scott and Marshall (2010).
6. Calvert *et al.* (1986), pp. 19, 24; Lunn *et al.* (2016), Figure 3; Ramsay and Stirling (1988), p. 615; Regehr *et al.* (2007b).
7. Stirling *et al.* (1977b).
8. Derocher and Stirling (1992, 1995a,b); Ramsay and Stirling (1988); Stirling and Lunn (1997); Stirling *et al.* (1977b).
9. Crockford (2015a,c).
10. Crockford (2015a,c); Derocher and Stirling (1992, 1995a,b); Stirling (1997, 2002); Stirling and Derocher (1993); Stirling *et al.* (1980b, 1982).
11. Shabecoff (1988).
12. Stirling and Derocher (1993).
13. Pratt (2016).
14. Stirling *et al.* (1999).
15. e.g. Etkin (1991); Hansen *et al.* (1988); Parkinson and Kellogg (1979).
16. Monnett and Gleason (2006).
17. Raver (2006).

Chapter 2 Conservation background

18. Aars *et al.* (2006).
19. Miller *et al.* (2012).
20. Cahill *et al.* (2013); Cronin *et al.* (1991, 2014); Cronin and Cronin (2015); Davison *et al.* (2011); Edwards *et al.* (2011); Lindqvist *et al.* (2010); Liu *et al.* (2014).
21. Dyck (2006); Fleck and Herrero (1988); Gjertz and Persen (1987); Herrero (1972, 1985, 2003); Herrero and Fleck (1990); Herrero *et al.* (2011); Jonkel (1978); Miller *et al.* (2015); Shelton (1997, 1998, 2001); Stenhouse *et al.* (1988).

22. Amstrup (2003); Brown *et al.* (2018); Citta *et al.* (2015); Cronin and Cronin (2015); Davis *et al.* (2008); Harington (2008); Stirling and Archibald (1977); Stirling and Ross (2011); Stirling *et al.* (1975, 1976, 1977a, 1981).

23. Aars (2018); Liu *et al.* (2014); Stirling (1974); Whiteman *et al.* (2015, 2018).

24. Amstrup (2003); Ferguson *et al.* (2000a); Mauritzen *et al.* (2001); Rode *et al.* (2014a, 2015a, 2018a); Rogers *et al.* (2015); Schliebe *et al.* (2008a); Stirling *et al.* (1977b, 1980a, 1993, 2004).

25.   Amstrup and Gardner (1994); Fedoseev (1975); Finley *et al.* (1983); Fischbach *et al.* (2007); Harington (1968); Larsen (1985); Lunn *et al.* (2004); Lydersen and Gjertz (1986); Mauritzen *et al.* (2001); Pilfold *et al.* (2012); Ramsay and Stirling (1988, 1990); Richardson *et al.* (2005); Smith and Stirling (1975, 1978); Stirling *et al.* (1975, 1977a); Van de Velde *et al.* (2003); Wiig *et al.* (1999).

26. Honderich (1991).

27. Honderich (1991), p. 104.

28. Bockstoce and Botkin (1982).

29. Elliott (1875); Elliott and Coues (1875); Klein and Sowls (2011).

30. Uspenski (1961); see https://en.wikipedia.org/wiki/Polar_bear.

31. Stirling (2011), p. 247–248.

32. Larsen (1972).

33. Paetkau *et al.* (1999).

34. Amstrup *et al.* (2001, 1986); Derocher and Stirling (1995a); Larsen (1986); Peacock *et al.* (2013); Stirling *et al.* (1977b, 1984); Taylor *et al.* (2008); Wiig *et al.* (1995).

35. Aars *et al.* (2009); Andersen and Aars (2016), p. 5.

36. Stirling (2011).

37. MOSJ (2018b).

38. Lønø (1970).

39. Schliebe *et al.* (2006b), p. 109.

40. COSEWIC (2008).

41. Derocher and Stirling (1995b), p. 1662.

42. Peacock (2017).

43. Paetkau *et al.* (1999), p. 1573.

44. Miller *et al.* (2012).

45. Baker *et al.* (1993); Bockstoce and Botkin (1982); Clapham *et al.* (1999); Sea Otter Recovery Team (2007); Weber *et al.* (2000).

46. Larsen and Stirling (2009); Marine Mammal Commission (2007).

47. Anonymous (1968).

48. Jonkel *et al.* (1976); Stirling (1986); Stirling *et al.* (1975, 1977a).

49. Aars *et al.* (2006).

50. Aars *et al.* (2006).

51. Aars *et al.* (2006), p. 61.

52. Wiig *et al.* (2015).

53. Aars *et al.* (2006); Schliebe *et al.* (2008b).

54. Schliebe *et al.* (2008b).

55. Siegel (2018).

56. Aars (2018).

57. Amstrup *et al.* (2006).
58. Taylor *et al.* (1985).
59. US Fish and Wildlife Service (2008).
60. Joling (2006).
61. Gleick *et al.* (2010).
62. Schliebe *et al.* (2006a).
63. US Fish and Wildlife Service (2008), p. 28213.
64. Derocher *et al.* (2004, 2013); Furevik *et al.* (2002); Stirling and Derocher (2012).
65. Adler (2008).
66. Adler (2008), p. 112.
67. e.g. Amstrup *et al.* (2007); Durner *et al.* (2007); Hunter *et al.* (2007); Regehr *et al.* (2006, 2007a).
68. Amstrup *et al.* (2007), p. 1.

Chapter 3 Sea ice and population predictions

69. Courtland (2008).
70. Serreze *et al.* (2003).
71. Earth Observatory (2009).
72. Lindsay and Zhang (2005); Serreze and Francis (2006).
73. NSIDC (2005).
74. Hassol (2004).
75. ACIA (2005); Hassol (2004); Holland *et al.* (2006); Solomon *et al.* (2007); Zhang and Walsh (2006).
76. Schliebe *et al.* (2006b).
77. Schliebe *et al.* (2008b); Wiig *et al.* (2007).
78. Hassol (2004).
79. Brazil and Goudie (2006).
80. Amstrup *et al.* (2007).
81. Durner *et al.* (2007).
82. IPCC (2007).
83. Parkinson (2014), p.4320; see also Durner *et al.* (2006), p. 47.
84. ACIA (2005); Amstrup *et al.* (2007); Durner *et al.* (2007); Hassol (2004); Holland *et al.* (2006); Stroeve *et al.* (2007); Zhang and Walsh (2006).
85. Regehr *et al.* (2016); Stern and Laidre (2016); Stroeve *et al.* (2014); Wang and Overland (2015); Whiteman *et al.* (2018).
86. MOSJ (2018a).
87. NSIDC (2017).
88. Amstrup *et al.* (2007), pp. 34–35.
89. Stroeve *et al.* (2007).
90. Durner *et al.* (2007), p. 1.
91. ACIA (2005), p. 193.
92. Durner *et al.* (2007), pp. 16, 44, 49.
93. Amstrup *et al.* (2008), p. 238. See also Stroeve *et al.* (2007).

94. Durner *et al.* (2007, 2009); IPCC (2007); Zhang and Walsh (2006).
95. Belikov (1995); Derocher *et al.* (1998), pp. 25, 29; Wiig *et al.* (1995), pp. 22, 24.
96. Aars *et al.* (2006), p. 34; Obbard *et al.* (2010); Wiig *et al.* (1995),p. 24.
97. Aars *et al.* (2006).
98. Aars *et al.* (2009); Wiig *et al.* (2015).
99. Amstrup *et al.* (2007), pp. 1, 6–8.
100. Amstrup *et al.* (2007); US Fish and Wildlife Service (2008).
101. Amstrup *et al.* (2007).
102. Amstrup *et al.* (2007); Durner *et al.* (2007); Regehr *et al.* (2007b).
103. Amstrup *et al.* (2007).
104. Aars *et al.* (2006).
105. Aars *et al.* (2006).
106. US Fish and Wildlife Service (2008), p. 28229.
107. Hunter *et al.* (2007, 2010).
108. Hunter *et al.* (2007, 2010).
109. Schliebe *et al.* (2006b); Wiig *et al.* (2007).
110. Aars *et al.* (2006).

Chapter 4 Testing the hypotheses

111. LiveScience (2008).
112. NSIDC (2016).
113. Frey *et al.* (2015); Hunter *et al.* (2007, 2010), p. 35, for 2003–2010; Meier *et al.* (2014), p. 4, for 2004–2012; Parkinson (2014), p. 4321, for 2013, Perovich *et al.* (2015), p. 39, for 2006–2015.
114. Galicia *et al.* (2016).
115. Castro de la Guardia *et al.* (2017); Cherry *et al.* (2016); Obbard *et al.* (2007, 2015, 2018).
116. Peacock *et al.* (2013); Rode *et al.* (2012); SWG (2016).
117. Stern and Laidre (2016).
118. Amstrup *et al.* (2007), p. 1.
119. AC SWG (2018); Matishov *et al.* (2014); Regehr *et al.* (2018).
120. NPI (2015).
121. Fauchald *et al.* (2014).
122. Aars *et al.* (2017).
123. Aars (2018); Aars *et al.* (2009); Andersen and Aars (2016); Andersen *et al.* (2012); Derocher (2005); Derocher *et al.* (2010); Larsen (1971); Wiig (1998).
124. Aars *et al.* (2009).
125. Regehr *et al.* (2018).
126. Aars *et al.* (2009).
127. Bromaghin *et al.* (2015).
128. Regehr *et al.* (2006).
129. Durner *et al.* (2018), p. 10.
130. Crockford (2019); Obbard *et al.* (2018).

131. Dyck *et al.* (2017).
132. Durner *et al.* (2018); Stapleton *et al.* (2014).
133. Regehr *et al.* (2016); Rode *et al.* (2014a, 2015a, 2018a,b); Wiig *et al.* (2015).
134. Durner *et al.* (2018); ECC (2017).
135. Durner *et al.* (2018); ECC (2017); Stapleton *et al.* (2016); SWG (2016).
136. Aars *et al.* (2006); Regehr *et al.* (2016); Wiig *et al.* (2015).
137. Crockford (2019).
138. SWG (2016).
139. Wiig *et al.* (2015).
140. Amstrup *et al.* (2007).
141. Armstrong *et al.* (2008).

Chapter 5 What went wrong?

142. Hopper (2017).
143. Whiteman *et al.* (2015, 2018).
144. Derocher *et al.* (2002); Obbard *et al.* (2016); Pilfold *et al.* (2012); Smith *et al.* (1975); Smith and Hammill (1981); Stirling (1974); Stirling and Archibald (1977); Stirling and Øritsland (1995); Stirling *et al.* (1975, 1977a, 1993, 2004).
145. Derocher *et al.* (2000); Obbard *et al.* (2016); Rode *et al.* (2015b).
146. Atwood *et al.* (2016b); Gormezano and Rockwell (2013a,b); Iles *et al.* (2013); Lønø (1970); Rode *et al.* (2015a); Rogers *et al.* (2015).
147. Lunn and Stirling (1985).
148. Rode *et al.* (2014a, 2015a, 2018a,b); Serreze *et al.* (2016).
149. Atwood *et al.* (2016b).
150. Aars *et al.* (2017); Crockford (2017d).
151. Aars (2018); Norwegian Polar Institute (2018).
152. Amstrup *et al.* (2007); Durner *et al.* (2007).
153. Amstrup *et al.* (2007).
154. Castro de la Guardia *et al.* (2017); Crockford (2019); Scott and Marshall (2010).
155. Regehr *et al.* (2007b); Stirling and Parkinson (2006).
156. Peacock *et al.* (2013); Rode *et al.* (2012, 2014a); Stapleton *et al.* (2016); SWG (2016).
157. Crockford (2015a,c); Derocher and Stirling (1992, 1995a,b); Stirling (2002); Stirling and Lunn (1997); Stirling *et al.* (1980b), p. 52; Stirling *et al.* (1982), p. 21.
158. Botkin (1995); Wu and Loucks (1995).
159. Derocher and Stirling (1992, 1995a,b); Stirling (1997, 2002); Stirling and Lunn (1997); Stirling *et al.* (1975, 1977a, 1980b), p. 52;' Stirling *et al.* (1982), p. 21.
160. Crawford and Quakenbush (2013); Crawford *et al.* (2015); Rode *et al.* (2014a).
161. Arrigo and van Dijken (2015); Cameron *et al.* (2010); George *et al.* (2015); Harwood and Stirling (1992); Kelly *et al.* (2010); Smith (1987); Smith and Hammill (1981).
162. Eurich (2019); Rode *et al.* (2018b).
163. Rode and Regehr (2010); Rode *et al.* (2014a).
164. Stapleton *et al.* (2016).

165. Joling (2018).
166. Sergeant (1976, 1991).
167. DFO (2014); Kovacs (2015); Stenson (2014).
168. Crockford (2019); Durner *et al.* (2018); Peacock *et al.* (2013).
169. Durner *et al.* (2018).
170. Aars *et al.* (2017); Andersen *et al.* (2012); Derocher (2005).
171. Aars *et al.* (2017).
172. Aars (2018).
173. Amstrup (2003).
174. Monnett and Gleason (2006).
175. Pilfold *et al.* (2017).
176. Durner *et al.* (2011).
177. Griffen (2018).
178. Lone *et al.* (2018).
179. Lone *et al.* (2018), p. 4.
180. Stirling and van Meurs (2015), p. 1303.
181. Castro de la Guardia *et al.* (2017); Obbard *et al.* (2016).
182. Cherry *et al.* (2009, 2016); Pagano *et al.* (2012); Pilfold *et al.* (2017).
183.   Derocher and Stirling (1992, 1995a,b); Stirling (1997, 2002); Stirling and Lunn (1997); Stirling *et al.* (1975, 1977b, 1980b), p. 52, Stirling *et al.* (1982), p. 21.
184. Ramseier *et al.* (1975); Stirling *et al.* (1975, 1981).
185.   Burns (1970); Burns *et al.* (1975); Calvert *et al.* (1986); DeMaster *et al.* (1980); Harwood and Stirling (1992); Harwood *et al.* (2000); Martinez-Bakker *et al.* (2013); Smith *et al.* (1975); Smith (1987); Stirling (1986, 1997, 2002); Stirling and Lunn (1997); Stirling *et al.* (1975, 1976, 1977a, 1980a,b, 1981, 1982, 1984).
186. Stirling *et al.* (1975).
187. Burns *et al.* (1975); Stirling *et al.* (1975, 1977a, 1985).
188. Stirling *et al.* (2008), p. 15.
189. Harwood *et al.* (2012, 2015); Pilfold *et al.* (2014, 2015); Stirling *et al.* (2008).
190. Regehr *et al.* (2006, 2007a); Stirling *et al.* (2008).
191. Regehr *et al.* (2006).
192. Regehr *et al.* (2006, 2007a).
193. Harwood *et al.* (2012); Stirling *et al.* (2008).
194. Bromaghin *et al.* (2013, 2015).
195. Bromaghin *et al.* (2015), pp. 646–647.
196. Bromaghin *et al.* (2015); Regehr *et al.* (2006).
197. Durner *et al.* (2018), p. 10.
198. COSEWIC (2008).
199. ACIA (2005); Hassol (2004).
200. Wiig *et al.* (2015).
201. Regehr *et al.* (2007b).
202. Obbard *et al.* (2007).
203. Derocher and Stirling (1992, 1995a,b); Ramsay and Stirling (1988); Stirling *et al.* (1977b).
204. Lunn *et al.* (2016); Regehr *et al.* (2007b); Stirling *et al.* (1977b).

205. Pratt (2016).
206. Stirling (2002); Stirling and Lunn (1997).
207. Derocher and Stirling (1992).
208. Holst *et al.* (1999).
209. Ferguson *et al.* (2005).
210. Stirling (2002); Stirling and Lunn (1997); Struzik (2010).
211. Stirling and Derocher (1993).
212. Stirling *et al.* (1999).
213. Regehr *et al.* (2007a); Stirling and Derocher (2007, 2012); Stirling and Parkinson (2006).
214. Derocher and Stirling (1995a,b); Stirling and Derocher (1993).
215. English (2016); Kelly *et al.* (2010); Pongracz *et al.* (2017); Popescu (2016); Post *et al.* (2013); Prigg (2016); Rohner (2016).
216. Clark (2000); COSEWIC (2012); Doup *et al.* (2007); McLoughlin *et al.* (2003); Nielsen *et al.* (2013); Rockwell *et al.* (2008).
217. Amstrup (2003); Taylor *et al.* (1985).
218. Amstrup *et al.* (2006); Derocher and Wiig (1999); Lunn and Stenhouse (1985); Stirling and Derocher (2012); Stirling and Ross (2011); Taylor *et al.* (1985).
219. Greshko (2016); National Geographic (2018).
220. Swaisgood and Sheppard (2010). p. 627.
221. Stanley-Becker (2019).
222. Atwood *et al.* (2016a).
223. Regehr *et al.* (2016); Wiig *et al.* (2015).

Chapter 6 Defending the model failure

224. Crockford (2017d).
225. Crockford (2018c).
226. Crockford (2018b).
227. Climate Feedback (2018).
228. Atwood *et al.* (2015).
229. Amstrup *et al.* (2007), p. 84 and Durner *et al.* (2007), p. 46.
230. Durner *et al.* (2009), p. 44.
231. Durner *et al.* (2007), p. 10.
232. US Geological Survey (2007).
233. See Durner *et al.* (2007), p. 4; the same figure used in Durner *et al.* (2009), p. 44.
234. Amstrup *et al.* (2007), p. 34–35.
235. Amstrup *et al.* (2007), p. 96.
236. Amstrup *et al.* (2008), p. 238.
237. Amstrup *et al.* (2008), plate 8.
238. Durner *et al.* (2007), p. 16.
239. Crockford (2017d).
240. Amstrup *et al.* (2007), Table 10.3.
241. Wiig *et al.* (2015), Supplement, Table 4.2.

242. Regehr *et al.* (2016).
243. Bromaghin *et al.* (2015).
244. Hunter *et al.* (2010).
245. Stirling *et al.* (2008), pp. 15–16.
246. Harwood *et al.* (2012, 2015).
247. Bromaghin *et al.* (2015); Hunter *et al.* (2010).
248. Burns *et al.* (1975); DeMaster *et al.* (1980); Harwood and Stirling (1992); Harwood *et al.* (2000, 2012); Ramseier *et al.* (1975); Smith (1987); Smith and Stirling (1978); Stirling (2002); Stirling and Archibald (1977); Stirling and Lunn (1997); Stirling *et al.* (1975, 1976, 1977a, 1980b, 1981, 1982, 1984, 2008).
249. Crawford and Quakenbush (2013); Crawford *et al.* (2015).
250. US Fish and Wildlife Service (2012a,b).
251. Kovacs (2015, 2016a,b); Lowry (2016).
252. Crockford (2017d, 2018c); Stirling *et al.* (2008).
253. Crockford (2015a,c); Ferguson *et al.* (2005); Ramsay and Stirling (1988); Stirling (2002).
254. Derocher and Stirling (1992, 1995a,b, 1996); Stirling (2002).
255. Derocher and Stirling (1992), p. 1155.
256. Derocher and Stirling (1995b).
257. Amstrup *et al.* (2010).
258. Crockford (2017d, 2018c).
259. Amstrup (2012a, 2014, 2018); Amstrup *et al.* (2007, 2008).
260. Crockford (2017d).

Chapter 7 Attacking the messenger

261. Harvey *et al.* (2018).
262. Mann (2017).
263. Harvey (2017); Kelly (2017).
264. Goode (2018).
265. Laframbroise (2018).
266. Corcoran (2017).
267. Tabuchi (2017).
268. Harvey *et al.* (2018); Stirling and Derocher (2007).
269. Crockford (2018c, 2014b,c).
270. Crockford (2017d).
271. Crockford (2017d).
272. US Fish and Wildlife Service (2008).
273. Crockford (2014b,c).
274. MacCracken *et al.* (2017); US Fish and Wildlife Service (2017a).
275. Collins and Evans (2002, 2007).
276. Rajan and Tol (2018).
277. e.g. Crockford (2015a,c, 2017d).
278. Crockford and Geist (2018).

279. Baker (2016); Horton (2015); Ioannidis (2005); but see Fanelli (2018).
280. Horton (2015), p. 1380.

Chapter 8 The rise and fall of the polar bear specialist

281. Aars *et al.* (2006); Derocher *et al.* (1998); Lunn *et al.* (2002); Wiig *et al.* (1995).
282. York (2015).
283. Amstrup *et al.* (2010); see also Amstrup (2011).
284. Amstrup (2018).
285. Regehr *et al.* (2016); Wiig *et al.* (2015).

Chapter 9 Climate science gutted by lost icon

286. Born (2018).
287. USGCRP (2017).
288. Cox (2018).
289. Carrington and Hilaire (2013a).
290. Carrington and Hilaire (2013b).
291. Orange (2013).
292. Gates (2013).
293. Johnston (2013).
294. Woollaston (2013).
295. Johnson (2013).
296. China Daily (2014).
297. Aars (2018); Ramsay and Stirling (1988).
298. Stirling (2013).
299. Graham (2013).
300. Aghbali (2015); Kelkar (2015); Newbern (2015).
301. National Geographic (2018).
302. Crockford (2018b); Mittermeier (2018).
303. 1–8 Amstrup (2003); Miller *et al.* (2006, 2015); Stirling (1974), p. 1196; 9–11 Calvert *et al.* (1986), p. 19, 24; Chambellant *et al.* (2012); Crawford *et al.* (2015); DeMaster *et al.* (1980); Derocher and Stirling (1992, 1995a,b); Ferguson *et al.* (2005); Obbard *et al.* (2018)[yearling cub survival in 2015]; Ramsay and Stirling (1988); Rode *et al.* (2013, 2014a, 2018b); Stirling (2002); Stirling and Lunn (1997); Stirling *et al.* (1975, 1977a).
304. Dyck *et al.* (2017); Obbard *et al.* (2018); Stapleton *et al.* (2014).
305. Obbard *et al.* (2018).
306. Amstrup (2003), p. 602.
307. Brean (2018); Lewandowsky and Whitmarsh (2018).
308. Crockford (2018b).
309. Stewart (2017).
310. AC SWG (2018); McLoughlin (2017); Regehr *et al.* (2018).
311. Nilsen (2019a,b); Stewart (2019).

312. BBC News (2014); Brodwin (2014); Jay and Fischbach (2008); National Geographic News (2014); Rosen (2010); Valentine (2014).
313. Crockford (2014b,c).
314. Joling (2017); US Fish and Wildlife Service (2017b).
315. MacCracken *et al.* (2017); US Fish and Wildlife Service (2017a).
316. Breum (2018); Riddoch (2018).
317. Kalvapalle (2018).
318. Osaka (2018).
319. Murphy (2018).
320. Discovery Institute (1998).
321. Nunatsiaq News (2019); Rose (2018).

Chapter 10 On population estimates, then and now

322. For example, Amstrup *et al.* (2001, 1986, 2005); Taylor *et al.* (2001, 2006, 2008).
323. Steele (2013).
324. Derocher *et al.* (1998), pp. 25, 29; Larsen (1972); Lønø (1970); Uspenski (1961).
325. Stapleton *et al.* (2016); Stirling *et al.* (2011); SWG (2016); Taylor and Lee (1995); Taylor *et al.* (2001, 2006, 2008).
326. Amstrup *et al.* (2001); Bromaghin *et al.* (2013, 2015); DeMaster *et al.* (1980); Derocher and Stirling (1995a); Dyck *et al.* (2017); Lunn *et al.* (2016); Regehr *et al.* (2007a,b, 2018); Stapleton *et al.* (2014); Stirling *et al.* (1977a, 1980a, 2004).
327. Clapham *et al.* (1999), p. 47.
328. Sea Otter Recovery Team (2007), p. 6; US Fish and Wildlife Service (2005).
329. Weber *et al.* (2000), p. 1287.
330. Baker *et al.* (1993).
331. Hamilton and Derocher (2019).
332. Hamilton and Derocher (2019), p. 84.
333. Harvey *et al.* (2018).
334. e.g Amstrup *et al.* (2007); Regehr *et al.* (2016).
335. Amstrup (2012b).
336. Derocher *et al.* (1998), p. 3.
337. Amstrup *et al.* (1986); Brooks and Lentfer (1965); Harington (1965); Jonkel (1969); Larsen (1972); Lentfer (1970); Scott *et al.* (1959); Uspenski (1961).
338. Scott *et al.* (1959).
339. Larsen (1972); Lønø (1970).
340. Uspenski and Kistchinski (1972); Uspenski (1961).
341. Larsen (1972), p. 163.
342. Cheek (2013).
343. Romm (2007).
344. Dykstra (2008).
345. Amstrup *et al.* (1986); Andersen and Aars (2016); Larsen (1986); Stirling *et al.* (1977b).
346. Taylor and Lee (1995), p. 151.

347. Aars *et al.* (2006); Obbard *et al.* (2010).

348. Hamilton and Derocher (2018).

349. AC SWG (2018); Regehr *et al.* (2018).

350. Bromaghin *et al.* (2015).

351. Wiig *et al.* (1995), p. 24.

352. http://polarbearscience.com/2014/12/19/challenging-noaas-arctic-report-card
-2014-on-polar-bears/.

353. Hamilton and Derocher (2018).

354. Amstrup *et al.* (2007).

355. Derocher *et al.* (1998), p. 27.

356. Matishov *et al.* (2014); Wiig *et al.* (2015).

357. Hamilton and Derocher (2018), p. 7.

358. Hamilton and Derocher (2018), p. 8.

359. Amstrup *et al.* (1986); Bromaghin *et al.* (2015); Lunn *et al.* (2016); Regehr *et al.*
(2006, 2007a,b); Stapleton *et al.* (2014); Stirling (1997); Stirling *et al.* (1999, 2004).

360. Anonymous (1968), p. 96.

Chapter 11 Concerns ahead for polar bears

361. Nunatsiaq News (2008).

362. Peacock *et al.* (2011), p. 374.

363. e.g. Lunn *et al.* (2016); McCall *et al.* (2015).

364. Aars *et al.* (2017); Obbard *et al.* (2018); Regehr *et al.* (2018); Rode *et al.* (2018b);
Stapleton *et al.* (2014); SWG (2016).

365. Peacock *et al.* (2011).

366. Rode *et al.* (2014b).

367. Madwar (2016); McCue (2017); Yong and Meyer (2016).

368. Bechshoft *et al.* (2016); Castro de la Guardia *et al.* (2017); Cherry *et al.* (2013,
2016); Lunn *et al.* (2016); McCall *et al.* (2015); Pilfold *et al.* (2017); Sciullo *et al.* (2016);
Towns *et al.* (2009).

369. Derocher and Stirling (1992, 1995a,b); Obbard *et al.* (2016).

370. Aars *et al.* (2017); Crockford (2018c).

371. Dyck *et al.* (2017).

372. Durner *et al.* (2018).

373. Stirling *et al.* (1980a).

374. Lentfer (1972).

375. Aars (2015); Vibe (1967).

376. Lentfer (1972).

377. Vinje (2001); Walsh *et al.* (2017).

378. Stirling and Kiliaan (1980).

379. Peacock *et al.* (2015).

380. Packard (1886); Rausch (1953); Smith *et al.* (1975); Stirling and Kiliaan (1980).

381. Honderich (1991); Sergeant (1976, 1991).

382. Ogilvie *et al.* (2000).

383. Mangerud and Svendsen (2018).
384. Aars (2015); Aars *et al.* (2017); Andersen *et al.* (2012); Barr (1985); Chernova *et al.* (2014); Derocher (2005); Descamps *et al.* (2017); Fauchald *et al.* (2014); Larsen (1972); Malenfant *et al.* (2016).
385. Amstrup *et al.* (2007, 2008); Derocher *et al.* (2011); Peacock *et al.* (2015).
386. Aars *et al.* (2017); Derocher *et al.* (2013); Malenfant *et al.* (2016).
387. Crockford (2012a,b); Harington (2008).
388. Taylor *et al.* (1997).
389. Stirling (1997, 2011); Stirling and Lunn (1997); Stirling *et al.* (1975, 1977a, 2008).
390. Cronin and Cronin (2015).
391. Arkell (2014); Kelly *et al.* (2011).
392. Chiu (2018); Pascus (2018); Rosenblatt (2018).
393. Briggs (2013); Durner *et al.* (2018), p. xxvi; Fouche (2016); Wilder *et al.* (2017).
394. Halls (2018).
395. Smyth (2007), in Manzo (2010), p. 197.
396. Amstrup (2012a).
397. Amstrup (2012a).
398. McLoughlin (2017); Rode and Regehr (2010); Uspenski and Kistchinski (1972).
399. Ramsay and Stirling (1988).
400. Stirling and Lunn (1997), p. 171.
401. Derocher *et al.* (2004); Stirling *et al.* (1999).
402. Durner *et al.* (2018), p. xxviii.
403. Dickie (2018); Wilder *et al.* (2017); Wootson, Jr. (2017); WWF Canada (2016).
404. Cecco (2018); Durner *et al.* (2018); Nunatsiaq News (2019); NWMB (2018); York *et al.* (2016); Zerehi (2016b).
405. Rose (2018); Tyrrell (2006).
406. Calvert *et al.* (1986); Kearney (1989); Stirling *et al.* (1977b); Towns *et al.* (2009).
407. Ferguson *et al.* (2000b); Harington (1968); Jonkel *et al.* (1972); Lunn *et al.* (2004); Messier *et al.* (1994); Ramsay and Stirling (1990); Richardson *et al.* (2005); Stirling *et al.* (1977b); Van de Velde *et al.* (2003); Yee *et al.* (2017).
408. Drolet (2018); Rogers (2018a).
409. Rogers (2018b).
410. Stirling *et al.* (1977b, 2004).
411. Gormezano and Rockwell (2013a,b); Iles *et al.* (2013); Russell (1975).
412. Lefebvre *et al.* (2017); Weber (2013, 2015).
413. Weber (2015).
414. CBC News (2018); Greer (2018a).
415. Fleck and Herrero (1988); Gjertz and Persen (1987); Gjertz *et al.* (1993); Stenhouse *et al.* (1988); Wilder *et al.* (2017).
416. Dickie (2018).
417. Greer (2018b).
418. Dickie (2018); Drolet (2018); Leavitt (2018).
419. Rose (2018).
420. Kearney (1989), p. :88; see also Fleck and Herrero (1988), p. 141.
421. Regehr *et al.* (2007b).

422. Kearney (1989); Stirling *et al.* (1977b); Towns *et al.* (2009).

423. Castro de la Guardia *et al.* (2017); Lunn *et al.* (2016); Scott and Marshall (2010).

424. Obbard *et al.* (2016).

425. Calvert *et al.* (1986); Kearney (1989); Ramsay and Stirling (1988); Stirling *et al.* (1977b).

426. Calvert *et al.* (1986); Cherry *et al.* (2013); Kearney (1989); Ramsay and Stirling (1988); Stirling *et al.* (1977b).

427. Dyck *et al.* (2017); Regehr *et al.* (2007b); Stapleton *et al.* (2014).

428. CBC News (2015, 2017a,b); Mercer (2018).

429. Truett (1993).

430. Campbell (2017); CBC News (2015, 2017a,b); Mercer (2018).

431. Polar Bears International (2011); RT (2013); Siberian Times (2018).

432. Stewart (2018).

433. Robinson (2016).

434. Arctic Journal (2016); Bailey (2012); Campbell (2017); CBC News (2015, 2016, 2018); Fouche (2016); Healey (2017); Ice People (2017); Martin (2014); Mills (2016); Newell (2017); Roberts (2018); Rose (2018); Tyrrell (2006).

435. Stirling and Øritsland (1995).

436. Martin (2014).

437. Mercer (2018).

438. Rose (2018).

439. Nilsen (2019a); Stewart (2019).

440. Stanley-Becker (2019).

441. Nilsen (2019b).

442. De Veer (1609).

443. Kearney (1989); Schmidt and Clark (2018); Stirling *et al.* (1977b); Towns *et al.* (2009).

444. Savikataaq Jr (2014); Zerehi (2016a).

445. WWF Canada (2016).

446. CBC News (2019).

447. Rose (2018).

448. Cheek (2013).

Chapter 12 Why I do what I do

449. Dobzhansky (1937, 1973).

450. Crockford (1997a).

451. Crockford (2018d); Crockford and Frederick (2011); Crockford *et al.* (1997); Crockford (2002).

452. Crockford and Pye. (1997); Crockford *et al.* (2011); Crockford (1997b, 2000a,b, 2012a,b); Koop *et al.* (2000).

453. Crockford (2002, 2003a,b, 2004, 2009).

454. Crockford and Frederick (2007, 2011); Crockford (2008a).

455. Buck (2007); see also Crockford (2008b).

456. Crockford (2017d).
457. Crockford (2015a,b,c, 2016, 2017a,b,c,d,e, 2018a,b,c, 2012a,b, 2014b,c).
458. Crockford (2014a).
459. Crockford (2015a).
460. Atwood *et al.* (2016a).

Appendix B: Additional notes on population estimates

461. AC SWG (2018); Matishov *et al.* (2014); Regehr *et al.* (2018); Wiig *et al.* (2015).
462. Regehr *et al.* (2016); Wiig *et al.* (2015).
463. Wiig *et al.* (1995), pp. 22, 24.
464. Derocher *et al.* (1998), pp. 25, 29.
465. Stirling *et al.* (2011).
466. SWG (2016).
467. Obbard *et al.* (2016, 2018).

Bibliography

Aars J (2015) Research on polar bears at Norwegian Polar Institute. Online seminar (webinar), January 14.

Aars J (2018) Population changes in polar bears: protected, but quickly losing habitat. Fram Forum Newsletter, Fram Centre, Tromso.

Aars J, Lunn NJ and Derocher A (2006) *Polar Bears: Proceedings of the 14th Working Meeting of the IUCN/SSC Polar Bear Specialist Group, Seattle, Washington, 20–24 June 2005.* Occasional paper of the IUCN Species Survival Commission 32, IUCN.

Aars J, Marques T, Buckland S *et al.* (2009) Estimating the Barents Sea polar bear subpopulation. *Marine Mammal Science*, 25, 35–52.

Aars J, Marques T, Lone K *et al.* (2017) The number and distribution of polar bears in the western Barents Sea. *Polar Research*, 36(1), 1374125.

AC SWG (2018) Chukchi-Alaska polar bear population demographic parameter estimation. Scientific Working Group: Report of the Proceedings of the 10th meeting of the Russian–American Commission on Polar Bears, 27–28 July 2018, US Fish and Wildlife Service. URL: https://www.fws.gov/alaska/fisheries/mmm/polarbear/bilateral.htm.

ACIA (2005) *Arctic Climate Impact Assessment: Scientific Report.* Cambridge University Press.

Adler J (2008) An animal to save the world: climate change and the polar bear. *The New Atlantis*, 21, 111–115.

Aghbali A (2015) Photographer of 'horribly thin' polar bear hopes to inspire climate change fight. *CBC News*, Canada, 17 September. URL: http://www.cbc.ca/news/trending/thin-bear-photo-kerstin-1.3232725.

Amstrup S (2003) Polar bear (*Ursus maritimus*). In: G Feldhamer, B Thompson and J Chapman (Eds.), *Wild Mammals of North America.* Johns Hopkins University Press.

Amstrup S (2011) Polar bears and climate change: certainties, uncertainties, and hope in a warming world. In: R Watson, T Cade, M Fuller, G Hunt and E Potapov (Eds.), *Gyrfalcons and Ptarmigan in a Changing World, Volume 1.* The Peregrine Fund.

Amstrup S (2012a) The future of polar bears. Submission to the Association of Zoos and Aquariums, no date. URL: https://web.archive.org/web/20160317002851/.

Amstrup S (2012b) A look at polar bear numbers. *Polar Bears International News*, 16 January. URL: https://polarbearsinternational.org/news/article-research/a-look-at-polar-bear-numbers/.

Amstrup S (2014) Cold weather in the US no solace for starving polar bears. *The Conversation*, 20 January. URL: https://theconversation.com/cold-weather-in-the-us-no-solace-for-starving-polar-bears-21942.

Amstrup S (2018) Polar bears listed as threatened 10 years ago. *Polar Bears International News*, 11 May. URL: https://polarbearsinternational.org/news/article-polar-bears/threatened/.

Amstrup S and Gardner C (1994) Polar bear maternity denning in the Beaufort Sea. *The Journal of Wildlife Management*, 58, 1–10.

Amstrup S, McDonald T and Stirling I (2001) Polar bears in the Beaufort Sea: a 30-year mark-recapture case history. *Journal of Agricultural, Biological, and Environmental Statistics*, 6, 221–234.

Amstrup S, Stirling I, Smith T *et al.* (2006) Recent observations of intraspecific predation and cannibalism among polar bears in the Southern Beaufort Sea. *Polar Biology*, 29, 997–1002.

Amstrup S, Marcot B and Douglas D (2007) *Forecasting the Rangewide Status of Polar Bears at Selected Times in the 21st Century*. Tech. rep., US Geological Survey.

Amstrup S, Marcot B and Douglas D (2008) A Bayesian network modeling approach to forecasting the 21st century worldwide status of polar bears. In: E DeWeaver, C Bitz and L Tremblay (Eds.), *Arctic Sea Ice Decline: Observations, Projections, Mechanisms, and Implications*. American Geophysical Union.

Amstrup S, DeWeaver E, Douglas D *et al.* (2010) Greenhouse gas mitigation can reduce sea-ice loss and increase polar bear persistence. *Nature*, 468, 955–958.

Amstrup SC, Stirling I and Lentfer JW (1986) Past and present status of polar bears in Alaska. *Wildlife Society Bulletin*, 14, 241–254.

Amstrup SC, Durner GM, Stirling I *et al.* (2005) Allocating harvests among polar bear stocks in the Beaufort Sea. *Arctic*, 58, 247–259.

Andersen M and Aars J (2016) Barents Sea polar bears (*Ursus maritimus*): population biology and anthropogenic threats. *Polar Research*, 35, 26029.

Andersen M, Derocher A, Wiig O *et al.* (2012) Polar bear (*Ursus maritimus*) maternity den distribution in Svalbard, Norway. *Polar Biology*, 35, 499–508.

Anonymous (1968) Proceedings of the First International Scientific Meeting on the Polar Bear, 6–10 September 1965 at Fairbanks, Alaska. US Dept. of the Interior and the University of Alaska.

Arctic Journal (2016) Scare tactics. *The Arctic Journal*, 18 February 2016. URL: https://web.archive.org/web/20160220100133/http://arcticjournal.com/culture/2162/scare-tactics.

Bibliography

Arkell H (2014) 'I tried to gouge the polar bear's eyes': Trip leader of Norway expedition where Eton schoolboy was tragically killed tells of horror of night-time attack. *Daily Mail*, 8 July. URL: http://www.dailymail.co.uk/news/article-2684735/I-tried-gouge -polar-bears-eyes-Trip-leader-Norway-expedition-Eton-schoolboy-tragically-kill ed-tells-horror-night-time-attack.html.

Armstrong J, Green K and Soon W (2008) Polar bear population forecasts: A public-policy forecasting audit. *Interfaces*, 38, 382–405.

Arrigo K and van Dijken G (2015) Continued increases in Arctic Ocean primary production. *Progress in Oceanography*, 136, 60–70.

Atwood T, Marcot B, Douglas D *et al.* (2015) *Evaluating and Ranking Threats to the Long-term Persistence of Polar Bears*. Open-File Report 2014–1254, US Geological Survey. URL: http://dx.doi.org/10.3133/ofr20141254.

Atwood T, Marcot B, Douglas D *et al.* (2016a) Forecasting the relative influence of environmental and anthropogenic stressors on polar bears. *Ecosphere*, 7(6), e01370.

Atwood T, Peacock E, McKinney M *et al.* (2016b) Rapid environmental change drives increased land use by an Arctic marine predator. *PLoS One*, 11, e0155932.

Bailey S (2012) Polar bear encounters on the rise in Newfoundland and Labrador. *The Star* via *The Canadian Press*, 6 April. URL: http://www.thestar.com/news/canada/20 12/04/06/polar_bear_encounters_on_the_rise_in_newfoundland_and_labrador.html.

Baker C, Perry A, Bannister J *et al.* (1993) Abundant mitochondrial DNA variation and world-wide population structure in humpback whales. *PNAS*, 90, 8239–8243.

Baker M (2016) 1,500 scientists lift the lid on reproducibility. *Nature*, 533, 452–454.

Barr S (1985) Franz Josef Land. Norwegian Polar Institute, Oslo.

BBC News (2014) Record haul-out for Pacific walrus. *BBC News*, 1 October. URL: http://www.bbc.com/news/science-environment-29450240.

Bechshoft T, Derocher A, Richardson E *et al.* (2016) Hair mercury concentrations in Western Hudson Bay polar bear family groups. *Environmental Science & Technology*, 50, 5313–5319.

Belikov S (1995) Status of polar bear populations in the Russian Arctic 1993. In: Ø Wiig, E Born and G Garner (Eds.), *Polar Bears: Proceedings of the 11th working meeting of the IUCN/SSC Polar Bear Specialist Group, Copenhagen, Denmark, 25–27 January 1993*. IUCN.

Bergen S, Durner G, Douglas D *et al.* (2007) *Predicting Movements of Female Polar Bears between Summer Sea Ice Foraging Habitats and Terrestrial Denning Habitats of Alaska in the 21st century: Proposed Methodology and Pilot Assessment*. Tech. rep., US Geological Survey.

Blix A (2016) An Roald Amundsens scientific achievements. *Polar Research*, 35, 31319.

Bockstoce J and Botkin D (1982) The harvest of Pacific walruses by the pelagic whaling industry, 1848 to 1914. *Arctic and Alpine Research*, 14, 183–188. The journal is now called *Arctic, Antarctic and Alpine Research*.

Born D (2018) Bearing witness? Polar bears as icons for climate change communication in *National Geographic*. *Journal of Environmental Communications*. URL: https://do i.org/10.1080/17524032.2018.1435557.

Botkin D (1995) *Our Natural History: The Lessons of Lewis and Clark*. Putnam.

Brazil J and Goudie J (2006) *A 5 Year Management Plan (2006–2011) for the Polar Bear (Ursus maritimus) in Newfoundland and Labrador*. Tech. rep., Wildlife Division, Department of Environment and Conservation. Government of Newfoundland and Labrador and the Department of Lands and Natural Resources, Nunatsiavut Government.

Brean J (2018) Stop using misleading images of polar bears and droughts to raise awareness of climate change, psychologists say. *National Post*, 9 October. URL: https://nati onalpost.com/news/world/scientists-should-stop-using-misleading-images-of-po lar-bears-and-droughts-to-raise-awareness-of-climate-change-psychologists-say.

Breum M (2018) How the narrative on polar bears has become a problem for Arctic environmental groups. *ArcticToday*, 21 October. URL: https://www.arctictoday.com/ narrative-polar-bears-become-problem-arctic-environmental-groups/.

Briggs H (2013) Close encounters with polar bears. *BBC News*, 11 March. URL: http: //www.bbc.co.uk/news/science-environment-21622349.

Brodwin E (2014) 35,000 walruses are all crowded together in one spot and it signals something ominous. *Business Insider*, 1 October. URL: http://www.businessinsider. com/35000-walruses-gathered-in-alaska-2014-10.

Bromaghin J, McDonald T and Amstrup S (2013) Plausible combinations: An improved method to evaluate the covariate structure of Cormack-Jolly-Seber mark-recapture models. *Open Journal of Ecology*, 3, 11–22.

Bromaghin J, McDonald T, Stirling I *et al.* (2015) Polar bear population dynamics in the southern Beaufort Sea during a period of sea ice decline. *Ecological Applications*, 25, 634–651.

Brooks J and Lentfer JW (1965) *The Polar Bear: a Review of Management and Research Activities in Alaska with Recommendations for Coordinated International Studies*. Unpublished report, Alaska Department of Fish and Game, Juneau.

Brown T, Galicia M, Thiemann G *et al.* (2018) High contributions of sea ice derived carbon in polar bear (*Ursus maritimus*) tissue. *PLoS One*, 13(1), e0191631.

Buck E (2007) *Polar Bears: Proposed Listing under the Endangered Species Act*. Tech. rep., Congressional Research Service. URL: https://fas.org/sgp/crs/misc/RL33941.p df. Report prepared for members and committees of Congress.

Burns J (1970) Remarks on the distribution and natural history of pagophilic pinnipeds in the Bering and Chukchi Seas. *Journal of Mammalogy*, 51, 445– 454.

Burns J, Fay F and Shapiro L (1975) The relationships of marine mammal distributions, densities, and activities to sea ice conditions (Quarterly report for quarter ending September 30, 1975, projects #248 and 249). In: *Environmental Assessment of the Alaskan Continental Shelf, Principal Investigators' Reports, July-September 1975*, vol. 1. NOAA Environmental Research Laboratories.

Cahill JA, Green RE, Fulton TL *et al.* (2013) Genomic evidence for island population conversion resolves conflicting theories of polar bear evolution. *PLoS Genetics*, 9(3), e1003345.

Calvert W, Stirling I, Schweinsburg R *et al.* (1986) Polar bear management in Canada 1982–84. In: *Polar Bears: Proceedings of the 9th meeting of the Polar Bear Specialist Group IUCN/SSC, Edmonton, Canada, 9–11 August 1985*. IUCN.

Cameron MF, Bengtson JL, Boveng JK *et al.* (2010) *Status Review of the Bearded Seal (Erignatha barbatus)*. Technical Memorandum NMFS-AFSC-211, NOAA.

Campbell M (2017) For Newfoundland kids, 'stranger danger' includes polar bears. *Maclean's Magazine*, 7 April. URL: http://www.macleans.ca/society/for-newfound land-kids-stranger-danger-includes-polar-bears/.

Carrington D and Hilaire E (2013a) The polar bear who died of climate change – big picture. *The Guardian*, 6 August 2013. URL: http://www.theguardian.com/environm ent/picture/2013/aug/06/polar-bear-climate-change-sea-ice.

Carrington D and Hilaire E (2013b) Starved polar bear perished due to record sea-ice melt, says expert. *The Guardian*, 6 August 2013. URL: http://www.theguardian.com/ environment/2013/aug/06/starved-polar-bear-record-sea-ice-melt.

Castro de la Guardia L, Myers P, Derocher A *et al.* (2017) Sea ice cycle in western Hudson Bay, Canada, from a polar bear perspective. *Marine Ecology Progress Series*, 564, 225–233.

CBC News (2015) Polar bears 'coming in all directions' in Black Tickle. *CBC News*, 25 February. URL: http://www.cbc.ca/news/canada/newfoundland-labrador/polar-bea rs-coming-in-all-directions-in-black-tickle-1.2970757.

CBC News (2016) 'Bear was looking right at him': Close encounters with polar bears in Labrador. *CBC News*, 6 February. URL: http://www.cbc.ca/news/canada/newfoundl and-labrador/polar-bear-encounters-labrador-1.3432312.

CBC News (2017a) Changing sea ice bad omen for province's polar bears: professor. *CBC News Newfoundland/Labrador*, 21 April. URL: http://www.cbc.ca/news/canada /newfoundland-labrador/davis-strait-polar-bears-ice-decline-1.4077164.

CBC News (2017b) Highway of ice: Easy route for polar bears chasing food, expert says. *CBC News Newfoundland/Labrador*, 12 April. URL: http://www.cbc.ca/news/canada /newfoundland-labrador/pack-ice-polar-bears-1.4065930.

CBC News (2018) Survivor recalls terrifying encounter with polar bears that left 1 dead. *CBC News*, 29 August. URL: https://www.cbc.ca/news/canada/north/polar-bear-ki mmirut-nunavut-death-1.4803481.

CBC News (2019) Igloolik elder won't be charged for killing polar bear and cub. CBC News, 18 February. URL: https://www.cbc.ca/news/canada/north/igloolik-hunter-c harges-kill-polar-bear-cub-1.5022763.

Cecco L (2018) Polar bear numbers in Canadian Arctic pose threat to Inuit, controversial report says. *The Guardian*, 13 November. URL: https://www.theguardian.com/wo rld/2018/nov/13/polar-bear-numbers-canadian-arctic-inuit-controversial-report.

THE POLAR BEAR CATASTROPHE THAT NEVER HAPPENED

Chambellant M, Stirling I, Gough W *et al.* (2012) Temporal variations in Hudson Bay ringed seal (*Phoca hispida*) life-history parameters in relation to environment. *Journal of Mammalogy*, 93, 267–281.

Cheek J (2013) A Nunavut perspective: the state of polar bears in Canada. *SciencePoles* (International Polar Foundation, Belgium), 27 February and 1 March. URL: http://www.sciencepoles.org/interview/a-nunavut-perspective-the-state-of-polar-bears-in-canada.

Chernova N, Friedlander A, Turchik A *et al.* (2014) Franz Josef Land: extreme northern outpost for Arctic fishes. *PeerJ*, 2, e692. URL: https://peerj.com/articles/692/.

Cherry S, Derocher A, Stirling I *et al.* (2009) Fasting physiology of polar bears in relation to environmental change and breeding behavior in the Beaufort Sea. *Polar Biology*, 32, 383–391.

Cherry S, Derocher A, Thiemann G *et al.* (2013) Migration phenology and seasonal fidelity of an Arctic marine predator in relation to sea ice dynamics. *Journal of Animal Ecology*, 82, 912–921.

Cherry S, Derocher A and Lunn N (2016) Habitat-mediated timing of migration in polar bears: an individual perspective. *Ecology and Evolution*, 6, 5032–5042.

China Daily (2014) Starved polar bear proof climate change deadly. *China Daily*, 8 August. URL: http://www.chinadaily.com.cn/photo/2013--08/08/content_16880716.htm.

Chiu A (2018) Killing of polar bear that attacked cruise employee on remote Arctic island sparks debate. *Washington Post*, 30 July. URL: https://www.washingtonpost.com/news/morning-mix/wp/2018/07/30/killing-of-polar-bear-that-attacked-cruise-employee-on-remote-arctic-island-sparks-debate/.

Citta J, Quakenbush L, Okkonen S *et al.* (2015) Ecological characteristics of core-use areas used by Bering–Chukchi–Beaufort (BCB) bowhead whales, 2006–2012. *Progress in Oceanography*, 136, 201–222.

Clapham PJ, Young S and Brownell Jr RT (1999) Baleen whales: conservation issues and the status of the most endangered populations. *Mammal Review*, 29, 35–60.

Clark D (2000) Recent reports of grizzly bears, *Ursus arctos*, in northern Manitoba. *Canadian Field Naturalist*, 114, 692–696. URL: http://www.biodiversitylibrary.org/item/106750#page/1/mode/thumb.

Climate Feedback (2018) *Financial Post* publishes misleading opinion that misrepresents science of polar bears' plight. *Climate Feedback*, 2 March. URL: https://climatefeedback.org/evaluation/financial-post-publishes-misleading-opinion-misrepresents-science-polar-bears-peril-susan-crockford/.

Collins H and Evans R (2002) The third wave of science studies: studies of expertise and experience. *Social Studies of Sciences*, 32, 235–296.

Collins H and Evans R (2007) *Rethinking Expertise.* University of Chicago Press.

Corcoran T (2017) Canadian finds polar bears are doing fine – and gets climate-mauled. *Financial Post*, 7 December. URL: http://business.financialpost.com/opinion/terence -corcoran-canadian-finds-polar-bears-are-doing-fine-and-gets-climate-mauled.

COSEWIC (2008) *Assessment and Update Status Report on the Polar Bear* Ursus maritimus *in Canada*. Tech. rep., Committee on the Status of Endangered Wildlife in Canada. URL: http://publications.gc.ca/collections/collection_2008/ec/CW69--14- -351--2008E.pdf.

COSEWIC (2012) *COSEWIC Assessment and Status Report on the Grizzly Bear* Ursus arctos *in Canada*. Tech. rep., Committee on the Status of Endangered Wildlife in Canada.

Courtland R (2008) Polar bear numbers set to fall. *Nature*, 453, 432–433.

Cox D (2018) It will take more than bear chow to keep the animals alive in the wild. NBC News, 26 February. URL: https://www.nbcnews.com/mach/science/scientists- hatch-bold-plan-save-polar-bears-ncna851356.

Crawford J and Quakenbush L (2013) Ringed seals and climate change: early predictions versus recent observations in Alaska. Presentation by Justin Crawford, 28th Lowell Wakefield Fisheries Symposium, March 26–29, Anchorage, AK. URL: http: //seagrant.uaf.edu/conferences/2013/wakefield-arctic-ecosystems/program.php.

Crawford J, Quakenbush L and Citta J (2015) A comparison of ringed and bearded seal diet, condition and productivity between historical (1975–1984) and recent (2003– 2012) periods in the Alaskan Bering and Chukchi seas. *Progress in Oceanography*, 136, 133–150.

Crockford S (2014a) Biological impacts. In: *Climate Change Reconsidered: The Report of the Nongovernmental International Panel on Climate Change*. SEPP, Heartland Institute, and Center for the Study of Carbon Dioxide and Global Change.

Crockford S (2015a) *The Arctic Fallacy: Sea Ice Stability and the Polar Bear*. Briefing 16, Global Warming Policy Foundation. URL: http://www.thegwpf.org/susan-crockfor d-the-arctic-fallacy-2/.

Crockford S (2015b) *EATEN: A Novel*. Amazon CreateSpace.

Crockford S (2015c) Unstable thinking about polar bear habitat. *The Arctic Journal*, 7 October. URL: journal.com/opinion/1869/unstable-thinking-about-polar-bear-ha bitat.

Crockford S (2016) *Polar Bear Facts and Myths*. Amazon CreateSpace.

Crockford S (2017a) The Death of a Climate Icon. GWPF TV. URL: http://www.theg wpf.org/gwpftv/?tubepress_item=XCzwFalI8OQ.

Crockford S (2017b) Polar Bear Scare Unmasked: The Saga of a Toppled Global Warming Icon. Global Warming Policy Foundation TV. URL: http://www.thegwpf.org/gw pftv/?tubepress_item=z6bcCTFnGZ0.

Crockford S (2017c) *Polar Bears: Outstanding Survivors of Climate Change*. Amazon CreateSpace.

Crockford S (2017d) Testing the hypothesis that routine sea ice coverage of 3–5m km^2 results in a greater than 30% decline in population size of polar bears (*Ursus maritimus*). *PeerJ Preprints*. URL: Doi:10.7287/peerj.preprints.2737v3.

Crockford S (2017e) *Twenty Good Reasons not to Worry about Polar Bears: An update*. Briefing 28, Global Warming Policy Foundation.

Crockford S (2018a) Polar bears keep thriving even as global warming alarmists keep pretending they're dying. *Financial Post*, 27 February. URL: http://business.financial post.com/opinion/polar-bears-keep-thriving-even-as-global-warming-alarmists-keep-pretending-theyre-dying.

Crockford S (2018b) The real story behind the famous starving polar bear video reveals more manipulation. *Financial Post*, 29 August. URL: https://business.financialpost .com/opinion/the-real-story-behind-the-famous-starving-polar-bear-video-reveal s-more-manipulation.

Crockford S (2018c) *State of the Polar Bear Report 2017*. Report 29, Global Warming Policy Foundation.

Crockford S (2018d) White Lie: The Cruel Abuse of a Starving Polar Bear. Video, Global Warming Policy Foundation. URL: https://www.youtube.com/watch?v=Z7KTfPlCr gY.

Crockford S (2019) *State of the Polar Bear Report 2018*. Report 32, Global Warming Policy Foundation.

Crockford S and Frederick G (2007) Sea ice expansion in the Bering Sea during the Neoglacial: Evidence from archaeozoology. *The Holocene*, 17, 699– 706.

Crockford S and Frederick G (2011) Neoglacial sea ice and life history flexibility in ringed and fur seals. In: T Braje and R Torrey (Eds.), *Human and Marine Ecosystems: Archaeology and Historical Ecology of Northeastern Pacific Seals, Sea Lions, and Sea Otters*. University of California Press.

Crockford S and Geist V (2018) Conservation Fiasco. *Range Magazine*, Winter 2017/2018, 26–27.

Crockford S and Pye C (1997) Forensic reconstruction of prehistoric dogs from the Northwest coast. *Canadian Journal of Archaeology*, 21, 149–153.

Crockford S, Frederick G and Wigen R (1997) A humerus story: albatross element distribution from two northwest coast sites, North America. *International Journal of Osteoarchaeology*, 7(4), 287–291.

Crockford S, Moss M and Baichtal J (2011) Pre-contact dogs from the Prince of Wales archipelago, Alaska. *Alaska Journal of Anthropology*, 9, 49–64.

Crockford SJ (1997a) Archaeological evidence of large northern bluefin tuna, *Thunnus thynnus*, in coastal waters of British Columbia and northern Washington. *Fishery Bulletin*, 95, 11–24.

Crockford SJ (1997b) *Osteometry of Makah and Coast Salish Dogs*. Archaeology Press.

Crockford SJ (2000a) A commentary on dog evolution: regional variation, breed development and hybridization with wolves. In: S Crockford (Ed.), *Dogs Through Time: An Archaeological Perspective*. Archaeopress.

Crockford SJ (2000b) Dog evolution: a role for thyroid hormone physiology in domestication changes. In: S Crockford (Ed.), *Dogs Through Time: An Archaeological Perspective*. Archaeopress.

Crockford SJ (2002) Animal domestication and heterochronic speciation: the role of thyroid hormone. In: N Minugh-Purvis and K McNamara (Eds.), *Human Evolution Through Developmental Change*. Johns Hopkins University Press.

Crockford SJ (2003a) Commentary: Thyroid hormones in Neandertal evolution: A natural or a pathological role? *Geographical Review*, 92, 73–88.

Crockford SJ (2003b) Thyroid hormone phenotypes and hominid evolution: a new paradigm implicates pulsatile thyroid hormone secretion in speciation and adaptation changes. *International Journal of Comparative Biochemistry and Physiology Part A*, 135, 105–129.

Crockford SJ (2004) *Animal Domestication and Vertebrate Speciation: A Paradigm for the Origin of Species*. Ph.D. thesis, University of Victoria, Canada.

Crockford SJ (2008a) Be careful what you ask for: archaeozoological evidence of mid-Holocene climate change in the Bering Sea and implications for the origins of Arctic Thule. In: G Clark, F Leach and S O'Connor (Eds.), *Islands of Inquiry: Colonisation, Seafaring and the Archaeology of Maritime Landscapes*. ANU EPress.

Crockford SJ (2008b) *Some Things We Know – and Don't Know – About Polar Bears*. Tech. rep., Science and Public Policy Institute.

Crockford SJ (2009) Evolutionary roots of iodine and thyroid hormones in cell-cell signaling. *Integrative and Comparative Biology*, 49, 155–166.

Crockford SJ (2012a) *Annotated Map of Ancient Polar Bear Remains of the World*. Spotted Cow Presentations. URL: http://polarbearscience/references/.

Crockford SJ (2012b) *A History of Polar Bears, Ringed Seals, and other Arctic and North Pacific Marine Mammals over the Last 200,000 Years*. Tech. rep., State of Alaska Department of Commerce, Community and Economic Development and The University of Alaska Fairbanks.

Crockford SJ (2014b) *On the Beach: Walrus Haulouts are Nothing New*. Briefing 11, Global Warming Policy Foundation. URL: http://www.thegwpf.org/susan-crockford-on-the-beach-2/.

Crockford SJ (2014c) The Walrus Fuss: Walrus Haulouts are Nothing New. Video, Global Warming Policy Foundation. URL: https://www.youtube.com/watch?v=cwaAwsS2OOY.

Cronin M, Amstrup S and Garner G (1991) Interspecific and intraspecific mitochondrial DNA variation in North American bears (Ursus). *Canadian Journal of Zoology*, 69, 2985–2992.

Cronin M, Rincon G, Meredith R *et al.* (2014) Molecular phylogeny and SNP variation of polar bears (*Ursus maritimus*), brown bears (*U. arctos*), and black bears (*U. americanus*) derived from genome sequences. *Journal of Heredity*, 105, 312–323.

Cronin TM and Cronin M (2015) Biological response to climate change in the Arctic Ocean: the view from the past. *Arktos*, 1, 1–18.

Davis CS, Stirling I, Strobeck C *et al.* (2008) Population structure of ice-breeding seals. *Molecular Ecology*, 17, 3078–3094.

Davison J, Ho S, Bray S *et al.* (2011) Late-Quaternary biogeographic scenarios for the brown bear (*Ursus arctos*), a wild mammal model species. *Quaternary Science Reviews*, 30, 418–430.

De Veer G (1609) *The Three Voyages of William Barents to the Arctic Regions.* The Hakluyt Society. URL: http://archive.org/details/cihm_18652. English translation.

DeMaster D, Kingsley M and Stirling I (1980) A multiple mark and recapture estimate applied to polar bears. *Canadian Journal of Zoology*, 58, 633–638.

Derocher A (2005) Population ecology of polar bears at Svalbard, Norway. *Population Ecology*, 47, 267–275.

Derocher A and Stirling I (1992) The population dynamics of polar bears in western Hudson Bay. In: DR McCullough and RH Barrett (Eds.), *Wildlife 2001: Populations.* Elsevier.

Derocher A and Stirling I (1995a) Estimation of polar bear population size and survival in western Hudson Bay. *Journal of Wildlife Management*, 59, 215–221.

Derocher A and Stirling I (1995b) Temporal variation in reproduction and body mass of polar bears in western Hudson Bay. *Canadian Journal of Zoology*, 73, 1657–1665.

Derocher A and Stirling I (1996) Aspects of survival in juvenile polar bears. *Canadian Journal of Zoology*, 74, 1246–1252.

Derocher A and Wiig Ø (1999) Infanticide and cannibalism of juvenile polar bears (*Ursus maritimus*) in Svalbard. *Arctic*, 52, 307–310.

Derocher A, Garner G, Lunn N *et al.* (Eds.) (1998) *Polar Bears: Proceedings of the 12th meeting of the Polar Bear Specialist Group IUCN/SSC, 3–7 February, 1997, Oslo, Norway.* IUCN.

Derocher A, Wiig Ø and Bangjord G (2000) Predation of Svalbard reindeer by polar bears. *Polar Biology*, 23, 675–678.

Derocher A, Wiig Ø and Andersen M (2002) Diet composition of polar bears in Svalbard and the western Barents Sea. *Polar Biology*, 25, 448–452.

Derocher A, Lunn N and Stirling I (2004) Polar bears in a warming climate. *Integrative and Comparative Biology*, 44, 163–176.

Derocher A, Andersen M, Wiig Ø *et al.* (2010) Sexual dimorphism and the mating ecology of polar bears (*Ursus maritimus*) at Svalbard. *Behavioral Ecology and Sociobiology*, 64, 939–946.

Derocher A, Andersen M, Wiig Ø et al. (2011) Sea ice and polar bear den ecology at Hopen Island, Svalbard. *Marine Ecology Progress Series*, 441, 273–279.

Derocher A, Aars J, Amstrup S et al. (2013) Rapid ecosystem change and polar bear conservation. *Conservation Letters*, 6, 368–3.

Descamps S, Aars J, Fuglei E et al. (2017) Climate change impacts on wildlife in a High Arctic archipelago – Svalbard, Norway. *Global Change Biology*, 23, 490–502.

DeWeaver E (2007) *Uncertainty in Climate Model Projections of Arctic Sea Ice Decline: An Evaluation Relevant to Polar Bears.* Tech. rep., US Geological Survey.

DFO (2014) *Status of Northwest Atlantic Harp Seals, Pagophilus groenlandicus.* Science Advisory Report 2014/011, Department of Fisheries and Oceans Canada, Canadian Science Advisory Secretariat.

Dickie G (2018) As Polar Bear Attacks Increase in Warming Arctic, a Search for Solutions. *Yale Environment 360*, 19 December. URL: https://e360.yale.edu/features/as-polar-bear-attacks-increase-in-warming-arctic-a-search-for-solutions.

Discovery Institute (1998) The Wedge. Center for Renewal of Science and Culture. URL: https://ncse.com/creationism/general/wedge-document.

Dobzhansky T (1937) *Genetics and the Origin of Species.* Columbia University Press.

Dobzhansky T (1973) Nothing in biology makes sense except in the light of evolution. *The American Biology Teacher*, 35, 125–129.

Doup J, England J, Furze M et al. (2007) Most northerly observation of a grizzly bear (*Ursus arctos*) in Canada: photographic and DNA evidence from Melville Island, Northwest Territories. *Arctic*, 60, 271–276.

Drolet M (2018) Declining ice blamed for rise in polar bear sightings after father killed while protecting kids. *Global News*, 13 July. URL: https://globalnews.ca/news/43314 45/sea-ice-polar-bear-kills-father/.

Durner G, Douglas D, Nielson R et al. (2006) *A Model for Autumn Pelagic distribution of Female Polar Bears in the Chukchi Sea, 1987–1994.* Tech. rep., US Geological Survey.

Durner G, Douglas D, Nielson R et al. (2007) *Predicting 21st-century Polar Bear Habitat Distribution from Global Climate Models.* Tech. rep., US Geological Survey.

Durner G, Douglas D, Nielson R et al. (2009) Predicting 21st-century polar bear habitat distribution from global climate models. *Ecology Monographs*, 79, 25–58.

Durner G, Whiteman J, Harlow H et al. (2011) Consequences of long-distance swimming and travel over deep-water pack ice for a female polar bear during a year of extreme sea ice retreat. *Polar Biology*, 34, 975–984.

Durner G, Laidre K and York G (Eds.) (2018) *Polar Bears: Proceedings of the 18th Working Meeting of the IUCN/SSC Polar Bear Specialist Group, 7–11 June 2016, Anchorage, Alaska.* IUCN.

Dyck M (2006) Characteristics of polar bears killed in defense of life and property in Nunavut, Canada, 1970–2000. *Ursus*, 17, 52–62.

Dyck M, Campbell M, Lee D *et al.* (2017) *2016 Aerial survey of the Western Hudson Bay Polar Bear Subpopulation.* Tech. rep., Nunavut Department of Environment, Wildlife Research Section, Iglolik, NU.

Dykstra P (2008) Magic number: A sketchy fact about polar bears keeps going... and going... and going. *Society of Environmental Journalists News Magazine*, Summer. URL: http://www.sejarchive.org/pub/SEJournal_Excerpts_Su08.htm.

Earth Observatory (2009) Arctic sea ice: 2002–2003. *NASA Earth Observatory*, Image of the day for 16 May 2009. URL: https://earthobservatory.nasa.gov/images/38521/a rctic-sea-ice-2002--2003.

ECC (2017) Maps of subpopulations of polar bears and protected areas. Environment and Climate Change Canada. URL: https://www.canada.ca/en/environment-climate -change/services/biodiversity/maps-sub-populations-polar-bears-protected.html.

Edwards C, Suchard M, Lemey P *et al.* (2011) Ancient hybridization and an Irish origin for the modern polar bear matriline. *Current Biology*, 21, 1251–1258.

Elliott H (1875) Polar bears on St. Matthew Island. *Harper's Weekly Journal of Civilization*, May 1.

Elliott H and Coues E (1875) A report upon the condition of affairs in the territory of Alaska. US Government Printing Office. URL: http://tinyurl.com/a8zk6yk.

English K (2016) Updating the bear facts: Public Editor. *The Star*, 30 June. URL: http s://www.thestar.com/opinion/public_editor/2016/06/30/updating-the-bear-facts-p ublic-editor.html.

Etkin D (1991) Break-up in Hudson Bay: its sensitivity to air temperatures and implications for climate warming. *Climatological Bulletin*, 25, 21–34.

Eurich J (2019) Seals seem to be adapting to shrinking sea ice off Alaska. *Alaska Daily News*, 11 February. URL: https://www.adn.com/alaska-news/wildlife/2019/02/11/so -far-seals-seem-to-be-adapting-to-shrinking-sea-ice-off-alaska/.

Fanelli D (2018) Opinion: Is science really facing a reproducibility crisis, and do we need it to? PNAS. URL: https://doi.org/10.1073/pnas.1708272114.

Fauchald P, Arneberg P, Berge J *et al.* (2014) *An Assessment of MOSJ – the State of the Marine Environment around Svalbard and Jan Mayen.* Tech. Rep. 145, Norwegian Polar Institute. URL: http://www.mosj.no/en/documents/.

Fedoseev G (1975) Ecotypes of the ringed seal (*Pusa hispida* Schreber, 1777) and their reproductive capabilities. In: K Ronald and A Mansfield (Eds.), *Biology of the Seal.* Conseil International Pour L'Exploration de la Mer.

Ferguson S, Stirling I and McLoughlin P (2005) Climate change and ringed seal (*Phoca hispida*) recruitment in Western Hudson Bay. *Marine Mammal Science*, 21, 121–135.

Ferguson SH, Taylor MK and Messier F (2000a) Influence of sea ice dynamics on habitat selection by polar bears. *Ecology*, 81, 761–772.

Ferguson SH, Taylor MK, Rosing Asvid A *et al.* (2000b) Relationships between denning of polar bears and conditions of sea ice. *Journal of Mammalogy*, 81, 1118–1127.

Finley K, Miller G, Davis R *et al.* (1983) A distinctive large breeding population of ringed seal (*Phoca hispida*) inhabiting the Baffin Bay pack ice. *Arctic*, 36, 162–173.

Fischbach AS, Amstrup SC and Douglas DC (2007) Landward and eastward shift of Alaskan polar bear denning associated with recent sea ice changes. *Polar Biology*, 30, 1395–1405.

Fleck S and Herrero SH (1988) *Polar Bear-Human Conflicts.* Tech. rep., Parks Canada and Department of Renewable Resources, Northwest Territories.

Fouche G (2016) As Norway's Arctic draws visitors, more polar bears get shot. Yahoo News via Reuters, 28 September. URL: https://ca.news.yahoo.com/norways-arctic-d raws-visitors-more-polar-bears-shot-121646372.html.

Frey K, Moore G, Cooper L *et al.* (2015) Divergent patterns of recent sea ice cover across the Bering, Chukchi, and Beaufort seas of the Pacific Arctic Region. *Progress in Oceanography*, 136, 32–49.

Furevik T, Drange H and Sorteberg A (2002) Anticipated changes in the Nordic Seas marine climate: Scenarios for 2020, 2050, and 2080. *Fisken og Havet*, 4, 1–13.

Galicia M, Thiemann G, Dyck M *et al.* (2016) Dietary habits of polar bears in Foxe Basin, Canada: possible evidence of a trophic regime shift mediated by a new top predator. *Ecology and Evolution*, 6, 6005–6018.

Gates S (2013) Starved polar bear in Norway may be a victim of climate change. *The Huffington Post UK*, 8 August. URL: http://www.huffingtonpost.com/2013/08/08/st arved-polar-bear-found-dead-norway-climate-change_n_3720236.html.

George J, Druckenmiller M, Laidre K *et al.* (2015) Bowhead whale body condition and links to summer sea ice and upwelling in the Beaufort Sea. *Progress in Oceanography*, 136, 250–262.

Gjertz I and Persen E (1987) Confrontations between humans and polar bears in Svalbard. *Polar Research*, 5, 253–256.

Gjertz I, Aarvik S and Hindrum R (1993) Polar bears killed in Svalbard 1987–1992. *Polar Research*, 12, 107–109.

Gleick P, Adams R and Amasino Rea (2010) Climate change and the integrity of science. *Science*, 328, 689–690.

Goode E (2018) Climate change denialists say polar bears are fine. Scientists are pushing back. *New York Times*, 10 April. URL: https://www.nytimes.com/2018/04/10/climate /polar-bears-climate-deniers.html.

Gormezano L and Rockwell R (2013a) Dietary composition and spatial patterns of polar bear foraging on land in western Hudson Bay. *BMC Ecology*, 13, 51.

Gormezano L and Rockwell R (2013b) What to eat now? Shifts in polar bear diet during the ice-free season in western Hudson Bay. *Ecology and Evolution*, 3, 3509–3523.

Graham C (2013) The poster boys of climate change thrive in the icy Arctic: Polar bears defy concerns about their extinction. *The Mail on Sunday*, 28 September. URL: http://www.dailymail.co.uk/news/article-2436882/The-poster-boys-climate-chang e-thrive-icy-Arctic-Polar-bears-defy-concerns-extinction.html.

Greer D (2018a) Naujaat man mauled to death by polar bear. *Nunavut News*, 5 September. URL: https://nunavutnews.com/nunavut-news/naujaat-man-mauled-to-death-by-polar-bear/.

Greer D (2018b) Rankin man shoots marauding polar bear. *Nunavut News*, 31 August. URL: https://nunavutnews.com/nunavut-news/rankin-man-shoots-marauding-polar-bear/.

Greshko M (2016) Exclusive video: polar bear cannibalizes cub. *National Geographic News*, 23 February. URL: http://news.nationalgeographic.com/2016/02/160223-polar-bears-arctic-cannibals-animals-science/.

Griffen B (2018) Modeling the metabolic costs of swimming in polar bears (*Ursus maritimus*). *Polar Biology*. URL: doi:10.1007/s00300-017-2209-x.

Halls M (2018) Why Arctic ecotourism should be allowed to flourish, despite the tragic shooting of a polar bear. Stuff (Opinion), 9 August (reprinted from *The Telegraph*, UK, 2 August). URL: https://www.stuff.co.nz/travel/news/106132155/why-arctic-ecotourism-should-be-allowed-to-flourish-despite-the-tragic-shooting-of-a-polar-bear.

Hamilton S and Derocher A (2018) Assessment of global polar bear abundance and vulnerability. *Animal Conservation*. URL: doi:10.1111/acv.12439.

Hamilton S and Derocher A (2019) Assessment of global polar bear abundance and vulnerability. *Animal Conservation*, 22(1), 83–95.

Hansen J, Fung I, Lacis A *et al.* (1988) Global climate changes as forecast by Goddard Institute for Space Studies three-dimensional model. *Journal of Geophysical Research*, 93(D8), 9341–9364.

Harington C (1965) The life and status of the polar bear. *Oryx*, 8, 169–176.

Harington C (2008) The evolution of Arctic marine mammals. *Ecological Applications*, 18(2), S23–S40.

Harington CR (1968) *Denning Habits of the Polar Bear (Ursus maritimus Phipps)*. Tech. Rep. 5, Canadian Wildlife Service.

Harvey C (2017) These scientists want to create 'red teams' to challenge climate research. Congress is listening. *Washington Post*, 29 March. URL: https://www.washingtonpost.com/news/energy-environment/wp/2017/03/29/these-climate-doubters-want-to-create-a-red-team-to-challenge-climate-science/.

Harvey J, van denBerg D, Ellers J *et al.* (2018) Internet blogs, polar bears, and climate-change denial by proxy. *Bioscience*, 68, 281–287.

Harwood L and Stirling I (1992) Distribution of ringed seals in the southeastern Beaufort Sea during late summer. *Canadian Journal of Zoology*, 70, 891–900.

Harwood L, Smith T and Melling H (2000) Variation in reproduction and body condition of the ringed seal (*Phoca hispida*) in western Prince Albert Sound, NT, Canada, as assessed through a harvest-based sampling program. *Arctic*, 53, 422–431.

Harwood L, Smith T, Melling H *et al.* (2012) Ringed seals and sea ice in Canada's western Arctic: harvest-based monitoring 1992–2011. *Arctic*, 65, 377–390.

Harwood L, Smith T, George J *et al.* (2015) Change in the Beaufort Sea ecosystem: Diverging trends in body condition and/or production in five marine vertebrate species. *Progress in Oceanography*, 136, 263–273.

Hassol S (2004) *Impacts of a Warming Arctic: Arctic Climate Impact Assessment Synthesis Report.* Cambridge University Press.

Healey J (2017) Pack ice produces polar bears. *The Telegram*, 10 April. URL: http://www.thetelegram.com/news/local/2017/4/10/pack-ice-produces-polar-bears.html.

Herrero S (1972) Aspects of evolution and adaptation in American black bears (*Ursus americanus Pallas*) and brown and grizzly bears (*U. arctos Linn*) of North America. *Bears – their Biology and Management*, 23, 221–231.

Herrero S (1985) *Bear Attacks: Their Causes and Avoidance.* 1st edn. Nick Lyon Books and Winchester Press.

Herrero S (2003) *Bear Attacks: Their Causes and Avoidance.* 2nd edn. McClelland & Stewart.

Herrero S and Fleck S (1990) Injury to people inflicted by black, grizzly or polar bears: recent trends and newer insights. *Bears: Their Biology and Management*, 8, 25–32.

Herrero S, Higgins A, Cardoza J *et al.* (2011) Fatal attacks by American black bears on people: 1900–2009. *The Journal of Wildlife Management*, 75, 596–602.

Holland M, Bitz C and Tremblay B (2006) Future reductions in the summer Arctic sea ice. *Geophysical Research Letters*, 33, L23503.

Holst M, Stirling I and Calvert W (1999) Age structure and reproductive rates of ringed seals (Phoca hispida) on the northwestern coast of Hudson Bay in 1991 and 1992. *Marine Mammal Science*, 15(4), 1357–1364.

Honderich J (1991) *Wildlife as a hazardous resource: an analysis of the historical interaction of humans and polar bears in the Canadian arctic.* Master's thesis, University of Waterloo, Ontario.

Hopper T (2017) The polar bears are fine: Certain populations coping with a warming Arctic better than expected. *National Post*, 2 March. URL: https://nationalpost.com/news/canada/despite-vanishing-sea-ice-canadas-polar-bears-appear-to-be-hanging-on-in-the-arctic-study-says.

Horton R (2015) Offline: What is medicine's 5 sigma? *The Lancet*, 385, 1380.

Hunter C, Caswell H, Runge M *et al.* (2007) *Polar Bears in the Southern Beaufort Sea II: Demography and Population Growth in Relation to Sea Ice Conditions.* Tech. rep., US Geological Survey.

Hunter C, Caswell H, Runge M *et al.* (2010) Climate change threatens polar bear populations: a stochastic demographic analysis. *Ecology*, 91, 2883–2897.

Ice People (2017) A bear of an all-nighter: trio of polar bears return to town Sunday, officials 'chase them as far as possible'. *IcePeople Svalbard*, 23 January. URL: http://icepeople.net/2017/01/23/a-bear-of-an-all-nighter-trio-of-polar-bears-return-to-town-sunday-officials-chase-them-as-far-as-possible/.

Iles D, Peterson S, Gormezano L *et al.* (2013) Terrestrial predation by polar bears: not just a wild goose chase. *Polar Biology*, 36, 1373–1379.

Ioannidis J (2005) Why most published research findings are false. *PLOS Medicine*, 2(8), e124.

IPCC (2007) *Climate Change 2007: The Physical Science Basis, Contribution of Working Group I to the Fourth Assessment Report of the Intergovernmental Panel on Climate Change*. Cambridge University Press.

Jay C and Fischbach A (2008) *Pacific Walrus Response to Arctic Sea Ice Losses*. Fact sheet 2008–3041, US Geological Survey. URL: http://pubs.usgs.gov/fs/2008/3041/pdf/fs20083041.pdf.

Johnson T (2013) Was this polar bear a victim of climate change? The Weather Channel, 12 August. URL: https://weather.com/science/environment/news/was-polar-bear-victim-climate-change-20130811.

Johnston I (2013) A victim of climate change? Polar bear found starved to death looked 'like a rug'. *NBC News*, 7 August. URL: http://worldnews.nbcnews.com/_news/2013/08/07/19909343-a-victim-of-climate-change-polar-bear-found-starved-to-death-looked-like-a-rug.

Joling D (2006) Polar bears may be turning to cannibalism. *Washington Post*, 12 June. URL: http://www.washingtonpost.com/wp-dyn/content/article/2006/06/12/AR2006061201266.html.

Joling D (2017) Walruses in Alaska may have died in stampede. *AP News*, 13 September. URL: http://www.apnewsarchive.com/2017/The-U-S-Fish-and-Wildlife-Service-says-64-walruses-died-on-a-northwest-Alaska-beach-and-the-animals-may-have-been-killed-in-stampedes/.

Joling D (2018) Quota raised for subsistence hunting of Chukchi polar bears. *National Post*, 3 August. URL: https://nationalpost.com/pmn/news-pmn/quota-raised-for-subsistence-hunting-of-chukchi-polar-bears.

Jonkel C (1969) *Polar Bear Research in Canada*. Progress Notes 13, Canadian Wildlife Service.

Jonkel C (1978) Black, Brown (grizzly), and polar bears. In: J Schmidt and D Gilbert (Eds.), *Big Game of North America: Ecology and Management*,. Stackpole Books.

Jonkel C, Kolenosky G, Robertson R *et al.* (1972) Further notes on polar bear denning habits. *Bears: Their Biology and Management*, 2, 142–158.

Jonkel C, Smith P, Stirling I *et al.* (1976) *Notes on the Present Status of the Polar Bear in James Bay and the Belcher Islands*. Occasional paper 26, Canadian Wildlife Service.

Kalvapalle R (2018) Trudeau's carbon tax on gas won't motivate Canadians to switch to fuel-efficient transportation: Ipsos poll. *Global News*, 27 December. URL: https://globalnews.ca/news/4778887/carbon-tax-gas-prices-ipsos-poll/.

Kearney S (1989) *The Polar Bear Alert Program at Churchill, Manitoba*. Tech. rep., Northwest Territories Department of Renewable Resources.

Kelkar K (2015) Are emaciated polar bears the new face of climate change? *Alaska Daily News*, 28 September. URL: http://www.adn.com/article/20150922/are-emaciated-polar-bears-new-face-climate-change.

Kelly B, Badajos O, Kunnasranta M *et al.* (2010) Seasonal home ranges and fidelity to breeding sites among ringed seals. *Polar Biology*, 33, 1095–1109.

Kelly J (2017) Michael Mann embarrasses himself before Congress. *National Review*, 30 March. URL: https://www.nationalreview.com/2017/03/michael-mann-house-testimony-climate-change-embarrassing-rude/.

Kelly T, Seamark M and Cohen T (2011) Eton pupil killed by polar bear: 17-year-old boy on £4,000 adventure trip is mauled to death as he sleeps in Arctic tent. *Daily Mail*, 6 August. URL: http://www.dailymail.co.uk/news/article-2022778/Polar-bear-attack-Norway-Eton-pupil-Horatio-Chapple-17-mauled-death.html.

Klein D and Sowls A (2011) History of polar bears as summer residents on the St. Matthew Islands, Bering Sea. *Arctic*, 64, 429–436.

Koop BF, Burbidge M, Byun A *et al.* (2000) Ancient DNA evidence of a separate origin for North American indigenous dogs. In: SJ Crockford (Ed.), *Dogs Through Time: An Archaeological Perspective*. Archaeopress.

Kovacs K (2015) *Pagophilus groenlandicus*. The IUCN Red List of Threatened Species, 2015.

Kovacs K (2016a) *Cystophora cristata*. The IUCN Red List of Threatened Species 2016.

Kovacs K (2016b) *Erignathus barbatus*. The IUCN Red List of Threatened Species 2016.

Laframbroise D (2018) Polar bears and the sleazy *New York Times*. *No Frakking Consensus*, 13 April. URL: https://nofrakkingconsensus.com/2018/04/13/polar-bears-and-the-sleazy-new-york-times/.

Larsen T (1971) Capturing, handling, and marking polar bears in Svalbard. *Journal of Wildlife Management*, 35, 27–36.

Larsen T (1972) Norwegian polar bear hunt, management and research. *Bears: Their Biology and Management*, 2, 159–164.

Larsen T (1985) Polar bear denning and cub production in Svalbard, Norway. *Journal of Wildlife Management*, 49, 320–326.

Larsen T (1986) Population biology of the polar bear (*Ursus maritimus*) in the Svalbard area. Skriter NR. 184. Monograph of the Norwegian Polar Institute, Oslo.

Larsen T and Stirling I (2009) *The Agreement on the Conservation of Polar Bears – Its History and Future*. Tech. Rep. 127, Norwegian Polar Institute.

Leavitt K (2018) There are parallels between the polar bear shot dead and the perils of climate change, University of Alberta researcher says. *The Star* (Edmonton), 1 August. URL: https://www.thestar.com/edmonton/2018/08/01/after-malnourished-polar-bear-attack-in-norway-canadian-expert-questions-walk-with-bears-tourism.html.

Lefebvre J, Gauthier G, Giroux JF et al. (2017) The greater snow goose *Anser caerulescens atlanticus*: Managing an overabundant population. *Ambio*, Suppl. 2(46), S262–S274.

Lentfer J (1970) Polar bear research and conservation in Alaska, 1968-1969. In: *Polar Bears: Proceedings of the 2nd Working Meeting of the Polar Bear Specialist Group, IUCN/SSC, 2-4 February 1970, Morges, Switzerland.* IUCN.

Lentfer J (1972) Alaska polar bear research and management, 1970–1971. In: *Polar Bears: Proceedings of the 3rd Working Meeting of the Polar Bear Specialist Group, IUCN/SSC, 7-10 February 1972, Morges, Switzerland.* IUCN.

Lewandowsky S and Whitmarsh L (2018) Climate communication for biologists: When a picture can tell a thousand words. *PLoS Biology*, 16(10), e2006004. URL: https://doi.org/10.1371/journal.pbio.2006004.

Linden E (2000) The big meltdown. *Time*, 156(10), 53–55. URL: http://www.cpp.edu/~aebresnock/aebres/ec435/Arctic%20Meltdown.htm.

Lindqvist C, Schuster S, Sun Y et al. (2010) Complete mitochondrial genome of a Pleistocene jawbone unveils the origin of polar bear. *Proceedings of the National Academy of Sciences USA*, 107, 5053–5057.

Lindsay R and Zhang J (2005) The thinning of Arctic sea ice, 1988-2003: have we passed a tipping point? *Journal of Climate*, 18, 4879–4894.

Liu S, Lorenzen E, Fumagalli M et al. (2014) Population genomics reveal recent speciation and rapid evolutionary adaptation in polar bears. *Cell*, 157, 785–794.

LiveScience (2008) Arctic sea ice melting faster than predicted. *LiveScience*, 11 January 2008. URL: https://www.livescience.com/4425-arctic-sea-ice-melting-faster-predicted.html.

Lone K, Kovacs K, Lydersen C et al. (2018) Aquatic behaviour of polar bears (*Ursus maritimus*) in an increasingly ice-free Arctic. *Scientific Reports*, 8, 9677.

Lønø O (1970) The polar bear (*Ursus maritimus* Phipps) in the Svalbard area. *Norsk Polarinstitutt Skrifter*, 149.

Lowry L (2016) *Pusa hispida*. The IUCN Red List of Threatened Species 2016.

Lunn N and Stenhouse G (1985) An observation of possible cannibalism by polar bears (*Ursus maritimus*). *Canadian Journal of Zoology*, 63, 1516–1517.

Lunn N and Stirling I (1985) The significance of supplemental food to polar bears during the ice-free period of Hudson Bay. *Canadian Journal of Zoology*, 63, 2291–2297.

Lunn N, Schliebe S and Born E (Eds.) (2002) *Polar Bears: Proceedings of the 13th working meeting of the IUCN/SSC Polar Bear Specialist Group, 23–28 June , 2001, Nuuk, Greenland.* IUCN.

Lunn N, Stirling I, Andriashek D *et al.* (2004) Selection of maternity dens by female polar bears in western Hudson Bay Canada and the effects of human disturbance. *Polar Biology*, 27, 350–356.

Lunn N, Servanty S, Regehr E *et al.* (2016) Demography of an apex predator at the edge of its range – impacts of changing sea ice on polar bears in Hudson Bay. *Ecological Applications*, 26, 1302–1320.

Lydersen C and Gjertz I (1986) Studies of the ringed seal (*Phoca hispida* Schreber 1775) in its breeding habitat in Kongsfjorden, Svalbard. *Polar Research*, 4, 57–63.

MacCracken J, Beatty W, Garlich Miller J *et al.* (2017) *Final Species Status Assessment for the Pacific Walrus* (Odobenus rosmarus divergens), May 2017. Tech. rep., US Fish & Wildlife Service.

Madwar S (2016) He speaks for the polar bears: no fearmongering, no exaggeration; for Ian Stirling, it's purely about the science. *Up Here Magazine*, February: 13–14. URL: http://uphere.ca/node/1899.

Malenfant R, Davis C, Cullingham C *et al.* (2016) Circumpolar genetic structure and recent gene flow of polar bears: a reanalysis. *PLoS One*, 11(3), e0148967.

Mangerud J and Svendsen J (2018) The Holocene Thermal Maximum around Svalbard, Arctic North Atlantic; molluscs show early and exceptional warmth. *The Holocene*, 28, 65–83.

Mann M (2017) Testimony to US Congress Committee on Science, Space and Technology. Full Committee Hearing: Climate science: assumptions, policy implications, and the scientific method, 29 March. URL: https://science.house.gov/legislation/hearings/full-committee-hearing-climate-science-assumptions-policy-implications-and.

Manzo K (2010) Beyond polar bears? Re-envisioning climate change. *Meteorological Applications*, 17, 196–208.

Marine Mammal Commission (2007) *The Marine Mammal Protection Act of 1972, as amended.* Tech. rep., National Marine Fisheries Service.

Martin H (2014) Hunters 5-Polar bears 0. *Arctic Journal*, 10 July. URL: journal.com/climate/773/hunters-5-polar-bears-0.

Martinez-Bakker M, Sell S, Swanson B *et al.* (2013) Combined genetic and telemetry data reveal high rates of gene flow, migration, and long-distance dispersal potential in Arctic ringed seals (*Pusa hispida*). *PLoS One*, 8, e77125.

Matishov G, Chelintsev N, Goryaev YI *et al.* (2014) Assessment of the amount of polar bears (*Ursus maritimus*) on the basis of perennial vessel counts. *Doklady Earth Sciences*, 458, 1312–1316.

Mauritzen M, Derocher A and Wiig Ø (2001) Space-use strategies of female polar bears in a dynamic sea ice habitat. *Canadian Journal of Zoology*, 79, 1704–1713.

McCall A, Derocher A and Lunn N (2015) Home range distribution of polar bears in western Hudson Bay. *Polar Biology*, 38, 343–355.

McCue D (2017) Polar bears in Churchill face bleak future, researchers warn. CBC News, 2 November. URL: http://www.cbc.ca/news/multimedia/polar-bears-in-chur chill-face-bleak-future-researchers-warn-1.4380568.

McLoughlin K (2017) Sheep grazing on a hill? No…it's 200 polar bears scrambling down a mountain slope to feast on a bloated whale carcass in the Arctic. *The Daily Mail*, 23 November. URL: http://www.dailymail.co.uk/news/article-5110801/Polar -bears-scramble-mountain-feast-whale.html.

McLoughlin P, Taylor M, Cluff H *et al.* (2003) Population viability of barren-ground grizzly bears in Nunavut and the Northwest Territories. *Arctic*, 56, 185–190.

Meier W, Hovelsrud G, vanOort B *et al.* (2014) Arctic sea ice in transformation: A review of recent observed changes and impacts on biology and human activity. *Reviews of Geophysics*, 52, 185–217.

Mercer G (2018) 'They're everywhere': has the decline of the seal hunt saved the polar bear? *The Guardian*, 24 May. URL: https://www.theguardian.com/world/2018/may /24/canada-polar-bears-labrador-rigolet-seal-hunt.

Messier F, Taylor M and Ramsay M (1994) Denning ecology of polar bears in the Canadian Arctic Archipelago. *Journal of Mammalogy*, 75, 420–430.

Miller S, Schliebe S and Proffitt K (2006) *Demographics and Behavior of Polar Bears Feeding on Bowhead Whale Carcasses at Barter and Cross Islands, Alaska, 2002-2004.* Alaska Outer Continental Shelf (OCS) Study MMS 2006-14, US Dept. of the Interior, Minerals Management Service, Anchorage.

Miller S, Wilder J and Wilson R (2015) Polar bear–grizzly bear interactions during the autumn open-water period in Alaska. *Journal of Mammalogy*, 96, 1317–1325.

Miller W, Schuster S, Welch A *et al.* (2012) Polar and brown bear genomes reveal ancient admixture and demographic footprints of past climate change. *Proceedings of the National Academy of Sciences*, 109, E2382–E2390.

Mills E (2016) Hungry polar bears go on food rampage in Russia. *The Daily Telegraph*, 10 March. URL: https://www.telegraph.co.uk/news/earth/wildlife/12189745/Hungr y-polar-bears-go-on-food-rampage-in-Russia.html.

Mittermeier C (2018) Nothing prepared me for what I saw. *National Geographic Magazine*, August, 36–37.

Monnett C and Gleason J (2006) Observations of mortality associated with extended open-water swimming by polar bears in the Alaskan Beaufort Sea. *Polar Biology*, 29, 681–687.

MOSJ (2018a) Fauna, Marine: Polar bear (*Ursus maritimus*). URL: http://www.mosj.n o/en/influence/hunting-trapping/polar-bear-bag.html.

MOSJ (2018b) Pressures: Polar bear take (*Ursus maritimus*). URL: http://www.mosj.n o/en/influence/hunting-trapping/polar-bear-bag.html.

Murphy R (2018) The UN climate-change panel that cried wolf too often. *National Post*, 12 October. URL: https://nationalpost.com/opinion/rex-murphy-the-un-climate-c hange-panel-that-cried-wolf-too-often.

National Geographic (2018) Editor's note. *National Geographic Magazine*, August, 37.

National Geographic News (2014) Biggest walrus gathering recorded as sea ice shrinks. *National Geographic News*, 14 October. URL: http://news.nationalgeographic.com/news/2014/10/141002-walruses-climate-change-science-global-warming-animals-alaska/.

Newbern E (2015) Starving polar bear photo: Don't blame (just) climate change. *LiveScience*, 16 September. URL: https://www.livescience.com/52179-polar-bears-climate-change-impact.html.

Newell D (2017) Highway of ice: easy route for polar bears chasing food, expert says. *CBC News Newfoundland and Labrador*, 12 April. URL: http://www.cbc.ca/news/canada/newfoundland-labrador/pack-ice-polar-bears-1.4065930.

Nielsen S, Cattet M, Boulanger J *et al.* (2013) Environmental, biological and anthropogenic effects on grizzly bear body size: temporal and spatial considerations. *BMC Ecology*, 13, 31.

Nilsen T (2019a) Declares emergency: Polar bears 'invade' military town. *Barents Observer*, 9 February. URL: https://thebarentsobserver.com/en/arctic/2019/02/declares-emergency-polar-bears-invades-military-town.

Nilsen T (2019b) Well-fed polar bears are not necessarily stuck at Novaya Zemlya due to climate change, experts say. Barent's Observer, 14 February. URL: https://thebarentsobserver.com/en/ecology/2019/02/well-fed-polar-bears-are-are-not-stuck-novaya-zemlya-due-climate-change-expert-says.

Norwegian Polar Institute (2018) *Polar Bear*. Marine fauna, monitoring of Svalbard and Jan Mayen (MOSJ), Norwegian Polar Institute. URL: http://www.mosj.no/en/fauna/marine/polar-bear.html.

NPI (2015) Polar bears in Svalbard in good condition – so far. Press release, Norwegian Polar Institute, 23 December 2015. URL: http://www.npolar.no/en/news/2015/12--23-counting-of-polar-bears-in-svalbard.html.

NSIDC (2005) Trends continue. NSIDC Newsroom, National Snow and Ice Data Center, September 28. URL: https://nsidc.org/news/newsroom/20050928_trendscontinue.html.

NSIDC (2016) Rapid ice growth follows the seasonal minimum, rapid drop in Antarctic extent. NSIDC Arctic Sea Ice News and Analysis, National Snow and Ice Data Center, 5 October. URL: http://nsidc.org/arcticseaicenews/2016/10/.

NSIDC (2017) Another record, but a somewhat cooler Arctic Ocean. NSIDC Arctic Sea Ice News and Analysis, National Snow and Ice Data Center, 11 April. URL: http://nsidc.org/arcticseaicenews/2017/04/.

Nunatsiaq News (2008) It's a great concern for Inuit. *Nunatsiaq News*, 8 May. URL: http://nunatsiaq.com/stories/article/Its_a_great_concern_for_Inuit/.

Nunatsiaq News (2019) Meet our newsmaker of the year: the polar bear. *Nunatsiaq News*, editorial, 2 January. URL: https://nunatsiaq.com/stories/article/meet-our-newsmaker-of-the-year-the-polar-bear/.

NWMB (2018) Nunavut Polar Bear Co-Management Plan. Nunavut Wildlife Management Board.

Obbard M, McDonald T, Howe E *et al.* (2007) *Polar Bear Population Status in Southern Hudson Bay, Canada.* Tech. rep., US Geological Survey.

Obbard M, Theimann G, Peacock E *et al.* (Eds.) (2010) *Polar Bears: Proceedings of the 15th meeting of the Polar Bear Specialist Group IUCN/SSC, 29 June–3 July, 2009, Copenhagen, Denmark.* IUCN.

Obbard M, Stapleton S, Middel K *et al.* (2015) Estimating the abundance of the Southern Hudson Bay polar bear subpopulation with aerial surveys. *Polar Biology,* 38, 1713–1725.

Obbard M, Cattet M, Howe E *et al.* (2016) Trends in body condition in polar bears (*Ursus maritimus*) from the Southern Hudson Bay subpopulation in relation to changes in sea ice. *Arctic Science,* 2, 15–32.

Obbard M, Stapleton S, Szor G *et al.* (2018) Estimating the abundance of the Southern Hudson Bay polar bear subpopulation with aerial surveys. *Arctic Science,* pp. 634–655.

Ogilvie A, Barlow L and Jennings A (2000) North Atlantic climate c. AD 1000: Millennial reflections on the Viking discoveries of Iceland, Greenland and North America. *Weather,* 55, 34–45.

Orange R (2013) Norwegian polar bear found starved to death. *The Local,* Norway, 7 August. URL: http://www.thelocal.no/20130807/polar-bear-starves-to-death-on-norways-svalbard.

Osaka S (2018) Move over polar bears: climate change has a new symbol. *Grist,* 23 July. URL: https://grist.org/article/move-over-polar-bears-climate-change-has-a-new-symbol/.

Packard A (1886) The former southern limits of the white or polar bear. *American Naturalist,* 20(7), 655–659.

Paetkau D, Amstrup S, Born E *et al.* (1999) Genetic structure of the world's polar bear populations. *Molecular Ecology,* 8, 1571–1584.

Pagano A, Durner G, Amstrup S *et al.* (2012) Long-distance swimming by polar bears (*Ursus maritimus*) of the southern Beaufort Sea during years of extensive open water. *Canadian Journal of Zoology,* 90, 663–676.

Parkinson C (2014) Spatially mapped reductions in the length of the Arctic sea ice season. *Geophysical Research Letters,* 41, 4316–4322.

Parkinson C and Kellogg W (1979) Arctic sea ice decay simulated for a CO_2-induced temperature rise. *Climatic Change,* 2, 149–162.

Pascus B (2018) A cruise line is facing public fury after one of its guards shot and killed a polar bear. *UK Business Insider,* 30 July. URL: http://uk.businessinsider.com/cruise-line-worker-kills-polar-bear-sparking-public-outrage-2018-7.

Peacock E, Derocher A, Thiemann G *et al.* (2011) Conservation and management of Canada's polar bears (*Ursus maritimus*) in a changing Arctic. *Canadian Journal of Zoology*, 89, 371–385.

Peacock E, Taylor M, Laake J *et al.* (2013) Population ecology of polar bears in Davis Strait, Canada and Greenland. *Journal of Wildlife Management*, 77, 463–476.

Peacock E, Sonsthagen S, Obbard M *et al.* (2015) Implications of the circumpolar genetic structure of polar bears for their conservation in a rapidly warming Arctic. *PLoS One*, 10(1), e112021.

Peacock L (2017) The harvest of polar bears across the circumpolar north. In: A Butterworth (Ed.), *Marine Mammal Welfare: Human Induced Change in the Marine Environment and its Impacts on Marine Mammal Welfare*. Springer.

Perovich D, Meier W, Tschudi M *et al.* (2015) Sea ice. In: M Jeffries, J Richter-Menge and J Overland (Eds.), *Arctic Report Card 2015*. NOAA. URL: http://www.arctic.noaa.gov/reportcard/index.html.

Pilfold N, Derocher A, Stirling I *et al.* (2012) Age and sex composition of seals killed by polar bears in the eastern Beaufort Sea. *PLoS One*, 7(7), e41429.

Pilfold N, Derocher A, Stirling I *et al.* (2014) Polar bear predatory behaviour reveals seascape distribution of ringed seal lairs. *Population Ecology*, 56, 129–138.

Pilfold N, McCall A, Derocher AE *et al.* (2017) Migratory response of polar bears to sea ice loss: to swim or not to swim. *Ecography*, 40, 189–199.

Pilfold NW, Derocher AE, Stirling I *et al.* (2015) Multi-temporal factors influence predation for polar bears in a changing climate. *Oikos*, 124, 1098–1107.

Polar Bears International (2011) Three polar bears killed in Russia. *PBI News*, 20 August. URL: https://polarbearsinternational.org/news/article-polar-bears/three-polar-bears-killed-in-russia/.

Pongracz J, Paetkau D, Branigan M *et al.* (2017) Recent hybridization between a polar bear and grizzly bears in the Canadian Arctic. *Arctic*, 70, 151–160.

Popescu A (2016) Love in the time of climate change: Grizzlies and polar bears are now mating. *Washington Post*, 23 May. URL: https://www.washingtonpost.com/news/animalia/wp/2016/05/23/love-in-the-time-of-climate-change-grizzlies-and-polar-bears-are-now-mating/.

Post E, Bhatt U, Bitz C *et al.* (2013) Ecological consequences of sea-ice decline. *Science*, 341, 519–524.

Pratt S (2016) Beyond the Polar Bear. *New Trail* (University of Alberta Alumni Magazine) Spring issue, pp. 30–33. URL: https://www.ualberta.ca/newtrail/spring-2016/features-dept/beyond-the-polar-bear.

Prigg M (2016) 'Pizzly' bear was NOT a hybrid: DNA tests find slaughtered animal was a 'blonde grizzly' and not part polar bear. *Daily Mail*, 23 June. URL: http://www.dailymail.co.uk/sciencetech/article-3657142/Pizzly-bear-NOT-hybrid-DNA-tests-slaughtered-animal-blonde-grizzly-not-polar-bear.html.

Rajan A and Tol R (2018) Lipstick on a bear: a comment on internet blogs, polar bears, and climate change denial by proxy. *Open Science Framework*, January 2018.

Ramsay M and Stirling I (1988) Reproductive biology and ecology of female polar bears (*Ursus maritimus*). *Journal of Zoology London*, 214, 601–624.

Ramsay MA and Stirling I (1990) Fidelity of female polar bears to winter den sites. *Journal of Mammalogy*, 71, 233–236.

Ramseier R, Vant M, Arsenault L *et al.* (1975) *Distribution of the Ice Thickness in the Beaufort Sea.* Beaufort Sea Technical Report 30, Canada Dept. of Environment, Victoria, BC.

Rausch R (1953) On the land mammals of St. Lawrence Island, Alaska. *Murrelet*, 34, 18–26.

Raver A (2006) With warmer weather, different decisions to make. *New York Times*, December 21. URL: https://www.nytimes.com/2006/12/21/garden/.

Regehr E, Amstrup S and Stirling I (2006) *Polar Bear Population Status in the Southern Beaufort Sea.* Tech. Rep. 2006–1337, US Geological Survey.

Regehr E, Hunter C, Caswell H *et al.* (2007a) *Polar Bears in the Southern Beaufort Sea I: Survival and Breeding in Relation to Sea Ice Conditions.* Tech. rep., US Geological Survey.

Regehr E, Lunn N, Amstrup S *et al.* (2007b) Effects of earlier sea ice breakup on survival and population size of polar bears in Western Hudson Bay. *Journal of Wildlife Management*, 71, 2673–2683.

Regehr E, Laidre K, Akçakaya H *et al.* (2016) Conservation status of polar bears (*Ursus maritimus*) in relation to projected sea-ice declines. *Biology Letters*, 12, 20160556.

Regehr E, Hostetter N, Wilson R *et al.* (2018) Integrated population modeling provides the first empirical estimates of vital rates and abundance for polar bears in the Chukchi Sea. *Scientific Reports*, 8(1).

Richardson E, Stirling I and Hik D (2005) Polar bear (*Ursus maritimus*) maternity denning habitat in western Hudson Bay: a bottom-up approach to resource selection functions. *Canadian Journal of Zoology*, 83, 860–870.

Riddoch L (2018) Why fake news is harming the Arctic. *The Scotsman*, 22 October. URL: https://www.scotsman.com/news/opinion/lesley-riddoch-why-fake-news-is-harming-the-arctic-1--4818036.

Roberts S (2018) Polar bear sightings continue. *Northern Pen*, 19 March. URL: http://www.northernpen.ca/news/polar-bear-sightings-continue-194734/.

Robinson J (2016) Scientists have been trapped inside an Arctic research lab for two weeks after POLAR BEARS 'besieged' it and ate their dog. *Daily Mail*, 14 September. URL: http://www.dailymail.co.uk/news/article-3788598/Scientists-trapped-inside-Arctic-research-lab-two-weeks-POLAR-BEARS-besieged-ate-dog.html.

Rockwell R, Gormezano L and Hedman D (2008) Grizzly bears, *Ursus arctos*, in Wapusk National Park, Northeastern Manitoba. *Canadian Field Naturalist*, 122, 323–326. URL: http://canadianfieldnaturalist.ca/index.php/cfn/article/view/639.

Rode K and Regehr E (2010) Polar bear research in the Chukchi and Bering Seas: A synopsis of 2010 field work. Unpublished report to the US Fish and Wildlife Service, Dept. Interior, Anchorage.

Rode K, Peacock E, Taylor M *et al.* (2012) A tale of two polar bear populations: ice habitat, harvest and body condition. *Population Ecology*, 54, 3–18.

Rode K, Douglas D, Durner G *et al.* (2013) Variation in the response of an Arctic top predator experiencing habitat loss: feeding and reproductive ecology of two polar bear populations. Oral presentation by Karyn Rode, 28th Lowell Wakefield Fisheries Symposium, March 26-29. Anchorage, AK.

Rode K, Regehr E, Douglas D *et al.* (2014a) Variation in the response of an Arctic top predator experiencing habitat loss: feeding and reproductive ecology of two polar bear populations. *Global Change Biology*, 20, 76–88.

Rode K, Robbins C, Nelson L *et al.* (2015a) Can polar bears use terrestrial foods to offset lost ice-based hunting opportunities? *Frontiers in Ecology and the Environment*, 13, 138–145.

Rode K, Wilson R, Regehr E *et al.* (2015b) Increased land use by Chukchi Sea polar bears in relation to changing sea ice conditions. *PLoS One*, 10, e0142213.

Rode KD, Amstrup S and Regehr E (2007) *Polar Bears in the Southern Beaufort Sea III: Stature, Mass, and Cub Recruitment in Relationship to Time and Sea Ice Extent between 1982 and 2006.* Tech. rep., US Geological Survey.

Rode KD, Pagano AM, Bromaghin JF *et al.* (2014b) Effects of capturing and collaring on polar bears: Findings from long-term research on the Southern Beaufort Sea population. *Wildlife Research*, 41, 311–322.

Rode KD, Olson J, Eggett D *et al.* (2018a) Den phenology and reproductive success of polar bears in a changing climate. *Journal of Mammalogy*, 99, 16–26.

Rode KD, Wilson RR, Douglas DC *et al.* (2018b) Spring fasting behavior in a marine apex predator provides an index of ecosystem productivity. *Global Change Biology*, 24, 410–423. URL: http://onlinelibrary.wiley.com/doi/10.1111/gcb.13933/full.

Rogers M, Peacock E, Simac K *et al.* (2015) Diet of female polar bears in the southern Beaufort Sea of Alaska: evidence for an emerging alternative foraging strategy in response to environmental change. *Polar Biology*, 38, 1035–1047.

Rogers S (2018a) Anger and grief hit Nunavut community following polar bear attack. *Nunatsiaq News*, 6 July. URL: http://nunatsiaq.com/stories/article/65674anger_and _grief_hit_nunavut_community_following_polar_bear_attack/.

Rogers S (2018b) Nunavut wildlife officials investigate illegal polar bear killings. *Nunatsiaq News*, 7 August. URL: http://nunatsiaq.com/stories/article/65674nunav ut_wildlife_officials_investigate_illegal_polar_bear_deaths/.

Rohner T (2016) Exotic bear harvested in Nunavut was a blonde grizzly: DNA analysis confirms no polar bear genetic material in female bear. *NunatsiaqNews*, 21 June. URL: http://www.nunatsiaqonline.ca/stories/article/65674exotic_bear_harvested_in_ nunavut_was_a_blonde_grizzly/.

Romm J (2007) On the myth that polar bear populations are flourishing. *Grist*, 11 September. URL: https://grist.org/article/will-polar-bears-go-extinct-by-2030-part -i/. Originally written for ClimateProgress.org, a project of the Center for American Progress Action Fund.

Rose D (2018) Why all you've been told about these polar bears could be WRONG. *The Mail on Sunday*, 30 December. URL: https://www.dailymail.co.uk/news/article-653 9067/Why-youve-told-polar-bears-WRONG-Inuits-different-story.html.

Rosen Y (2010) Global warming may be harming Pacific walrus: scientists. *Reuters*, 3 October. URL: https://www.reuters.com/article/us-usa-walrus-climate-idUSTRE6 920W820101003.

Rosenblatt K (2018) Did cruise ship guards have to kill polar bear? Experts say maybe – but blame climate change. *NBC News*, 30 July. URL: https://www.nbcnews.com/ science/environment/did-cruise-ship-guards-have-kill-polar-bear-experts-say-n8 95796.

RT (2013) Bear scare: crowds of polar predators 'besiege' Russian Far East town. *RT News*, 11 November. URL: http://rt.com/news/polar-bears-siege-chukotka-russia- 539/.

Russell R (1975) The food habits of polar bears of James Bay and southwest Hudson Bay in summer and autumn. *Arctic*, 28, 117–129.

Savikataaq Jr J (2014) *Operation Arviat Polar Bear Summary Report*. Tech. rep., Government of Nunavut, Department of Environment, Wildlife Management, Iqaluit.

Schliebe S, Evans T, Johnson K *et al.* (2006a) *Range-wide Status Review of the Polar Bear (Ursus maritimus)*. Tech. rep., US Fish and Wildlife Service.

Schliebe S, Wiig Ø, Derocher A *et al.* (2006b) *Ursus maritimus*. The IUCN Red List of Threatened Species 2006.

Schliebe S, Rode K, Gleason J *et al.* (2008a) Effects of sea ice extent and food availability on spatial and temporal distribution of polar bears during the fall open-water period in the southern Beaufort Sea. *Polar Biology*, 31, 999–1010.

Schliebe S, Wiig Ø, Derocher A *et al.* (2008b) *Ursus maritimus*. The IUCN Red List of Threatened Species 2012. URL: https://www.iucnredlist.org/es/species/22823/93911 71.

Schmidt A and Clark D (2018) 'It's just a matter of time': Lessons from agency and community responses to polar bear inflicted human injury. *Conservation and Society*, 16, 64–75.

Sciullo L, Thiemann G and Lunn N (2016) Comparative assessment of metrics for monitoring the body condition of polar bears in western Hudson Bay. *Journal of Zoology*, 300, 45–58.

Scott J and Marshall G (2010) A step-change in the date of sea-ice breakup in western Hudson Bay. *Arctic*, 63, 155–164.

Scott RF, Kenyon KW, Buckley JL *et al.* (1959) Status and management of the polar bear and Pacific walrus. *Transactions of the Twenty-Fourth North American Wildlife Conference*, 24, 366.

Sea Otter Recovery Team (2007) Recovery strategy for the sea otter (*Enhydra lutris*) in Canada. Species at Risk Act Recovery Strategy Series. Fisheries and Oceans Canada, Vancouver.

Sergeant D (1976) History and present status of populations of harp and hooded seals. *Biological Conservation*, 10, 95–118.

Sergeant D (1991) *Harp Seals, Man and Ice.* Canadian Special Publication of Fisheries and Aquatic Sciences 114, Fisheries and Oceans Canada.

Serreze M and Francis J (2006) The Arctic amplification debate. *Climatic Change*, 76, 241–264.

Serreze M, Maslanik J, Scambos T *et al.* (2003) A record minimum arctic sea ice extent and area in 2002. *Geophysical Research Letters*, 30(3), 1110.

Serreze M, Crawford A, Stroeve J *et al.* (2016) Variability, trends, and predictability of seasonal sea ice retreat and advance in the Chukchi Sea. *Journal of Geophysical Research: Oceans*, 121, 7308–7325.

Shabecoff P (1988) Global warming has begun, expert tells senate. *New York Times*, 24 June. URL: https://www.nytimes.com/1988/06/24/us/global-warming-has-begun-expert-tells-senate.html.

Shelton J (1997) *Bear Encounter Survival Guide.* Pallister Publishing.

Shelton J (1998) *Bear Attacks: The Deadly Truth.* Pallister Publishing.

Shelton J (2001) *Bear Attacks II: Myth and Reality.* Pallister Publishing.

Siberian Times (2018) 25 polar bears plus cubs besiege village of Ryrkaypiy in Chukotka. *Siberian Times News*, 7 November. URL: https://siberiantimes.com/other/others/news/25-polar-bears-plus-cubs-besiege-village-of-ryrkaypiy-in-chukotka/.

Siegel K (2018) Keeping fossil fuels in the ground is the only way to save polar bears ravaged by climate change. *The Hill*, 26 May. URL: http://thehill.com/opinion/energy-environment/389493-keeping-fossil-fuels-in-the-ground-is-the-only-way-to-save-polar.

Smith P, Stirling I, Jonkel C *et al.* (1975) *Notes on the Present Status of the Polar Bear (Ursus maritimus) in Ungava Bay and Northern Labrador.* Progress Notes 53, Canadian Wildlife Service.

Smith T (1987) *The Ringed Seal,* Phoca hispida, *of the Canadian Western Arctic.* Tech. Rep. 216, Canadian Bulletin of Fisheries and Aquatic Science.

Smith T and Stirling I (1975) The breeding habitat of the ringed seal (*Phoca hispida*): the birth lair and associated structures. *Canadian Journal of Zoology*, 53, 1297–1305.

Smith T and Stirling I (1978) Variation in the density of ringed seal (*Phoca hispida*) birth lairs in the Amundsen Gulf, Northwest Territories. *Canadian Journal of Zoology*, 56, 1066–1071.

Smith TG and Hammill MO (1981) Ecology of the ringed seal, *Phoca hispida*, in its fast ice breeding habitat. *Canadian Journal of Zoology*, 59, 966–981.

Smyth D (2007) Special Report: Global Warming. *British Journal of Photography* 15 August.

Solomon S, Qin D, Manning M *et al.* (Eds.) (2007) *Climate Change 2007: The Physical Science Basis. Contribution of Working Group I to the 4th Assessment Report of the Intergovernmental Panel on Climate Change.* Cambridge University Press. URL: https://www.ipcc.ch/publications_and_data/ar4/wg1/en/spm.html.

Stanley Becker I (2019) A 'mass invasion' of polar bears is terrorizing an island town. Climate change is to blame. Washington Post, 11 February. URL: https://www.washingtonpost.com/nation/2019/02/11/mass-invasion-polar-bears-is-terrorizing-an-island-town-climate-change-is-blame/.

Stapleton S, Atkinson S, Hedman D *et al.* (2014) Revisiting Western Hudson Bay: using aerial surveys to update polar bear abundance in a sentinel population. *Biological Conservation*, 170, 38–47.

Stapleton S, Peacock E and Garshelis D (2016) Aerial surveys suggest long-term stability in the seasonally ice-free Foxe Basin (Nunavut) polar bear population. *Marine Mammal Science*, 32, 181–201.

Steele J (2013) *Landscapes and Cyles: An Environmentalist's Journey to Climate Scepticism.* CreateSpace.

Stenhouse GB, Lee L and Poole KG (1988) Some characteristics of polar bears killed during conflicts with humans in the Northwest Territories, 1976–86. *Arctic*, 41, 275–278.

Stenson G (2014) *The Status of Harp and Hooded Seals in the North Atlantic.* Tech. Rep. SCR Doc. 14/026, Serial No. N6321, Northwest Atlantic Fisheries Organization.

Stern H and Laidre K (2016) Sea-ice indicators of polar bear habitat. *Cryosphere*, 10, 2027–2041.

Stewart W (2017) Incredible moment more than 230 polar bears descend on a Russian beach to feast on a giant whale carcass. *The Sun* (UK), 29 September. URL: https://www.thesun.co.uk/news/4577222/incredible-moment-more-than-230-polar-bears-descend-on-a-russian-beach-to-feast-on-a-giant-whale-carcass/.

Stewart W (2018) Incredible footage shows man fleeing a POLAR BEAR in Russian town that is under siege from the animals that locals worry want to EAT them. *DailyMail*, 16 October. URL: https://www.dailymail.co.uk/news/article-6281361/Russian-town-siege-polar-bears-try-eat-residents.html.

Stewart W (2019) State of emergency is declared after more than 50 polar bears invade Russian town and 'chase terrified residents'. *Daily Mail* (UK), 10 February. URL: https://www.dailymail.co.uk/news/article-6687731/State-emergency-declared-50-polar-bears-invade-Russian-town.html.

Stirling I (1974) Midsummer observations on the behavior of wild polar bears (*Ursus maritimus*). *Canadian Journal of Zoology*, 52, 1191–1198.

Stirling I (1986) Research and management of polar bears, *Ursus maritimus*. *Polar Record*, 23(143), 167–176.

Stirling I (1988) *Polar Bears*. University of Michigan Press.

Stirling I (1997) The importance of polynyas, ice edges, and leads to marine mammals and birds. *Journal of Marine Systems*, 10, 9–21.

Stirling I (2002) Polar bears and seals in the eastern Beaufort Sea and Amundsen Gulf: a synthesis of population trends and ecological relationships over three decades. *Arctic*, 55(Suppl. 1), 59–76.

Stirling I (2011) *Polar Bears: The Natural History of a Threatened Species*. Fitzhenry and Whiteside.

Stirling I (2013) Dead polar bear in Svalbard. *Polar Bears International*, 8 August 2013. URL: http://www.polarbearsinternational.org/news-room/news/dead-polar-bear-s valbard.

Stirling I and Archibald W (1977) Aspects of predation of seals by polar bears. *Journal of Fisheries Research Board of Canada*, 34, 1126–1129.

Stirling I and Derocher A (1993) Possible impacts of climatic warming on polar bears. *Arctic*, 46, 240–245.

Stirling I and Derocher A (2007) Melting under pressure. *The Wildlife Professional*, Fall, 24–27, 43.

Stirling I and Derocher A (2012) Effects of climate warming on polar bears: a review of the evidence. *Global Change Biology*, 18, 2694–2706.

Stirling I and Kiliaan H (1980) *Population Ecology Studies of the Polar Bear in Northern Labrador*. Occasional paper 42, Canadian Wildlife Service.

Stirling I and Lunn N (1997) Environmental fluctuations in arctic marine ecosystems as reflected by variability in reproduction of polar bears and ringed seals. In: SJ Woodin and M Marquiss (Eds.), *Ecology of Arctic Environments*. Blackwell Science.

Stirling I and Øritsland NA (1995) Relationships between estimates of ringed seal (*Phoca hispida*) and polar bear (*Ursus maritimus*) populations in the Canadian Arctic. *Canadian Journal of Fisheries and Aquatic Science*, 52, 2594–2612.

Stirling I and Parkinson C (2006) Possible effects of climate warming on selected populations of polar bears (*Ursus maritimus*) in the Canadian Arctic. *Arctic*, 59, 261–275.

Stirling I and Ross J (2011) Observations of cannibalism by polar bears (*Ursus maritimus*) on summer and autumn sea ice at Svalbard, Norway. *Arctic*, 64, 478–482.

Stirling I and van Meurs R (2015) Longest recorded underwater dive by a polar bear. *Polar Biology*, 38, 1301–1304.

Stirling I, Andriashek D, Latour P *et al.* (1975) *Distribution and Abundance of Polar Bears in the Eastern Beaufort Sea*. Beaufort Sea technical report 2, Department of the Environment, Victoria, BC.

Stirling I, Pearson A and Bunnell F (1976) Population ecology studies of polar and grizzly bears in northern Canada. In: *Transactions of the North American Wildlife and Natural Resources Conference*, vol. 41, pp. 421–429.

Stirling I, Archibald R and DeMaster D (1977a) Distribution and abundance of seals in the Eastern Beaufort Sea. *Journal of the Fisheries Research Board of Canada*, 34, 976–988.

Stirling I, Jonkel C, Smith P *et al.* (1977b) *The Ecology of the Polar Bear (Ursus maritimus) along the Western Coast of Hudson Bay*. Occasional paper 33, Canadian Wildlife Service.

Stirling I, Calvert W and Andriashek D (1980a) *Population Ecology Studies of the Polar Bear in the Area of Southeastern Baffin Island*. Occasional paper 44, Canadian Wildlife Service.

Stirling I, Schweinsburg R, Kolenosky G *et al.* (1980b) Research on polar bears in Canada 1976–1978. In: *Polar Bears: Proceedings of the 7th meeting of the Polar Bear Specialist Group IUCN/SSC, 30 January–1 February, 1979, Copenhagen, Denmark.* IUCN.

Stirling I, Cleator H and Smith T (1981) *Marine Mammals*. Occasional paper 45, Canadian Wildlife Service.

Stirling I, Kingsley M and Calvert W (1982) *The Distribution and Abundance of Seals in the Eastern Beaufort Sea, 1974–79*. Occasional paper 47, Canadian Wildlife Service.

Stirling I, Calvert W and Andriashek D (1984) Polar bear ecology and environmental considerations in the Canadian High Arctic. In: R Olson, F Geddes and R Hastings (Eds.), *Northern Ecology and Resource Management*. University of Alberta Press.

Stirling I, Schweinsburg R, Kolenosky G *et al.* (1985) Research on polar bears in Canada 1978–80. In: *Polar Bears: PROCEEDINGS of the 8th meeting of the Polar Bear Specialist Group IUCN/SSC, Oslo, Norway, 15–19 January 1981.* IUCN.

Stirling I, Andriashek D and Calvert W (1993) Habitat preferences of polar bears in the western Canadian Arctic in late winter and spring. *Polar Record*, 29, 13–24.

Stirling I, Lunn N and Iacozza J (1999) Long-term trends in the population ecology of polar bears in Western Hudson Bay in relation to climate change. *Arctic*, 52, 294–306.

Stirling I, Lunn N, Iacozza J *et al.* (2004) Polar bear distribution and abundance on the southwestern Hudson Bay coast during open water season, in relation to population trends and annual ice patterns. *Arctic*, 57, 15–26.

Stirling I, Richardson E, Thiemann G *et al.* (2008) Unusual predation attempts of polar bears on ringed seals in the southern Beaufort Sea: possible significance of changing spring ice conditions. *Arctic*, 61, 14–22.

Stirling I, McDonald T, Richardson E *et al.* (2011) Polar bear population status in the northern Beaufort Sea, Canada, 1971–2006. *Ecological Applications*, 21, 859–876.

Stroeve J, Holland M, Meier W *et al.* (2007) Arctic sea ice decline: Faster than forecast. *Geophysical Research Letters*, 34, L09501.

Stroeve J, Markus T, Boisvert L *et al.* (2014) Changes in Arctic melt season and implications for sea ice loss. *Geophysical Research Letters*, 41, 1216–1224.

Struzik E (2010) On thin ice. *Edmonton Journal*, 18 December.

Swaisgood R and Sheppard J (2010) The culture of conservation biologists: show me the hope! *BioScience*, 60, 626–630.

SWG (2016) *Re-Assessment of the Baffin Bay and Kane Basin Polar Bear Subpopulations: Final Report to the Canada-Greenland Joint Commission on Polar Bear*. Tech. rep., Scientific Working Group to the Canada-Greenland Joint Commission on Polar Bear. URL: http://www.gov.nu.ca/documents-publications/349.

Tabuchi H (2017) How climate change deniers rise to the top in Google searches. *New York Times*, 29 December. URL: https://www.nytimes.com/2017/12/29/climate/google-search-climate-change.html.

Taylor K, Mayewski P, Alley R *et al.* (1997) The Holocene–Younger Dryas Transition Recorded at Summit, Greenland. *Science*, 278, 825–827.

Taylor M and Lee J (1995) Distribution and abundance of Canadian polar bear populations: a management perspective. *Arctic*, 48, 147–154.

Taylor M, Larsen T and Schweinsburg R (1985) Observations of intraspecific aggression and cannibalism in polar bears (*Ursus maritimus*). *Arctic*, 38, 303–309.

Taylor M, Akeeagok S, Andriashek D *et al.* (2001) Delineating Canadian and Greenland polar bear (*Ursus maritimus*) populations by cluster analysis of movements. *Canadian Journal of Zoology*, 79, 690–709.

Taylor M, Lee J, Laake J *et al.* (2006) *Estimating Population Size of Polar Bears in Foxe Basin, Nunavut, using Tetracycline Biomarkers*. Tech. rep., Government of Nunavut, Department of Environment.

Taylor M, Laake J, McLoughlin P *et al.* (2008) Mark-recapture and stochastic population models for polar bears of the High Arctic. *Arctic*, 61, 143–152.

Towns L, Derocher A, Stirling I *et al.* (2009) Spatial and temporal patterns of problem polar bears in Churchill, Manitoba. *Polar Biology*, 32, 1529–1537.

Truett JC (1993) *Guidelines for Oil and Gas Operations in Polar Bear Habitats*. Tech. Rep. 93-0008, Minerals Management Service Alaska, US Dept. of the Interior.

Tyrrell M (2006) More bears, less bears: Inuit and scientific perceptions of polar bear populations on the west coast of Hudson Bay. *Études/Inuit/Studies*, 30, 191–208.

US Fish and Wildlife Service (2005) Endangered and threatened wildlife and plants; determination of Threatened Status for the Southwest Alaska distinct population segment of the northern sea otter (*Enhydra lutris kenyoni*); final rule. *Federal Register*, 70, 46366.

US Fish and Wildlife Service (2008) Determination of threatened status for the polar bear (*Ursus maritimus*) throughout its range. *Federal Register*, 73, 28212–28303.

US Fish and Wildlife Service (2012a) Threatened status for the Arctic, Okhotsk and Baltic subspecies of the ringed seal. *Federal Register*, 77, 76706–76738.

US Fish and Wildlife Service (2012b) Threatened status for the Beringia and Okhotsk distinct population segments of the *Erignathus barbatus nauticus* subspecies of the bearded seal. *Federal Register*, 77, 76740–76768.

US Fish and Wildlife Service (2017a) Endangered and threatened wildlife and plants; 12-month findings on petitions to list 25 species as endangered or threatened. *Federal Register*, 82, 46618–46645.

US Fish and Wildlife Service (2017b) Pacific walruses haul out near Point Lay earlier than in previous years. Press release, 16 August. URL: https://www.fws.gov/news/S howNews.cfm?ref=pacific-walruses-haul-out-near-point-lay-earlier-than-in-prev ious-years-&_ID=36121.

US Geological Survey (2007) *Executive Summary, USGS Science Strategy to Support US Fish and Wildlife Service Polar Bear Listing Decision*. Administrative report, US Geological Survey.

USGCRP (2017) *Climate Science Special Report: Fourth National Climate Assessment, Volume I*. Tech. rep., US Global Change Research Program.

Uspenski S and Kistchinski A (1972) New data on the winter ecology of the polar bear (*Ursus maritimus*, Phipps) on Wrangel Island. *Bears: Their Biology and Management*, 2, 181–197.

Uspenski SM (1961) Animal population estimates in the Soviet Arctic. *Priroda*, 8, 3341. Reprinted in 1962 as *Polar Record*, 71(11): 195196.

Valentine K (2014) Stranded walrus are a 'new phenomenon' and we don't know how bad it will get. *Think Progress*, 1 October. URL: http://thinkprogress.org/climate/20 14/10/01/3574540/walrus-stranding-adaptation-questions/.

Van de Velde F, Stirling I and Richardson E (2003) Polar bear (*Ursus maritimus*) denning in the area of the Simpson Peninsula, Nunavut. *Arctic*, 56, 191–197.

Vibe C (1967) Arctic Animals in Relation to Climatic Fluctuations. *Meddelelser om Grønland*, 170(5).

Vinje T (2001) Anomalies and trends of sea-ice extent and atmospheric circulation in the Nordic Seas during the period 1864–1998. *Journal of Climate*, 14, 255–267.

Walsh J, Fetterer F, Stewart J et al. (2017) A database for depicting Arctic sea ice variations back to 1985. *Geographical Review*, 107, 89–107.

Wang M and Overland J (2015) Projected future duration of the sea-ice-free season in the Alaskan Arctic. *Progress in Oceanography*, 136, 50–59.

Weber DS, Stewart BS, Garza JC et al. (2000) An empirical genetic assessment of the severity of the northern elephant seal population bottleneck. *Current Biology*, 10, 1287–1290.

Weber R (2013) Too many geese big honking problem for North: scientists. *The Globe and Mail*, 23 June. URL: http://www.theglobeandmail.com/news/national/too-many -geese-big-honking-problem-for-north-scientists/article12767802/.

Weber R (2015) Exploding Arctic snow geese numbers stabilizing, but still high. *CBC News*, 1 June. URL: https://www.cbc.ca/news/canada/north/exploding-arctic-snow -geese-numbers-stabilizing-but-still-high-1.3095247.

Whiteman J, Harlow H, Durner G *et al.* (2015) Summer declines in activity and body temperature offer polar bears limited energy savings. *Science*, 349, 295–298.

Whiteman JP, Harlow H, Durner G *et al.* (2018) Phenotypic plasticity and climate change: can polar bears respond to longer Arctic summers with an adaptive fast? *Oecologia*, 186(2), 369–381.

Wiig Ø (1998) Survival and reproductive rates for the polar bears at Svalbard. *Ursus*, 10, 2532.

Wiig Ø, Born E and Garner G (1995) *Polar Bears: Proceedings of the 11th Working Meeting of the IUCN/SSC Polar Bear Specialist Group, Copenhagen, Denmark, 25–27 January 1993.* Occasional paper of the IUCN Species Survival Commission 43, IUCN.

Wiig O, Derocher AE and Belikov S (1999) Ringed seal (*Phoca hispida*) breeding in the drifting pack ice of the Barents Sea. *Marine Mammal Science*, 15, 595– 598.

Wiig Ø, Aars J, Belikov S *et al.* (2007) *Ursus maritimus.* The IUCN Red List of Threatened Species 2007. URL: http://www.iucnredlist.org/details/full/22823/1.

Wiig Ø, Amstrup S, Atwood T *et al.* (2015) *Ursus maritimus.* The IUCN Red List of Threatened Species 2015. URL: http://www.iucnredlist.org/details/22823/0.

Wilder J, Vongraven D, Atwood T *et al.* (2017) Polar bear attacks on humans: implications of a changing climate. *Wildlife Society Bulletin*, 41, 537–547.

Woollaston V (2013) Is this starved polar bear which died as 'skin and bones' the 'categorical proof' that climate change is wiping out the species? *Daily Mail*, 7 August. URL: https://www.dailymail.co.uk/sciencetech/article-2385930/Starved-polar-bear -dead-Norway-categorical-proof-climate-change-wiping-species-say-experts.htm l.

Wootson, Jr C (2017) Polar bears hurt by climate change are more likely to turn to a new food source humans. *Washington Post*, 13 July. URL: https://www.washingtonpost.c om/news/animalia/wp/2017/07/13/polar-bears-hurt-by-climate-change-are-more -likely-to-turn-to-a-new-food-source-humans/.

Wu J and Loucks O (1995) From balance of nature to hierarchical patch dynamics: a paradigm shift in ecology. *Quarterly Review of Biology*, 70, 439–466.

WWF Canada (2016) Polar bear patrols keep bears and Arctic communities safe. WWF Canada News and Reports, 22 February. URL: http://www.wwf.ca/newsroom/?201 61/Polar-bear-patrols-keep-bears-and-Arctic-communities-safe.

Yee M, Reimer J, Lunn N *et al.* (2017) Polar bear (*Ursus maritimus*) migration from maternal dens in western Hudson Bay. *Arctic*, 70, 319–327.

Yong E and Meyer R (2016) Busy times at the world's largest polar bear prison. *The Atlantic*, December. URL: https://www.theatlantic.com/science/archive/2016/12/tr ouble-in-polar-bear-capital/510839/.

York G (2015) On International Polar Bear Day, hope for an iconic species. *Huffington Post*, 27 February. URL: https://www.huffingtonpost.com/geoff-york/on-internation al-polar-be_b_6770010.html.

York J, Dowsley M, Cornwell A *et al.* (2016) Demographic and traditional knowledge perspectives on the current status of Canadian polar bear subpopulations. *Ecology and Evolution*, 6, 2897–2924.

Zerehi S (2016a) Arviat polar bear patrols reduce bear deaths, says WWF-Canada. CBC News, 24 February. URL: https://www.cbc.ca/news/canada/north/polar-bear-patrol -arviat-1.3460947.

Zerehi S (2016b) Nunavut's polar bear problem growing in Hudson Bay communities. CBC News, 6 April. URL: https://www.cbc.ca/news/canada/north/problem-polar-b ears-hudson-bay-nunavut-1.3522375.

Zhang X and Walsh J (2006) Toward a seasonally ice-covered Arctic Ocean: Scenarios from the IPCC AR4 model simulations. *Journal of Climate*, 19, 1730–1747.

About the GWPF

The Global Warming Policy Foundation is an all-party and non-party think tank and a registered educational charity which, while openminded on the contested science of global warming, is deeply concerned about the costs and other implications of many of the policies currently being advocated.

Our main focus is to analyse global warming policies and their economic and other implications. Our aim is to provide the most robust and reliable economic analysis and advice. Above all we seek to inform the media, politicians and the public, in a newsworthy way, on the subject in general and on the misinformation to which they are all too frequently being subjected at the present time.

The key to the success of the GWPF is the trust and credibility that we have earned in the eyes of a growing number of policy makers, journalists and the interested public. The GWPF is funded overwhelmingly by voluntary donations from a number of private individuals and charitable trusts. In order to make clear its complete independence, it does not accept gifts from either energy companies or anyone with a significant interest in an energy company.

Views expressed in the publications of the Global Warming Policy Foundation are those of the authors, not those of the GWPF, its trustees, its Academic Advisory Council members or its directors.

Made in the USA
Middletown, DE
17 July 2020